In Excess

IN EXCESS

Studies of Saturated Phenomena

JEAN-LUC MARION

Translated by ROBYN HORNER
AND VINCENT BERRAUD

Fordham University Press
New York

Perspectives in Continental Philosophy No. 27
ISSN 1089-3938

Library of Congress Cataloging-in-Publication Data

Marion, Jean-Luc, 1946–
  [De surcroît. English]
  In excess : studies of saturated phenomena / Jean-Luc Marion ;
translated by Robyn Horner and Vincent Berraud.
      p.   cm.—(Perspectives in continental philosophy ; no. 27)
  Includes bibliographical references and index.
   ISBN 0-8232-2216-0 (hardcover)—ISBN 0-8232-2217-9 (pbk.)
   1. Phenomenology.   I. Title.   II. Series.
  B2430. 283 D413   2002
  194—dc21   2002009757

Printed in the United States of America
04   05   06   5   4   3   2

CONTENTS

TRANSLATOR'S ACKNOWLEDGMENTS

The traces of many others are woven throughout this text, including those of John D. Caputo, who persistently and patiently cajoled me to undertake this work, which has indeed become a labor of love; Kevin Hart, mentor and friend, who first introduced me to Jean-Luc Marion; Marion himself, not least because this work is born from his book, but also because he supported and encouraged me in the project; my co-translator for chapters 1–5, Vincent Berraud, without whose expertise I would have been lost, and who shared a lot of chocolate, cheese, and good Australian red; Jeffrey L. Kosky, whose work with previous versions of chapters 1 and 6 and other Marion texts was a constant and inspiring reference point and who, in making his translation of "In the Name: How to Avoid Speaking of Negative Theology" available electronically, saved me an enormous amount of new work; Thomas A. Carlson, whose translations of Marion were an invaluable resource; my friend and colleague Stephen Curkpatrick, who completed all the transliterations and translations of the Greek, who proofread the text as a whole and made valuable editorial suggestions, and whose understanding of and excitement about the text deepened and reinforced my own; my good friend Peter Howard, who translated the Latin; my colleagues and friends at the Melbourne College of Divinity and Monash University, who made space for this sometimes omnipresent work, and especially Anne Collopy, who was often called upon to locate resources for me, and whose friendship unfolded along with the delights of Marion's book; my newer colleagues at Australian Catholic University, who were a supportive part of the final stages of preparation; the highly professional team at Fordham University Press; Paul Caputo, who did the artwork; and not least my family and friends—my parents, Damian, Meg, Julie, and Bosco—whose faithfulness overwhelms me, and whose love enables me to fly.

Robyn Horner
April 2002

TRANSLATOR'S INTRODUCTION

Jean-Luc Marion frequently shapes his work in trilogies, and with this volume he seeks to complete the phenomenological trilogy that began with *Réduction et donation* in 1989 and was continued with *Étant donné* in 1997.[1] In this respect it not only concludes a series but also bears traces of many of the debates evoked by the earlier works. These debates have centered on the nature and role of phenomenology and, in particular, on the relationship phenomenology might bear to theology. This is in spite of the fact that Marion himself would argue for the trilogy's strictly phenomenological focus. Nevertheless, in working out the consequences of two main insights—givenness as the sole horizon of phenomena, and the possibility of phenomena that saturate intuition to such an extent that all horizons are shattered—he seems inevitably to return to questions about phenomena of revelation. Because of this fascination, his phenomenological works resonate to some degree with his theological ones, although, as I have argued at length elsewhere, and as Thomas A. Carlson insists with clarity and brevity in his introduction to *The Idol and Distance,* this is not to say that the relationship between Marion's phenomenology and his theology is straightforward or lacking in subtlety.[2] Two basic complaints correspond to Marion's central insights: that his emphasis on givenness implies a divine Giver and that his saturated phenomenon allows him to smuggle theological

---

[1] Jean-Luc Marion, *Réduction et donation: Recherches sur Husserl, Heidegger, et la phénoménologie* (Paris: Presses Universitaires de France, 1989); *Reduction and Givenness: Investigations of Husserl, Heidegger, and Phenomenology,* trans. Thomas A. Carlson (Evanston: Northwestern University Press, 1998); Jean-Luc Marion, *Étant donné: Essai d'une phénoménologie de la donation* (Paris: Presses Universitaires de France, 1997); *Being Given: Toward a Phenomenology of Givenness,* trans. Jeffrey L. Kosky (Stanford: Stanford University Press, forthcoming).

[2] Robyn Horner, *Rethinking God as Gift: Marion, Derrida, and the Limits of Phenomenology,* Perspectives in Continental Philosophy 19 (New York: Fordham University Press, 2001); Thomas A. Carlson, "Translator's Introduction," in *The Idol and Distance: Five Studies,* Perspectives in Continental Philosophy 17 (New York: Fordham University Press, 2001), xi–xxxi.

objects into phenomenology.[3] While at various times Marion has responded to these assertions, *In Excess* is a response of a different order. The compelling phenomenological analyses undertaken here provide a new perspective on his entire project, focusing his theses and his evidence very precisely. In short, while it also has its own work to do, *In Excess* is a tight rearticulation and reformulation of the main thrust of Marion's argument across the trilogy.

Following his basic thesis from *Réduction et donation,* Marion once again argues for the legitimacy of the claim that phenomenology is first philosophy. In an expanded form of an article that appeared in English in *Critical Inquiry* in 1999, he again makes a case for the rehabilitation of Husserl as the thinker who opens a way beyond metaphysics. The first part of this argument relies on the failure of metaphysics as first philosophy where it is defined as the "divine science." This occurs whether metaphysics is understood on the basis of *ousia* (read either as substance or essence), ontology, or cause, since none of these meanings adequately enables a thinking of God or sustains primacy. These failures in turn lead to a focus on the possible primacy of epistemology. Nevertheless, Marion argues that grounding philosophy on the transcendental *I* is also problematic. In this we see nothing new, although the material is sketched with a deftness that emerges typically from Marion's close knowledge of the history of philosophy. It is the second part of the argument that marks his distinctive contribution to the debate. Here he re-presents his thesis that one of the four formulas used to define the scope of phenomenology allows for a thinking of phenomenology as first philosophy, since it escapes the problems of metaphysics. This is the formula that emphasizes the importance of the phenomenological reduction: "*Autant de réduction, autant de donation* (As much reduction, as much givenness)."[4] With the exclusion, by way

---

[3] See, for example, the arguments presented in John D. Caputo and Michael Scanlon, eds., *God, the Gift, and Postmodernism* (Bloomington: Indiana University Press, 1999); Dominique Janicaud, *La phénoménologie éclatée* (Combas: Éditions de l'éclat, 1998); Dominique Janicaud, *Le tournant théologique de la phénoménologie française* (Combas: Éditions de l'Éclat, 1991); Dominique Janicaud, "'Veerings' from *The Theological Turn of French Phenomenology*," in *The Religious,* ed. John D. Caputo (Oxford: Blackwell, 2002), 145–58; Dominique Janicaud, Jean-François Courtine, Jean-Louis Chrétien, Jean-Luc Marion, Michel Henry, and Paul Ricoeur, *Phenomenology and the "Theological Turn": The French Debate,* Perspectives in Continental Philosophy 15 (New York: Fordham University Press, 2001).

[4] This formula is often translated "So much reduction, so much givenness," which is perfectly legitimate. Nevertheless, I prefer "as much" for *autant,* since it underlines

of the reduction, of all that does not give itself "in person," Marion
maintains that we are left with phenomena given in complete certainty.
Consciousness becomes the screen upon which given phenomena show
themselves instead of the origin and measure of objective thought.

In the final part of the argument in the first chapter, Marion deals
with some of the objections that have been raised to it, largely, although by no means exclusively, by Jacques Derrida and Dominique
Janicaud. The first objection is that this reading of phenomenology
opens it to a theological interpretation: in emphasizing the givenness
of the given, particularly insofar as it relies on a type of passivity of
consciousness, he could be arguing that givens are simply the effects
of a theological cause. In response, Marion argues that even if this were
the case, it would not be a legitimate move to make theologically, since
"in revealed theology, causality is applied to God in such a way that
God nevertheless does not become comprehensible by God's effects."[5]
Further, the reduction eliminates all transcendence in any case. Finally,
and this is something of an aside, notwithstanding that elimination of
transcendence, Marion argues that a thinking of God's immanence
would nevertheless not preclude God from phenomenological consideration. It is primarily Janicaud who is the focus of these rebuttals, and
while he may have a significant point to make in the context of the
possibility of phenomena of revelation, it would seem that his objections to givenness as such are no more than a general allegation of bias
on the basis of Marion's other interests.[6]

A second objection, put forward by Derrida and amounting to the
same thing, is that the translation of Husserl's *Gegebenheit* using the
French *donation* (which, at Marion's insistence, has become "givenness" rather than "donation" in English) forces a gap between the act
and the fact of being given.[7] In other words, it complicates the given
with the possibility of a giver. On the face of it this seems a reasonable
point to make, especially in the context of Marion's earlier work. Nev-

---

the proportionality of the formula: the more strictly the reduction is applied, givenness
increases.

[5] Below, p. 23.

[6] See Horner, *Rethinking God as Gift*, for a detailed discussion of the debate. It is
important to note that it is not just Marion who is the target of Janicaud's accusation
but also figures like Emmanuel Levinas and Michel Henry.

[7] One of the complicating factors in this debate is, of course, the extent to which
even the author can argue for authorial intention. Marion claims not to be positing an
origin; Derrida might say that the text nevertheless opens onto this question.

ertheless, even if there are various other theological complications, this
is not a gap that Marion ever actually exploits in the phenomenological
trilogy. It seems to have more of a linguistic function: in the same way
that to see something as an object means to see it according to its
objectivity, to see something as given is to see it according to its givenness. Marion uses givenness—as he asserts in his response—to reinforce the fact that a phenomenon is given rather than to put in question
its origin.

Significant is Marion's resistance here to translating *Gegebenheit*
with *présence,* owing to its metaphysical resonance, not because it is
a point newly made in *In Excess* but because he deals much more
comprehensively in the current work with issues relating to presence.[8]
This is important because what is really at issue is the status of phenomenology as such. Is phenomenology inevitably compromised, as
Derrida claims, by its pretension to making phenomena present by way
of the reduction, or does it succeed in evading metaphysics, as Marion
would have us believe? Clearly, Marion would like to argue that a
rehabilitated phenomenology involves a reduction to givenness rather
than to presence, and therefore that even if Husserl was not entirely
successful in completing the counter-metaphysical move, the potential
was always there for phenomenology to go beyond the metaphysical
impasse. Derrida would maintain in response that, on the one hand,
since the reduction cannot reduce to presence, it must fail along with
phenomenology, and on the other, that metaphysics is in any case not
so easily sidestepped.[9]

The validity of these responses is better assessed in the consideration
of a phenomenon. To consider the first response, we leap forward to
the beginning of chapter 5, where Marion begins by considering the
phenomenon of his box of tobacco. Following a typically Husserlian
analysis, he notes that the constitution of the object depends not only
on its presentation but also on the intentional use of appresentation (by
way of anticipation or by memory). Now, the inevitable rupture in the
presence of the object (it is never simply present but can only be constituted with reference to the past and the future) is one of the factors

---

[8] This is in spite of several disclaimers about dealing with the issue of presence.

[9] See, for example, Derrida in "On the Gift: A Discussion between Jacques Derrida
and Jean-Luc Marion," in Caputo and Scanlon, eds., *God, the Gift, and Postmodernism,* 54–78, 71; and "Implication: Interview with Henri Ronse," in *Positions,* trans.
Alan Bass (Chicago: University of Chicago Press, 1981), 3–14, 12.

highlighted by Derrida in his critique of phenomenology: the reduction is never actually a reduction to presence. Marion does not reject this critique, but instead he goes on to emphasize it in further considering those aspects of constitution where, given the dimensions of space and time, visibility always "conceals and reveals an invisibility."[10] This is so spatially because of the incompatibility of lived experiences: not all the faces of the box can be simultaneously manifest. It is so temporally because, as Husserl had admitted, objects are basically undefined and are only constituted over time: we learn to see the object as a tobacco box. Further, because objects not only change through time (the tobacco box ages and deteriorates) but are offered through successive temporalizations, no object ever gives rise to the same lived experience twice. Yet there is a further aspect of constitution that renders problematic its presentation of objects: an object intentionality is only one of the possible intentionalities that could be applied to the phenomenon that gives itself.[11] By stepping back from Husserl's effective preoccupation with object intentionality and exploiting the incessant rupture of presence that disturbs constitution, Marion aims to set out a phenomenology that functions in spite of Derrida's critique. What we have, in fact, is a phenomenology that has recognized shortcomings and must be explicitly supplemented by hermeneutics.

This brings us to consider the second response, which has to do with the capacity of phenomenology to go beyond metaphysics. Conscious of Marion's detailed and fine analyses of the nature of medieval and modern metaphysics that appear elsewhere, it is nevertheless primarily a Heideggerian and post-Heideggerian critique of metaphysics that will form the basis of my characterization here.[12] In very broad strokes, metaphysics in this sense is (or involves elements of) a conception in terms of being as presence, with a claim to some kind of absoluteness, on the foundation of a transcendental I, whose existence and certainty is guaranteed by a term posited beyond the conceptual system: metaphysics is "onto-theo-logy." Given that Derrida is profoundly influenced by Heidegger's analysis, he is still able to maintain that

---

[10] See below, p. 105

[11] See below, p. 108.

[12] See, for example, the first chapter of Jean-Luc Marion, *On Descartes's Metaphysical Prism,* trans. Jeffrey L. Kosky (Chicago: University of Chicago Press, 1999); *Sur le prisme métaphysique de Descartes. Constitution et limites de l'onto-théo-logie de la pensée cartésienne* (Paris: Presses Universitaires de France, 1986).

Heidegger does not entirely escape the metaphysical snare. More importantly, he argues that it would be virtually impossible for anyone to think without some kind of metaphysical compromise, and so he never makes the claim that he, for example, has done so. What Derrida pursues, however, is what interrupts the metaphysical pretension to absoluteness, and he does this by way of *différance* as well as by the aporia of the impossible. In the context of this all too brief sketch, we return to Marion's claim that phenomenology allows philosophy to go beyond the metaphysical impasse. Now, the striking thing about *In Excess* is that its phenomenological analyses are riddled with *différance* even where it is not so named. In other words, in terms of what has just been observed in the consideration of the tobacco box, what is emphasized is what prevents constitution from being absolute. This could be read either in Derrida's terms as the failure of phenomenology, which attempts to disguise its reliance on hermeneutics and so is always metaphysically implicated, or in Marion's terms as the successful orientation of thought by phenomenology always to the brink of its own need for supplementation. On my reading, Marion would claim to exceed metaphysics in the signaling toward excess, while admitting the limited and probably metaphysical nature of any particular hermeneutic of that excess. This is confirmed by his acknowledgment at various points in the book that what is said will always need to be unsaid, or in Levinasian terms, that the Saying will always be compromised when it is hardened into a Said. The question then becomes: to what extent does Marion succeed in walking this fine line, in "signaling toward" without assuming to directly refer to "the" excess, and without absolutizing his hermeneutics? It is in the light of this question that I turn to his phenomenological analyses.

Although it will be evident from the example of the tobacco box given above that Marion will argue for a kind of excessiveness in the giving of all phenomena, the focus of *In Excess* is on saturated phenomena, or paradoxes, those that so exceed the Kantian categories of quantity, quality, relation, or modality that they interrupt or even blind the intentional aim. Marion considers in each chapter in turn the saturated phenomena of the event (which saturates according to quantity, being unable to be accounted for), the idol (which saturates according to quality, being unbearable by the look), flesh (which saturates according to relation, being absolute), the icon (which saturates according to modality, being unable to be looked at), and Revelation (which saturates according to all four categories at once), always attentive to the *self* of the phenomenon that gives itself there and the extent to which what is given is also shown.

In chapter 2, under the title of saturated phenomenon as event, Marion examines the historical event, friendship, death, time, and birth. He distinguishes between the event and the object on three grounds: the event has the character of facticity (it has always already occurred), accomplishment (it is uniquely achieved, "this time, once and for all"), and endlessness (its hermeneutic can never be completed); yet it also has other characteristics similarly typical of saturated phenomena, including that it involves anamorphosis, cannot be repeated, cannot be accorded a unique cause, and cannot be foreseen. Further, while what gives itself will often necessarily first show itself, events like death or birth actually only show themselves in the mode of being given. The event is a *fait accompli,* irremediably striking the one who receives it. And this recipient is not the transcendental I, not the *ego,* but the *adonné,* the one "given over," gifted, or devoted to the self-giving phenomenon, the one who receives itself from what it receives. As Marion points out, this seems to involve a performative contradiction, in that in giving priority to the self of the phenomenon and demoting the I to a *me,* he seems to have done away with the operator of the reduction. Nevertheless, he argues that this is simply to do as Husserl would insist, to include the I itself in the overall sweep of the reduction. This context provides Marion with an opportunity to explore in further detail the character of *l'adonné* and how it functions to reveal the given. What he seeks is a description that goes beyond activity and passivity, particularly since he aims not merely to replace the transcendental I with an empirical me. As he has done in *Étant donné,* he refers to this reduced "self" as the screen upon which the self of the unseen is projected or against which it is crushed.[13] In phenomenalizing the unseen, the one who phenomenalizes is simultaneously phenomenalized. But there are important developments from earlier texts. Here there is no reference to *l'attributaire* (the assigned) or *l'interloqué* (the interlocuted), and at this point at least, no reference to a call. There is only *l'adonné,* whose name is, admittedly, sufficiently ambiguous to maintain something of the religious interest of which Marion has so often been accused (*s'adonner* is "to give oneself over to"; "to devote

---

[13] Marion, *Étant donné,* 365.

oneself"). Nevertheless, the absence of the other names and of the device of the call suggests that Marion has moved to limit this resonance. In this setting, revelation occurs in a process of offering resistance: in its resistance to the given, *l'adonné* enables it to be revealed. "The revealed does not thus define an extreme stratum or a particular region of phenomenality, but rather the universal mode of phenomenalization of what gives *itself* in what shows *itself*."[14] Having carefully circumscribed the religious connotations of his description, however, Marion concludes the chapter by turning once again to the possibility of phenomena of Revelation. This is a cleverly executed maneuver, attacking Janicaud's accusation head-on. One question remains. In spite of Marion's explicit avowal that "philosophy has neither the authority nor the competence to say more," is it possible even to speak of phenomena of Revelation without having made a decision about their existence? While elsewhere I have suggested that this is not the case, it seems to me that the ground in this instance is far better prepared.[15] Here, Marion's description of revelation does not require a commitment in advance to the possibility of Revelation, although it remains a possibility, and will later be analyzed in terms of its saturation of saturation.[16]

Although the theme of the idol has been prominent in many of Marion's works, the analysis found in chapter 3 of *In Excess* is far and away the most powerful. This is due in large part to the extraordinary passages dealing, on the one hand, with the unrelenting wash of visibility, and on the other, with particular works of art. Marion's descriptions are never simple, but they are compelling. With them he makes an important contribution to a phenomenology of art, one in which an ethical component is not missing. He is also able to articulate the role of the artist as one who "tries to receive, in his or her frame, a newcomer, a new seen, and to hold it there in reducing it without remainder to its pure visibility."[17] Marion's previous analyses of the idol (except perhaps in *La croisée du visible*) tend to focus on it negatively as what fills the aim and mirrors the limits of the observer, in contrast to the icon, which shatters the aim and reverses intentionality. Here the exces-

---

[14] See below, p. 52.

[15] This is the question I raise in Horner, *Rethinking God as Gift,* 157.

[16] This move seems to take Marion beyond the impasse of Revelation/revealability described by Derrida in "On the Gift," 73, 76.

[17] See below, p. 69.

sive quality of the idol is emphasized and celebrated: no one look can capture what is made visible; art demands a multiplicity of intentional aims, not only from the one person, but from many. At the same time, the problem of the representation of the other person is raised, and this again leads to a consideration of the icon—not in an explicitly religious sense, but as the face of the other, a theme that is pursued in chapter 5.

Drawing extensively from Husserl, but integrating his detailed knowledge of Descartes and Pascal, with an eye to the work of Michel Henry and something of a debt to Levinas, Marion devotes all of chapter 4 to a consideration of flesh. This is his first extended piece on the theme, and in it he makes a careful distinction between flesh and body. Reminiscent to some degree of Levinas's analyses of insomnia, nausea, and suffering, Marion's description of the *ego* fixed to itself in flesh—or better, riveted to itself and unable to be phenomenalized in the world otherwise—is another very powerful passage.[18] Of particular interest is the way in which Marion considers the relationship between flesh and time: "*time,* especially according to the having-been, *does not pass,* but . . . accumulates. . . . The past is . . . accumulated in the flesh of my members, muscles and bones. . . . Above all, the weight of time is accumulated there where my flesh is most openly visible—on my face."[19] Or again: "accomplished time only manifests itself in taking flesh in mine, which it defeats, affects, marks. It takes flesh in me."[20] Time, in other words, is phenomenologically given in flesh. A second important focus is on the question of individuation. What individualizes is not thought or bodily extension but the tension between them that is played out in flesh and that is given absolutely as a saturated phenomenon. Flesh gives the *ego* to itself. Possibly the most innovative feature of the chapter, however, is the list of questions at the end, which opens not only onto the ongoing discussion of "who comes after the subject" and the consequent problem of intersubjectivity but also onto the theological issue of the Incarnation. This last question is not one that Marion pursues (and he again risks being typecast as a phenomenologist for the sake of theology), but I would hope that he takes it up in a different context.

---

[18] See, for example, Emmanuel Levinas, *Existents and* Existence, trans. Alphonso Lingis (The Hague: Martinus Nijhoff, 1978); *De l'évasion* (Paris: Fata Morgana, 1982); or *Totality and Infinity: An Essay on Exteriority,* trans. Alphonso Lingis (Pittsburgh: Duquesne University Press, 1969).

[19] See below, p. 95.

[20] See below, p. 96.

I have already referred in some detail to at least part of chapter 5. Following on from the analysis of the tobacco box and the recognition that all phenomena to some extent exceed our capacity to constitute them, Marion returns to a thinking of *l'invu* (the unseen) and the task of phenomenology, through the reduction, to phenomenalize it, even where this can only be done asynchronously and even then incompletely. What he seeks to do here is signal toward another type of invisibility, one that remains invisible although given. He returns to a quasi-Levinasian thematic of the face and of the counter-intentionality of the face which means that it can function iconically.[21] Marion focuses on the eyes as a point of recession to infinity, and precisely the infinite point from which a counter-intentionality operates. The face looks at me with a silent command, the injunction not to kill, a command that is issued in the Saying, as Levinas would have it, rather than the Said. It is here that Marion reintroduces the theme of the call; clearly, in this instance, he is not assigning it any particularly divine origin. Undoubtedly conscious of the difficulties that have been raised by John Milbank and others with regard to the question of counter-intentionality, Marion proceeds to consider whether or not the face is unevisageable. Why would the counter-intentionality of the other person not presuppose my own intentional aim? This is both because the face of the other never expresses a single meaning that could be constituted, even to itself, and because the other person only appears to me at the point when I am prepared to give up mastering or constituting him or her. The face of the other demands an infinite hermeneutic, proceeding from its priority in appearing to me as saturated phenomenon. Whether or not this is an entirely asymmetrical relationship, Marion does not question, although he suggests the possibility that the call does not rely simply or only on an ethical exigency. In other words, while Marion does not clarify one of Levinas's problems, which is whether or not my face might in turn be the place of an iconic call for another, he at least opens up what Levinas limits to ethics.

For one so concerned to keep the boundaries between his phenomenology and his theology clear, Marion makes an interesting move at the end of chapter 5. In the context of the demand for an infinite herme-

---

[21] See, for example, Marion, *Étant donné; La croisée du visible*, rev. ed. (Paris: Éditions de la Différence, 1996); *Prolégomènes à la charité*, 2nd ed. (Paris: Éditions de la Différence, 1991).

neutic of the face as icon, he contemplates what this might mean for each discipline. For theology, he says, to wait for the full manifestation of the other is akin to waiting for the return of Christ, which means that an infinite hermeneutic operates with faith that on that day all will be revealed. For phenomenology, such faith is an inappropriate tool. Nevertheless, following the Kantian argument for moral progress toward the infinite, Marion suggests that the demand for an infinite hermeneutic of the face can be similarly sustained: "The face of the other person compels me to believe in my own eternity, like a need of reason or, what comes back to the same thing, as the condition of its infinite hermeneutic."[22] There is something very appealing about this argument, especially since it affirms the ultimate meaningfulness of love, but it seems to me to rely on its own form of philosophical faith.

We arrive at the final chapter having experienced something of a shift in gears. This is the chapter on the saturated phenomenon of Revelation, the phenomenon that, Marion argues, performs the saturation of saturation, combining all the other types. In large part, what Marion has to say here is not new: it formed the text of a paper he delivered at Villanova in 1997 and was published as part of the volume *God, the Gift, and Postmodernism* in 1999.[23] It has already been part of public debate, and I do not propose to repeat in this setting my earlier remarks on its contents.[24] What is significant here is the new context of its presentation and the minor revisions Marion has made to the text. With regard to the former, it is once again reasonable to wonder at the extent to which Marion wants to insist on the distinction between his phenomenology and his theology, since the phenomenological trilogy is concluded with such a sustained piece on phenomena of Revelation. At the same time, however, if Marion indeed manages to argue successfully for saturated phenomena that resist any decidable reference, and therefore any commitment in advance as to their meaning, then he has not gone beyond the limits of phenomenology but has rather brought it to its brink. I would maintain not only that he has done this but that in setting this chapter in the context of a book that deals far more explicitly with hermeneutics than do his previous volumes, he has resolved any lingering doubts that the Villanova version occasioned. With re-

---

[22] See below, p. 127.
[23] Caputo and Scanlon, eds., *God, the Gift, and Postmodernism.*
[24] Horner, *Rethinking God as Gift.*

gard to the second point, then, about the minor revisions: these only reinforce Marion's attempts to implicate an infinite hermeneutics. There are a number of points slightly amplified or clarified throughout the text. Most importantly, the additions tend to reinforce the incomprehensibility and unknowability of God and the way in which mystical theology functions *pragmatically.* Two examples will briefly illustrate the interest of the latter. First: "With the third way, not only is it no longer a matter of saying (or denying) something about something, it is also no longer a matter of saying or unsaying, but of referring to the One who is no longer touched by nomination, *a matter no longer of saying the referent, but of pragmatically referring the speaker to the inaccessible Referent.*"[25] Second: "By '*pragmatic* theology of absence,' therefore, I mean not the non-presence of God but the fact that the name that God is given, the name that gives God . . . serves to shield God from presence."[26] While Marion uses the word "pragmatic" a number of times in the earlier version of the paper (and this is noted by Derrida), he pointedly increases its use in the revision.[27] It seems to me that he tries to emphasize its use to further disrupt the possibility of direct reference. For all intents and purposes, the use of the Name gives an orientation to prayer, but it is always a misorientation; it is a pragmatic strategy that cannot be over-invested. I have no doubt, however, that this will be a point long argued.

A final comment must be made about the work of translation itself. Marion's text is extraordinarily complex, and while choices have been made on occasion to simplify sentence structure, I have kept closer to his turn of phrase than to lucid English expression. This sometimes makes for hard work on the part of the reader, but effort is, in this case, always rewarded. That said, I have chosen to translate Marion's text using inclusive language where at all possible, although I have very often left his quotes of others as he translated them into French. Ambiguous or highly fertile expressions are often included in the original language in brackets.

---

[25] See below, p. 142, emphasis added to indicate additional text.

[26] See below, p. 156, emphasis added to indicate additional text and Marion's emphasis removed.

[27] Jacques Derrida, in his response to Marion's "In the Name," Caputo and Scanlon, eds., *God, the Gift and Postmodernism,* 45.

FOREWORD

Here it is a question of the excess [*le surcroît*, the addition, increase, extra], of the excess [*l'excès*] of intuition over the concept, of the saturated phenomenon and of its givenness outside the norm—and in excess [*de surcroît*]—once more.[1]

To begin with, the question of the excess. Do phenomena always appear according to the calm adequation in them of intuition with one or several significations, or following a deficit measured from one on the other? Or instead, do not some among them—paradoxes—appear thanks to (or in spite of) an irreducible excess of intuition over all the concepts and all the significations one would assign to them? This question, although then remaining implicit, was inevitably being shaped in the wake of my attempt to radically re-envisage the whole phenomenological project beginning with the primacy in it of givenness.[2] In this way, once the principle "As much reduction, as much givenness" was acquired, the question of the saturated phenomenon could only become explicit: it became so, in effect, quite quickly.[3] But the excess of intuition over signification and over the concept could only take all its importance, in my view decisive, by virtue of the givenness that is accomplished there in exemplary fashion—that is to

---

[1] Émile Littré: "Surcroît: *s.m.* 1. That which, added to something, increases in it the force, the number, the quality [. . .]. 3. De surcroît: *loc. adv.* Extra." *Dictionnaire de la langue française* (Paris, 1875), vol. 4, p. 2096.

[2] *Réduction et donation: Recherches sur Husserl, Heidegger, et la phénoménologie* (Paris: Presses Universitaires de France, 1989); *Reduction and Givenness: Research on Husserl, Heidegger, and Phenomenology,* trans. Thomas A. Carlson (Evanston: Northwestern University Press, 1998).

[3] "Le phénomène saturé," in Jean-François Courtine, ed., *Phénoménologie et théologie* (in collaboration with Jean-Louis Chrétien, Michel Henry and Paul Ricoeur) (Paris: Critérion, 1992); "The Saturated Phenomenon," trans. Thomas A. Carlson, in Dominique Janicaud, Jean-François Courtine, Jean-Louis Chrétien, Michel Henry, Jean-Luc Marion, and Paul Ricoeur, *Phenomenology and the "Theological Turn": The French Debate* (New York: Fordham University Press, 2000), pp. 176–216. This first essay still confused, in the fourth type of saturated phenomenon, the icon and Revelation; they will be finally distinguished in 1997, with indispensable differences of phenomenological status (see below, p. 29 and pp. 111ff.).

say, being given as rigorous as possible an account of the relation between what gives *itself* and what shows *itself*.[4] Nevertheless, *Étant
donné* would still only furnish a very approximative review of the four
types of saturated phenomena (§23) and of the saturated phenomenon
par excellence, that of Revelation (§24). As soon as the opportunity
arose, it was appropriate to start the description again, systematically.
Moreover [*de surcroît*], it was necessary to deal with the excess [*du
surcroît*] in its diverse figures.

The occasion of this addition [*ce surcroît*] was accorded to me by
demands for explication and exposition that the theses presented by *Étant
donné* aroused. The studies collected here were drafted in order to respond to academic invitations, all friendly and prestigious.[5] But they
were not, nevertheless, conceived without preparation. Since the publica-
tion of *Étant donné,* and precisely because it had appeared clearly that
the theses were not always glimmering there with the evidence with
which they had appeared to me, the project was quickly undertaken to
organize interventions in advance, according to a clear and simple plan:
to repeat the primacy of givenness in all phenomenality (chapter 1); next,
to review with more precision each of the four types of saturated phenomena (chapters 2–5); and finally, to try to confirm the possibility of a
saturated phenomenon *par excellence,* that of Revelation (chapter 6).

I am hoping, in doing this, not only to render more clear the very
idea of the saturated phenomenon and to confer on it sufficient credibil-
ity for its reception into phenomenology, but to conclude, with *In Excess,* the trilogy begun by *Reduction and Givenness* and continued in
Étant donné. This work nevertheless scarcely begins to render to givenness the attention that is owed to it—an unending task by definition,
since it is like ". . . a gold coin from which you never stop giving
change" (Henri Bergson).[6] Such is the character of the excess.

---

[4] *Étant donné: Essai d'une phénoménologie de la donation* (Paris: Presses Universitaires de France, 1997), but I will refer to the edition of 1998, where the most obvious
typographical errors have been corrected. [This text will soon be available as *Being
Given: Toward a Phenomenology of Givenness,* trans. Jeffrey L. Kosky (Stanford:
Stanford University Press).]

[5] I am thus happy to express my gratitude here to the Institut Catholique de Paris
and to Father Philippe Capelle, to the University "La Sapienza" of Rome and to Professor Marco M. Olivetti, to the Deutsche Gesellschaft für phänomenologische For-
schung and to Professor Rudolf Bernet, to the Divinity School of Harvard University
and to Professor Ronald F. Thiemann, to Villanova University and to Professor John D.
Caputo, to the Université Laval and to Professors J.-M. Narbonne and T. de Koninck.

[6] *La pensée et le mouvant,* in *Œuvres,* ed. André Robinet (Paris: Presses Universitaires de France, 1959), p. 1395.

1

Phenomenology of Givenness and First Philosophy

1. OF PRIMACY IN PHILOSOPHY

However dated it may be, the very theme of "first philosophy" remains full of issues, as much real as symbolic, indeed, full of polemics and passions. And that should not be surprising, since the pretension to a "first philosophy," the decision about its identity and its establishment, remains neither optional nor foreign to philosophy taken as such. In effect, philosophy only remains a simply possible knowledge in remaining useful, thus in seeming irreplaceable as such by any science—or, if it lays claim to the role of science, by any *other* science. But in what manner would contemporary sciences demand the least help from philosophy? The ancient model that attributed to philosophy, as first, the role of inquiring into the "principles" and "foundations" of the sciences seems out of date since the "end of metaphysics."

And this for at least two reasons. Certainly, first because each of the sciences has gained, at different moments, but always according to an irrepressible forward motion, an apparently definitive autonomy from philosophy, in such a way that not only no single one acknowledges toward philosophy any other debt than a historical one (having begun in this sense in its heart and progressively escaping it, following a chronology that the history of the sciences learns to establish more and more finely), but that inversely, all the positive areas having found a taker, the question would rather be to see if there remains a proper area for philosophy itself anymore. This is to the extent that philosophy itself seems in doubt of what is first, when it redefines itself as being, on the one hand, a knowledge at the second degree of science (epistemology), or as being, on the other hand, a simple inquiry into the forms of a correct use of language ("language analysis," "linguistic turn," and so on). But it is especially so because the contemporary sciences—far from seeking their "principles" from philosophy, because they determine them themselves—exempt themselves strongly from having, or even from researching, "principles" in general. What would still be stigmatized, in the first third of the twentieth century, as a "crisis of foundations" did not prevent mathematics and particle physics from progressing, as we know. For under the regime of the "end of metaphysics"—and it is that which, among other symptoms, characterizes it—neither the "principles" nor the "foundations" are found to be required any longer by any science. Or, instead, each science decides them by itself, freely and provisionally, according to its needs and its hypotheses, without ever claiming to attain a definitive apodicticity that would enable it to reach whatever "things themselves" there might be, nor wanting to attain them. The ascendancy of method over science,[1] today having become that of technology over what one persists in calling, for convenience, "the sciences," actually exempts them from conceiving the possibility and the interest of a foundation of absolute truth; it suffices, and amply, that an effective result occurs, whatever it is, in order that the question of truth is cut short, or rather, evacuated.

In this situation, philosophy as such would disappear because it would disappear as "first philosophy," responsible for securing not a further science but the "principles" and "foundations" of sciences. Consequently, it becomes vital for philosophy to maintain, even today, a claim of primacy, or at least of a certain type of primacy, in its very definition, failing which it will disappear not only as "first philosophy" in relation to other sciences, which do not cease to take up this challenge (the physics of the two last centuries, the biology of today), but simply as philosophy. It is only in claiming, essentially, the rank of "first philosophy" that philosophy remains in conformity with its proper essence. For a second philosophy would either become a regional science (in this way already the science—φυσιχή [*physikē, physics*]—of Aristotle) or instead simply lose its status as philosophy. In fact, the two terms are equal—without the adjective, the substantive

---

[1] Friedrich Nietzsche: "It is not the triumph of science that characterizes our nineteenth century, but the triumph of scientific method over science. . . ." *Wille zur Macht,* §466, ed. Peter Gast (Stuttgart: Kröner Verlag, 1964), p. 329; *Werke: Kritische Gesamtausgabe,* ed. Giorgio Colli and Mazzino, div. VIII, vol. 3: *Nachgelasrene Fragmente 1888–1889* (Berlin: de Gruyter, 1972), 15 [51], p. 236. To be fair, this last triumph most likely goes back to René Descartes and his generation.

would disappear. One could scarcely reproach philosophy for claiming—in whatever manner, even desperate—the primacy without which it would disappear as such. Thus, if the primacy of philosophy presupposes "first philosophy," then the difficulty will consist less in the legitimacy of this claim of primacy than in the determination of its type. And immediately, the difficulty changes in nature: it is henceforth a question of defining and establishing the primacy that philosophy must exercise in order to remain itself. I will no longer ask if "first philosophy" remains thinkable, but rather which determination of primacy can legitimately be exercised there.

Therefore, the question becomes more formidable and also more simple: does philosophy have at its disposal a domain and operations which, on the one hand, would be absolutely proper to it, such that no other science could either confiscate them from it or be born infiltrating it in order ultimately to dispossess it, and which, on the other hand, impose themselves as the condition of possibility of all other knowledge? This double question implies, on the evidence, that one at once redefine the field of primacy and the range of possibility.

2. THE TWO PRIMARY FIRST PHILOSOPHIES

The phrase "first philosophy" derives, as we know, from Aristotle. He introduces it in a development, where in another place, as I have indicated, the same term φιλοσοφία [*philosophia,* philosophy] only gives the common sense of an item of knowledge, more precisely of "knowledge bearing on. . . ." It is thus a question, in the famous text of *Metaphysics* E 1, of placing items of knowledge in a hierarchy, according to that on which they bear. They can bear on three areas: (i) nature, which considers moving, thus indeterminate, but at least separate, bodies; (ii) mathematics, which considers non-separate realities that are thus ontically incomplete but at least unchanging and thus knowable; (iii) finally, the φύσις τὶς μία [*physis tis mia,* one source, origin], the divine, which, if such can be found, would be at once unchanging, and thus epistemologically perfectly knowable, and separate, as a complete entity. In these conditions, primacy must be accorded to the φιλοσοφία that considers such an unchanging and separated domain. It is well known that the interpretative tradition, as much Greek as medieval and even modern (Werner Jaeger, Martin Heidegger, up to Pierre Aubenque), has here privileged the question of knowing if such a first philosophy, directly linked to a domain that is exceptional by definition (separated, unchanging and divine), could claim to assume all philosophical primacy, following a universality without remainder—say, the hermeneutic of the enigmatic formula justifying, for Aristotle, the primacy of the divine science, καθόλου οὕτωα ὅτι πρώτη [*katholou houtōs hoti prōtē*], universal in this way—because first. As famous and, without any doubt, decisive as it is, this debate must not hide another, for the universalization of the φιλοσοφία πρώτη [*philosophia prōtē, first philosophy*] only becomes a subject of debate if it first satisfies a prior, still more essential condition: it is necessary not only that the οὐσία [*ousia, substance, essence*] on which it bears can be universalized or universalize its authority, but, especially, that such an οὐσία be simply given. And Aristotle actually poses this condition of first philosophy: εἰ δ᾽ ἔστι τις οὐσία ἀκίνηντος [*ei d' esti tis ousia akinēntos*],[2] if, in any case, there is such an immutable essence.

Evidently, this reserve must not be understood as an indication of atheism, here anachronistic to the point of being self-contradictory. On the other hand, it can be understood in another way, perhaps strange to Aristotle, but surely not to our modern—thus necessarily nihilistic—attitude in this respect. What does such an οὐσία ἀκίνητη [*ousia akinētē,* immutable essence] signify for us? I am not envisaging here the aporias that the existence of such an entity could raise, nor its immutable, thus divine, character, precisely because even insofar as they are aporias, they have been entirely distanced from my questioning.[3] Let us consider the difficulty of the immovable essence in its simple guise of οὐσία: the Latin metaphysical usage has utilized at least two translations to explain it, from which it has imposed doublets in all modern philosophical languages—as *substance* or as *essence.* This division

---

[2] *Metaphysics* E 1, 1026a 29–31 and following, which will not be separated from the parallel of *Metaphysics* K 7 (on this point, I am following Emmanuel Martineau, "De l'inauthenticité du livre E de la *Métaphysique* d'Aristote," *Conférence* 5 (Autumn 1997). The equivocal nature of the primacy appears as early as its definition in *Metaphysics* Δ 11, where the list is concluded correctly by primacy according to the οὐσία (1019a 3ff.): but what is a last primacy, a primacy in the last instance? On these difficulties, see Pierre Aubenque, *Le problème de l'être chez Aristote: Essai sur la problématique aristotélicienne* (Paris: Presses Universitaires de France, 1962), pp. 38ff., 49–50, etc.

[3] As Rémi Brague has powerfully demonstrated in *La sagesse du monde: Histoire de l'expérience humaine de l'univers* (Paris: Fayard, 1999).

lacks, without any doubt, the Aristotelian stake of οὐσία, which is opposed to substrate (thus to materiality), such that it allows categorial predication and is accomplished by the passage from δυνάμι ζ [dynamis, power] to ἐνεργεία [energeia, agency, force], in a non-predicative unity. The dual translation suffices to render inaccessible what Aristotle had thought indissolubly, if not unitarily, in resolving the first difficulties from book Z by recourse to ἐνεργεία in the last chapters of Z and especially in book Θ.[4] Because the translation by substance will, in the end, impose itself completely without division, and because the concept of substance, in the light of the Cartesian (and already medieval) critique, will privilege the interpretation as substrate and according to predication, the aporia of origin will be all the more damaging. But the most patent aporia of such an οὐσία reduced to substance comes from an argument consecrated by René Descartes, which he already knew from the medieval authors: substance cannot be conceived without its attributes, but only the latter are knowable by us directly (here, extension and thought), such that substance, as such ". . . does not affect us."[5] Substance remains unknown as such, except according to its epistemological dependence on its attributes and its accidents. There is nothing more logical, then, than that David Hume and especially Immanuel Kant in the end only admitted it as a mere function of the understanding (concept of the understanding, no longer category of being [étant]) and therefore strictly limited its validity to phenomena alone, that is to say, exactly to that which οὐσία had to surpass for Aristotle. Its final disqualification by Friedrich Nietzsche went without saying: with substance it is only a question of a phantom concept that it would be appropriate to dismiss at the same time as the other metaphysical idols. Do we attempt to avoid this aporia by no longer under-

---

[4] As has been demonstrated, without truly affecting the "consecrated" usage, by the remarkable work of Rudolf Boehm, *Das Grundlegende und das Wesenliche* (The Hague: Martinus Nijhoff, 1965); *La "Métaphysique" d'Aristote: Le fondamental et l'essentiel,* trans. Emmanuel Martineau, with a note by Jean-François Courtine (Paris: Gallimard, 1976).

[5] *Principa Philosophiae* 1, §52, revisiting at least John Duns Scotus, *Ordinatio,* I, d. 3, p. 1, q. 3, n. 139 (*Opera omnia,* ed. Carolus Balic [Civitas Vaticana: Typis polyglottis vaticanis, 1950–54], vol. 3, p. 87); Francisco de Tolet, *Commentaria [. . .] in "De Anima,"* I, 1, 11, q. 6 (ed. Venice, 1574, in Étienne Gilson, *Index scolastico-cartésien* [Paris: F. Alcan, 1913], p. 280); Francisco Suarez, *Disputationes Metaphysicae* XXXVIII, s. 2, n. 8 (*Opera omnia,* ed. Charles Berton [Paris, 1856], vol. 26, p. 503). See my *Questions cartésiennes II* (Paris: Presses Universitaires de France, 1996), chapter III, §2, pp. 99ff.

standing the οὐσία as substance (substrate) but as an essence? But what remains today of the notion of essence, after the Cartesian refusal of substantial form (and, indissolubly, of final causality), after the rejection of inner ideas by John Locke and Hume (reducing essences to abstraction from general ideas), after the denegation of all "platonism" of significations in the second philosophy of Ludwig Wittgenstein? And finally, even if, in this context, we could imagine being able to hold onto something of the originally Aristotelian meaning of οὐσία, we would still expose ourselves to the stronger argument against it: in its intimate resonance with παρουσία [*parousia*, presence, advent], οὐσία thus reduces the being of the being to the primacy in it of presence, thus of permanence, that is to say, it declines being (*l'être*) to the benefit of that which persists in it, being (*l'étant*). By this means it is οὐσία itself, in its hypothetical unity, that engages the forgetting of being to the benefit of the inflation of being. Ousiology has taken over the question of the being of being and, even and especially when it is accomplished, it transforms into mere certitude of presence the primacy that wanted first to be focused on being and to be enriched with being's dignity.

I thus conclude that the justification of "first philosophy" by its attention to οὐσία seems weak, not only because it claims to bear on an unmoving and separate (divine) authority, which remains hypothetical even for Aristotle, but simply because it allows that such an authority can, as such (simply as οὐσία), be defined and understood, even though it does not manage to do so. Consequently, οὐσία can neither guarantee nor style a primacy for philosophy.

It can reasonably be objected that the real institution of the idea of "first philosophy," just like, for that matter, that of "metaphysics," proceeds less from Aristotle than from his descendants. Since I am evidently not claiming here to sketch a detailed history of philosophy, I will consider straightaway the position of Thomas Aquinas. Or, more precisely, I will follow his attempt to redefine the three different meanings of the unique science that are attributed to Aristotle under the borrowed and undecided title of "metaphysics": "It is called, in fact, divine science or *theology*, insofar as it considers substances said to be preliminary (*praedictae substantiae*). [It is called] *metaphysics*, insofar as it considers being (*l'étant*) and what follows from it. It is also called *first philosophy,* insofar as it considers the causes of things."[6] It could be understood in this way: the divine science, which is based on substances (and which suffers, for us moderns, from the impracticability of οὐσία in general), can and must be reinforced by two other sciences. First, by the science of being insofar as being (*l'étant*), already established by Aristotle in *Metaphysics* Γ 1, but which here receives the title of *metaphysica,* taken in a restrained sense. We know that this innovation, which essentially goes back to Thomas Aquinas, will have a determining importance on two counts: first, it will end in the science of *ontology;* next, it will concentrate in itself the ambiguity of onto-theology. But it is very clear that these two characteristics appear quite problematic today: first, ontology will only be historically deployed in the seventeenth century, as a science of being not insofar as it is, but insofar as it is known, quite the opposite of what Aristotle initiated in *Metaphysics* Γ 1; next, because the onto-theo-logy that flourishes here, far from consecrating the primacy of a "first philosophy," exposes it to a difficult compatibility with the other primacy, that of the divine, such that far from assuring the primacy of philosophy, it redoubles and weakens it. There remains, to make up for it, the third of the new sciences, the second of those here added to the *theologia,* which is defined not only explicitly as a *philosophia prima* but above all in terms astonishingly different from those of the φιλοσοφία πρώτη: it is no longer a question of considering an οὐσία, but the *causae* of things, of οὐσίαι [*ousiai*] from now on separated from "first philosophy" by the supplementary step of the cause. Now, as God causes not only created beings (ontic causality) but also their beingness and even their *esse* (ontological causality), the consideration of causes by *philosophia prima* will lead, in another mode, to that which φιλοσοφία πρώτη already took into account—God. Nevertheless, Aquinas fixes a limit to this approach: in God, cause does without οὐσία and is exercised as (coming from) pure *esse* [to be, act of being]. Does this displacement nevertheless suffice to validate, *for us,* "first philosophy," or more precisely, a primacy for philosophy? It can doubtlessly be contested: the concept of cause, as, for that matter, all the categories of metaphysics, had to be withdrawn from the things themselves and fall

---

[6] Thomas Aquinas, *In duodecim libros Metaphysicorum Aristotelis expositio.* ed. M. R. Cathala (Taurini, Rome: Marietti, 1964), p. 2.

back on the mere "simple natures" (Descartes) or "concepts of the understanding" (Kant).[7] The illegitimacy of their transcendent usage beyond the limits of possible experience, concretely beyond the limits of sensible intuition, follows; as a consequence, causality can neither attain the divine nor, therefore, here assure a "first philosophy." More generally, cause no longer allows us to secure any primacy at all, since the possibility of reversing the priority between the cause (which "explains") and the effect (which alone "proves") has been shown—and thus, in fact, existence precedes cause, which only comments on it (as Descartes and Nietzsche have established).[8] And, besides, did Aquinas not agree with this when, after having reached God following the guiding thread of causality, he vigorously refused to conceive God according and subject to cause, in rejecting the pertinence of any *causa sui* [cause of itself] and in leaving the divine *esse incausatum* [being uncaused]?[9] It is therefore necessary to conclude, here again, that no more than οὐσία, *cause* can neither guarantee nor qualify a primacy for philosophy.

3. THE THIRD FIRST PHILOSOPHY

Nevertheless, do these two denegations of "first philosophy" not designate, as if in spite of themselves, a completely different result—a way open in an opposing sense? Against the two first exceptions from primacy, they argue, in effect, from another anteriority, from another primacy, that of the noetic over cause and over οὐσία, which lose their primacy before—precisely—conditions of knowledge henceforth held

---

[7] See my study "Konstanten der kritischen Vernunft" in Hans Friedrich Fulda and Rolf-Peter Hortsmann, eds., *Vernunftbegriffe in der Moderne.* Veröffentlichung der Internationalen Hegel-Vereinigung 20 (Stuttgart: Klett Cotta, 1994), reprinted as "Constances de la raison critique—Descartes et Kant," in *Questions cartésiennes II,* chapter VIII, §4, pp. 298ff.

[8] René Descartes, *Discours de la Méthode,* in *Oeuvres de Descartes, publiées par Charles Adam et Paul Tannery* (Paris: L. Cerf, 1897–1913) [hereafter AT] VI, 6–22, p. 76; and Friedrich Nietzsche, "Les quatre grandes erreurs," §§1–5, *Crépuscule des idoles,* trans. Henri Albert (Paris: Flammarion, 1985).

[9] On Thomas, see my study "Saint Thomas d'Aquin et l'onto-théo-logie," *Revue Thomiste* 14, no. 1 (1995): 31–66. On this debate in general, see Albert Zimmermann, *Ontologie oder Metaphysik? Die Diskussion über den Gegenstand der Metaphysik im 13. und 14. Jahrhundert, Texte und Untersuchungen* (Leiden/Cologne: E. J. Brill, 1965).

forever to be prior. From that point on, why not envisage defining primacy directly by the priority of knowledge, substituting in this way the primacy of the noetic for that of the ontic? Would it not then become possible to establish a third figure of "first philosophy" on this new primacy? These hypotheses are justified all the more that they define the explicit tactic put to work by Descartes, like Kant.

When he justifies the title of his ". . . *Meditationes de prima Philosophia . . . ,*" Descartes specifies without any ambiguity his very new concept of "first philosophy": ". . . I scarcely treat in particular of God and the soul, but in general of all the first things that can be known in philosophizing"; repeating the same thesis in another letter, he even adds there: ". . . in philosophizing in order."[10] Thus he redefines the primacy, no longer starting with certain ontically privileged οὐσίαι or αἰτίαι [*aitiai,* causes, reasons] (separate essences, essences in act, the divine, and so on), but following a purely noetic anteriority: the order of acts of knowledge, according to the "order of reasons," which disposes ". . . all things in certain series, certainly not insofar as they are referred to a certain type of being *(ad aliquod genus entis),* as the Philosophers had divided them, following their categories, but insofar as they are able to be known, the one from the others *(unae ex aliis cognosci possunt)."*[11] That which can first be known for certain (simple natures) is first in philosophy, without presupposing anything, and whatever this sole truth might be (their combinations)—whether it is a question of a finite truth *(ego sum* [I am]), an abstract truth *(ego cogito* [I think]), a formal truth (equation, figure, equality, and so on), or even an empty truth *(ego dubito* [I doubt]), rather than existent, infinite, or physical truths, and so on, which would become known by deduction from others, more abstract and more simple. For ontic excellence gives way to noetic excellence in the hierarchization of first terms, which only become first in being known, never again insofar as they are beings.

When Kant, a Cartesian in spite of himself, claims that ". . . the proud name of an ontology, which claims to give synthetic knowledge

---

[10] René Descartes, *Lettres à Mersenne,* 11 novembre 1640, AT III, p. 235, 15–18, and p. 239, 2–7.

[11] René Descartes, *Regulae ad directionem ingenii,* VI, AT X, p. 381, 10–14; *René Descartes: Regles utiles et claires pour la direction de l'esprit en la recherche de la vérité,* trans. Jean-Luc Marion and Pierre Costabel (The Hague: Martinus Nijhoff, 1977), p. 17.

a priori of things in general in a systematic doctrine (for example, the principle of causality), yields its place to a straightforward analytic of the pure understanding,"[12] he accordingly ratifies the passage of the two former primacies to that of knowledge; but in fact, he only dismisses the former ontic (and etiological) primacy of the οὐσία in paradoxically recovering the sense of the modern *ontologia* that he thinks he has ruined. In effect, Johannes Clauberg, who had definitively consecrated the term in metaphysics after its still imprecise introduction by Rudolph Goclenius (in 1613), justifies the privileged object of this new science—the *intelligibile* [rational] rather than the *aliquid* [something] or the substance—by the argument that it is necessary to begin ". . . universal philosophy with the cogitable being, in the same way that first philosophy, beginning with the singular, considers nothing before cogitating thought."[13] Noetic primacy in this way allows not

---

[12] Immanuel Kant, *Critique de la raison pure*, A247/B303.

[13] Johannes Clauberg: "Entis initio statim tres distinguendae significationes. Nam vel denotat omne quod cogitari potest (distinctionis causa nonnullis vocatur *Intelligibile*) et huic non potest opponi quicquam; vel notat id, quod revera *Aliquid* est, nemine etiam cogitante, cui opponitur Nihil; vel significat *Rem,* quae per se existit, ut Substantia, cui solent opponi Accidentia. / Quamvis autem Ens in tertia significiatione acceptum, sit potissimum illud, quod in Ontologia per sua attributa ac divisiones explicatur, tamen *ad meliorem* hujus *notitiam* comparandam nonnulla de Ente prima et secunda acceptione praetermittemus, incohaturi universalem philosophiam ab *Ente cogitabili,* quemadmodum a singularis incipiens* prima philosophia nihil prius considerat *Mente cogitante.*" The note* referred to here sends us back explicitly to Descartes: "[*Prima philosophia*] sic dicta non propter universalitatem objecti, de quo agit; sed quod serio philosophaturus ab ea debeat incipere. Nempe a cogitatione suae mentis et Dei, etc. Haec prima philosophia sex Meditationibus Cartesii continetur. Summam ejus etiam prima pars Principiorum exhibet." *Metaphysica de Ente quae rectius Ontosophia.* . . . (Groningen, 1647; Amsterdam, 1663), §§4–5, in *Opera philosophica omnia,* vol. 1 (Amsterdam, 1691; reprint Darmstadt, 1968), p. 283. Here it is remarkable that the "potissimum" ontology, which is about being (thus the Aristotelian project), is found explicitly opposed and submitted to the ontology of the one who "philosophizes seriously" (according to the order of reason) and must begin with the intelligible, that is to say, with the *Mens cogitans:* henceforth, the concept of "ontology" is thus divided in itself and dismisses the οὐσία in itself. Kant will ratify this decision: "The first and the most important question of ontology is to know how *a priori knowledge* is possible. . . . [T]he supreme concept of all *human knowledge* is the concept of an object in general, *not that of being and non-being.*" *Vorlesungen über Metaphysik und Rationaltheologie,* ed. M. Pölitz, AK, A., 28.2,1 (Berlin: de Gruyter, 1970), p. 540, 54; *Leçons de métaphysique: Emmanuel Kant,* trans. Monique Castillo, Le Livre de Poche (Paris: Librarie Générale Française, 1993), pp. 133–35, my emphasis. It could not be said more clearly: ontology, in the metaphysical sense, is not the science of being, but the science of science itself. The noetic primacy of "first philosophy" leads to criticism, in no way to beings insofar as being (*l'étant*).

only the refounding of "first philosophy" but also the reconnecting of first philosophy with ontology, or rather with that which metaphysics has always understood under its modern name—the science of the *knowledge* of being in general, insofar as it is reduced to what is intelligible, that is to say to the *cogitabile* [conceivable], such that it responds to the *a priori* conditions of its appearance to an *ego cogito*. Noetic primacy of this last type finally founds an unshakable "first philosophy."

It is seen immediately that this transfer to and this refoundation of primacy on the noetic authority alone themselves rely entirely on the primacy of the *I*. But can the *I* itself be founded in a sufficiently radical way to ensure of its primacy that of "first philosophy"? Can it justify its claim to as inaugural a primacy? There precisely is that which philosophy has never ceased, in its march toward and within nihilism, to put in question. Two major arguments are at work in this regard. First, the *I* can only legitimately exercise its noetic primacy in assuming a transcendental status—not that of one object among others, even transcendent, but of a unique, non-objectlike authority, which fixes the conditions of possibility of the knowledge of objects. Now, this status necessarily separates the transcendental *I* from the empirical *I* and opposes to it the object-ness hostile to the me; that which, in me, can be known according to space and time becomes an object, thus cannot be confused with that which *I,* insofar as transcendental, am. Inversely, this *I* that I am cannot nor should not, by definition, be known as an object; thus, *I* do not coincide with the *me* that I know, and I do not know the *I* that I am. Between being and self-knowledge, the *ego* must choose—and in both cases, be lost. This dichotomy will never be surpassed by modern (post-Cartesian) metaphysics, not even with Husserl, because it will initially be defined by it. Further still: just as this truly first *I,* because transcendental, is not known to me, it leaves me universal; it is not sufficiently able to individualize me (in space and time or otherwise); thus, in stripping me of my individuality, it renders me unfit for any access to another person—except in reducing the other to the rank of an object, in the manner of my empirical me. The transcen-

---

Many of the defenses today, reactive to "ontology," are unaware of this original ambiguity and thus uphold the misinterpretation they destroy, or destroy that which they believe they maintain. See Vincent Carraud, "L'ontologie peut-elle être cartésienne?" in Theo Verbeek, ed., *Johannes Clauberg (1622–1665) and Cartesian Philosophy in the Seventeenth Century* (Dordrecht: Kluwer, 1999).

dental turn of the *I,* on the one hand, leaves it without ontic determination (the *I* is not anyone), and on the other separates it from itself (the *I* is completely unfamiliar with the empirical me). It could even be ventured that, until the nonspecific universality of *Dasein,* this split does not suffer any exceptions. As a consequence, noetic primacy has a price: the disappearance or the putting in parenthesis of the one who plays the role of first, without being [*l'être*].

Supposing that this primacy can be accomplished even without the ontic individuation of the *I,* it would still be exposed to a second, more severe argument: noetic primacy, the possible base of all modern "first philosophy," implies perhaps no single thematized primacy in any *I* whatever—just because, by its own avowal, it does not claim any individuality, any identity, any *haecceitas* [this-ness]. Even if knowledge is deployed without precedent and without any foundation other than itself, it can be deployed, although (or because) it thinks following an anonymous process, without origin or assignable subject. Or, if one wants absolutely to maintain that a subject thinks everywhere where thought is being thought, then why would it be more the author of it than the screen and the place of welcome for it? Two reasons favor this hypothesis: (a) first, the impossibility, even uselessness, of attributing any substantiality to the *ego.* Kant denied it with precision in the *paralogisms,* but by doing so he only accomplished the aporias already recognized by Descartes, Locke, and Bishop Berkeley: the concept of substance cannot be applied univocally to finite subjectivity facing the infinite, precisely because it is deduced from the latter, which precedes it.[14] (b) Next, finite subjectivity, even if it thinks all the thinkable, unthinkable without it, could produce it, or rather re-produce it, re-think it in an empirical mode without giving rise to it. For the thinkable depends, more originally than on its performance in the time of history and of intersubjectivity, on that which is proposed to thought as intrinsically rational: logical, formal, or even structural demands not only decide on well-constructed propositions, alone given sense, but also

---

[14] See my *Questions cartésiennes I: Méthode et métaphysique* (Paris: Presses Universitaires de France, 1991), chapter III, §4, pp. 108ff.; *Cartesian Questions,* trans. Jeffrey L. Kosky, John Cottingham, and Stephen Voss (Chicago: University of Chicago Press, 1999), pp. 65ff.; and *Sur le prisme métaphysique de Descartes: Constitution et limites de l'onto-théo-logie de la pensée cartésienne* (Paris: Presses Universitaires de France, 1986), chapter III, §13, pp. 180ff.; *On Descartes' Metaphysical Prism: The Constitution and the Limits of Onto-theo-logy in Cartesian Thought,* trans. Jeffrey L. Kosky (Chicago: University of Chicago Press, 1999), pp. 169ff.

assess the admissible validity of vagueness, approximations, and quasi-formulations of everyday discourse ("effects of language," "gossip of the They," and so on). The empirical me is limited to repetition, most often approximative, of the thinkable, without ever drawing from it the least primacy, neither, of course, ontic (not having claimed, for a long time, the role of οὐσία)[15] nor even noetic: this is thought within me, who officiates behind the scenes, without inaugurating or mastering the thought. Let us not stress this argument, since it has been put to work *ad nauseam* so much since Nietzsche and Michel Foucault by the "human sciences" and the ideologies that go with that.

These few reflections will suffice at least to pose the inevitable conclusion: none of the types of primacy that metaphysics has ever been able to propose—by οὐσία, by cause, and by the noetic—can assure, today and for us, the legitimacy of any primacy for philosophy, in short, of a "first philosophy."[16]

4. PHENOMENOLOGY AS THE POSSIBILITY OF ANOTHER FIRST PHILOSOPHY

Nevertheless, this conclusion did not prevent Husserl, at the historical moment of the indisputable advent of nihilism, from claiming the traditional title of "first philosophy" for phenomenology. The famous course of 1923–24 that bears this title makes this clear from the beginning: "If I pick up the expression coined by Aristotle, it is because I rightly draw profit and advantage from that which has fallen into disuse and no longer evokes for us anything but its strictly literal meaning, and not the numerous, varied sediments, put down by the historical tradition, which mix confusedly under the vague concept of metaphysics the memories of diverse types of metaphysics of the past." This is a strange argument: it is precisely because one can no longer remember

---

[15] The same demonstration could be repeated, without difficulty and without other references, with regard to the relinquishing of the function of αἰτία, that the *ego* cannot assure, seeing that this concept has neither transcendental validity (Kant), nor physical efficacy (Nicolas de Malebranche, Werner Karl Heisenberg).

[16] As a complement to these analyses, see my essay "La science toujours recherché et toujours manquante" in Jean-Marc Narbonne and Luc Langlois, eds., *La métaphysique: Son histoire, sa critique, ses enjeux* (Acts of the 27th Congress of the Association des sociétés de philosophie de langue française) (Paris: J. Vrin; Laval: Les Presses de l'Université Laval, 1999), pp. 13–36.

anything of its real accomplishments (*philosophia prima,* φιλοσοφία πρώτη) that one can maintain all the more the principle of a "first philosophy," redefined very formally as "a scientific discipline of the beginnings." How is it to be understood? By the complete equivocity of the phrase? But Husserl immediately dismisses this hypothesis in maintaining that ". . . with the breakthrough of the new transcendental phenomenology a first breakthrough of a true and authentic *first philosophy* was already accomplished."[17] In short, phenomenology takes up again (or claims to take up again) the entire project of "first philosophy" and is in this way constituted as the philosophy with which it is necessary to begin, in order then to put to work the second philosophies or regional sciences. Let us therefore proceed to another hypothesis: the unequivocal renewal of this science would escape the metaphysical aporias (οὐσία, *causa,* subjectivity), because phenomenology would no longer belong to metaphysics. This pretension remains to be justified, since it is not at all obvious. Note that the successors of Husserl hesitated to taint their essays—which expressed a rupture with metaphysics [*essai de rupture avec la métaphysique*]—with this apparently heavily metaphysical comment, "first philosophy." Even Heidegger, although he had at one time wanted to maintain a "[fundamental] ontology" and the use of "metaphysics," before giving it up, never risked claiming the title of "first philosophy." Nor did Jean-Paul Sartre, Maurice Merleau-Ponty, Paul Ricoeur, and Michel Henry, not to mention Jacques Derrida. Nevertheless, one of Husserl's successors, and not the least (was he not the first to win France over to his thought?), Emmanuel Levinas, took explicitly as his responsibility the revindication of Husserl. For in bringing to the foreground the fundamental dignity of ontology, or rather in order to threaten it better, he concluded his demonstration in these terms: "Ethics is not a branch of philosophy, but first philosophy."[18] There would therefore not have been any proper

---

[17] Edmund Husserl, *Erste Philosophie (1923–24). Erste Teil: Kritische Ideengeschichte,* in *Husserliana* [hereafter Hua.] VII, ed. Rudolph Boehm (The Hague: Martinus Nijhoff, 1956), §1, pp. 3, 5; *Philosophie première,* trans. Arion L. Kelkel (Paris: Presses Universitaires de France, 1970), I, §1, pp. 3, 5.

[18] Emmanuel Levinas, *Totalité et infini: Essai sur l'extériorité* (The Hague: Martinus Nijhoff, 1961; Paris: Livre de Poche, Librairie Générale Française, 1990); *Totality and Infinity: An Essay on Exteriority,* trans. Alphonso Lingis (Pittsburgh: Duquesne University Press, 1969), p. 304 (penultimate paragraph of the conclusion). This is confirmed by a later text: "First philosophy is an ethics." *Ethique et infini: Dialogues avec Philippe Nemo* (Paris: Fayard, 1982), p. 81; *Ethics and Infinity: Dialogues with*

incompatibility between phenomenology and "first philosophy." To claim it and to be scandalized by it only proves a poor attention to the texts or a frankly ideological afterthought. Each of them leaves me indifferent. Besides, it could be that in order to attribute "first philosophy" even to phenomenology, it is not necessary to compromise it with the reflux of metaphysics or make it regress toward onto-theo-logy, but, completely the opposite, clarify radically its nature and project. For phenomenology—which claims to be a "breakthrough," a "new start," even one of the dominant figures of all contemporary philosophy—must inevitably recognize a primacy, or at least agree to have a primacy attributed to it. But has this primacy been sufficiently explicated? Its rupture with the metaphysical face of philosophy, a rupture always to be reconquered and consolidated, demands that it define anew its new primacy—and in terms that repeat nothing of the three metaphysical definitions of primacy. To try to clarify the sense and the bearing of another meaning of "first philosophy," assigned to phenomenology, will not mean to fold it back on what it wants to go beyond, but to try a crucial experiment on the type and the mode of its primacy, in order to establish if and in what drastic conditions it earns that to which it lays claim, to see if it accomplishes what it promises: it means nothing less than to recommence philosophy in the time of nihilism. It is not a question of going back to metaphysics, but of determining if the figure of "first philosophy" that phenomenology sometimes assumes allows it to find the new ground of an unconditioned primacy, without which it would escape the title of philosophy—the title, and the very thing itself. To this end, I will proceed in four stages: (a) to determine the principle of phenomenology; (b) to expose the recourse to givenness in its relationship to the reduction; (c) to raise some objections against the intelligibility of givenness; and (d) to assure the primacy of the new domain of givenness.

Philippe Nemo, trans. Richard A. Cohen (Pittsburgh: Duquesne University Press, 1985), p. 77. This is to be compared with: "The relation with the Other is thus not an ontology." "L'ontologie est-elle fondamentale?" *Revue de métaphysique et de morale* 56, no. 1 (1951), reprinted in *Entre Nous: Essais sur le penser-à-l'autre* (Paris: Éditions Grasset et Fasquelle, 1991), p. 20; "Is Ontology Fundamental?" *Entre Nous: Thinking-of-the-Other*, trans. Michael B. Smith and Barbara Harshav (New York: Columbia University Press, 1998), pp. 1–11, 7. Whence is drawn the title of the collection *Emmanuel Levinas: L'éthique comme philosophie première*, ed. Jean Greisch and Jacques Rolland (Paris: Presses Universitaires de France, 1993). (I thus give up willingly, in the opinion of Jean Greisch, my reserve on the first state of this text.)

To determine the principle of phenomenology can seem, at first
glance, all the easier since Husserl mobilized many explicit formulas
to reach it; but this very multiplication can also cause disquiet: a single
formula suffices for a principle to be first; on the other hand, many
formulas confuse primacy. Let us proceed, then, to review the three
formulas used by Husserl. The first, "as much appearing, as much
being," keeps a clearly metaphysical origin: first, because it derives
from metaphysics, in the case of Johann Friedrich Herbart.[19] This is
especially because it makes use of the couple seeming/being, the perfectly metaphysical scope of which it limits itself to reversing (as
Nietzsche sometimes does, for that matter): seeming accedes to the
rank of being, but their duality subsists intact. Finally, this principle
exposes neither why nor how this operation is practiced—in other
words, by the reduction, ostensibly absent here. The second formulation, "Return to the things themselves!,"[20] suffers from a double imprecision, first concerning the identity of these things (are they empirical
realities or "matters" at stake?) and then concerning the operation of
inversion that would allow this return itself; in short, in both cases the
reduction is always missing, by fault of which the slogan would quickly

[19] Edmund Husserl, *Cartesianische Meditationen und Pariser Vorträge,* in Hua. I,
ed. Stephen Strasser (The Hague: Martinus Nijhoff, 1973), §46, p. 133; *Méditations
cartésiennes,* trans. Marc B. de Launay, Jean-Luc Marion, et al. (Paris: Presses Universitaires de France, 1994), pp. 152 etc.; *Cartesian Meditations,* trans. Dorion Cairns
(The Hague: Martinus Nijhoff, 1970), p. 103 ["so much illusion, so much being"],
and taken up again by Martin Heidegger, *Sein und Zeit,* 7th ed. (Tübingen: Niemeyer,
1953), §7, p. 36; *Gesamtausgabe* [hereafter GA] II (Frankfurt am Main: Klostermanon,
1977), p. 48; *Being and Time,* trans. John Macquarrie and Edward Robinson (Oxford:
Blackwell, 1960), p. 60 ["so much semblance, so much 'Being'"]; [see also the newer
translation by Joan Stambaugh (Albany: State University of New York Press, 1996),
p. 32: "where there is semblance there is 'being'"]. See Johann Friedrich Herbart,
Hauptpunkte der Metaphysik (Göttingen: J. F. Danckwerts, 1808), in *Sämmliche
Werke,* ed. Carl Kehrbach et al. (Aalen: Scientia, 1964), p. 187, and Marion, *Étant
donné,* p. 19.
[20] Edmund Husserl, *Ideen zu einer reinen Phänomenologie und phänomenologischen Philosophie. Erstes Buch: Allgemeine Einführung in die reine Phänomenologie,*
in Hua. III, ed. Walter Biemel (The Hague: Martinus Nijhoff, 1950), §19, pp. 42–43;
*Idées directrices pour une phénoménologie, Première Livre: Introduction générale à
la phénoménologie,* trans. Paul Ricoeur (Paris: Gallimard, 1950), pp. 63–64 etc.;
Ideas: General Introduction to Pure Phenomenology, Book 1, trans. W. R. Boyce
Gibson (London: Allen and Unwin, 1972), pp. 82–83 [see also the newer translation
by Frederick I. Kersten, *Ideas Pertaining to a Pure Phenomenology and to a Phenomenological Philosophy,* vol. 2 of *Edmund Husserl, Collected Works* (The Hague, Boston,
London: Martinus Nijhoff, 1982)].

sink into a-theoretical cynicism: let us not bother with concepts and distinctions, the "things" are found before us (a refusal to reason)! Regarding the famous third formula—incidentally, the only one qualifying for the title of "principle of principles" and alone invented by Husserl—it postulates that ". . . every giving intuition is a proper source for knowledge, that all that which is offered originally to us in intuition . . . must be simply received as that which is given."[21] Its authority cannot, accordingly, be contested, but it must be limited: (i) According to what right does intuition decide all phenomenality? Does this Kantian presupposition, even corrected by the addition of the vision of essences and of categorial intuition, not submit all phenomena to that which intuition fulfills, that is to say, to the condition of all intuition of fulfillment—intentionality? Now, would intentionality not first or even exclusively be defined by the object at which it aims? Would phenomenology thus limit itself only to object-ness? Would it be strictly limited from its beginning? (ii) Furthermore, what is a principle linked to intuition especially worth if it intervenes *before,* thus also perhaps *without,* the operation (and the simple mention) of the reduction? How are we to accord to it the least priority if it ignores the operation about which Husserl did not cease to repeat, until the end, that it conditions the entire phenomenological enterprise which its omission also ruins irretrievably? (iii) Finally, what role does givenness play here: explicitly utilized as the criterion and the achievement of the phenomenality that intuition delivers, it nevertheless remains undetermined as such. Givenness here comes into view at once as the last criterion and as the absolute uninterrogated.

These obvious insufficiencies have led me to propose a fourth and last formulation of a possible first principle of phenomenology: "As much reduction, as much givenness."[22] I base it on, among many other texts, two sequences from Husserl, drawn from the very work that first made the theory of the reduction, *The Idea of Phenomenology* (1907). First: "It is through a *reduction,* which we would now like to call the phenomenological reduction, that I gain an *absolute givenness* not owing anything to transcendence." Next: ". . . the *givenness of a re-*

[21] Husserl, Hua. III, §24, p. 52; *Idées directrices,* I, p. 78; *Ideas,* I, p. 92.

[22] See Marion, *Réduction et donation,* p. 303; *Reduction and Givenness,* p. 203, commented on and deepened by Michel Henry in "Quatre principes de la phenomenology," *Revue de métaphysique et de morale* 96, no. 1 (January 1991): 3–26. This analysis has been developed in Marion, *Étant donné,* §1, "Le dernier principe," pp. 13–31.

duced phenomenon in general is an absolute and indubitable givenness."[23] In this way confirmed by the Husserlian letter,[24] my formula
henceforth reveals its essential interest: it alone explicitly thinks the
givenness of the given—givenness, where in fact the appearing passes
into being [*l'être*] (first formula), where one returns effectively to the
matters at stake (second formula), and where intuition authorizes to
appear (third formula), but from now on always starting from the operation that provokes it, the reduction. No givenness without reduction,
no reduction that does not lead to a givenness. Now, the reduction
eliminates all transcendence, that is to say, the intentional ecstasy of
consciousness toward its objective, which alone allows knowledge
of it, but also incertitude, error, illusion, and so on; thus the givenness
of the given, on the express condition that it is already reduced, reduced
to the pure given, becomes absolutely indubitable. Doubt can only be
instilled in a not-yet-reduced perception, where one takes equally and
confusedly for granted that which is not truly given and that which
the reduction has brought back to a given without remainder, without
shadow, without aura. The reduction alone gives the phenomenon, be-

---

[23] Edmund Husserl, *Die Idee der Phänomenologie: Fünf Vorlesungen,* in Hua. II,
ed. Walter Biemel (The Hague: Martinus Nijhoff, 1973), pp. 44 and 50; *L'idée de la
phénoménologie: Cinq leçons,* trans. Alexandre Lowith (Paris: Presses Universitaires
de France, 1970), pp. 68 and 76 (my emphasis); *The Idea of Phenomenology,* trans.
William P. Alston and George Nakhnikian (The Hague: Martinus Nijhoff, 1964), pp.
34 and 40 [see also the newer translation by Lee Henly, in *Edmund Husserl: Collected
Works,* vol. 8, ed. Rudolf Bernet (Dordrecht: Kluwer Academic, 1999)]. The French
translation, otherwise excellent, renders improperly *"donation* [fr.], *Gegebenheit,"* by
"presence" (pp. 68 and 76)—whereas it is precisely a question here of going beyond
it, if we intend, by phenomenology, to get rid of the "metaphysics of presence" (see
below, chapter 6, §1, pp. 128ff.).

[24] Except, of course, refusing to read the texts by declaring, without further ado, that
"[. . .] *The Idea of Phenomenology* is not a reliable text [why?] and thus cannot,
without precautions [which?] play the role that it is made to play in . . . *Étant
donné.* . . ." [insertions by Jean-Luc Marion—Trans.] Denis Fisette, "Phénoménologie
et métaphysique: remarques à propos d'un débat recent," in Jean-Marc Narbonne and
Luc Langlois, eds., *La métaphysique: Son histoire, sa critique, ses enjeux,* p. 101. Is it
necessary to restate that, in front of a text, it is not a question of making it play a role,
whatever that may be, but of reading it and of admitting what one understands of
it—and of not, oneself, playing the least role, especially not that of the suspicious one?
As for the reliability of this text, let us remember that Husserl considered it to be his
Critique of Pure Reason (*The Idea of Phenomenology,* part VII) and as ". . . a new
beginning, which, unfortunately, has not been understood and welcomed by my stu-
dents as I had hoped" (cited by Lowith in the "Foreword to the Reader" of his excellent French translation, p. 33, after Walter Biemel). The readers have not all changed
since.

cause it dissolves in it the semblances of a given, just as a distillation leads to a reduced solution. None of the reproaches banally addressed to the supposed intuitionism of phenomenology, to its so-called naive confidence in the evidence or to its supposed complaisance with subjectivity, could sustain a moment's attention if the radicality of the reduction were taken really seriously, such that it suspends precisely in each of these cases the transcendences that make the given fragile. If philosophy is deployed immanently (which is often claimed, but without always taking the means to think it through), then phenomenology, following the principle "As much reduction, as much givenness," merits, *par excellence,* the title of philosophy.

The intimate interconnection between reduction and givenness thus defines the principle of phenomenology. What appears gives itself, that is to say, it appears without restraint or remainder; it thus comes about [*ad-vient*], happens, and imposes itself as such, not as the semblance or the representative of an absent or dissimulated in-itself, but as itself, in person and in the flesh; what appears is emptied totally, so to speak (with its essential being [*estance*], its innermost depth of substance, its material individuation, and so on), to the point of passing from the rank of image, from simple seeming or bereft appearance, to the one unique thing at stake. And if the phenomenon did not give itself as such, it would remain simply the other of being [*être*]. But then, how does it succeed in giving itself and not remain the simple image of itself without itself? Because the reduction eliminates from the process of appearing all that which is not given without reserve: semblances and confusions, inventions or given memories, all linked to transcendences that merge the lived experience (possibly intentional) with the object intended (by definition only sketched), are marked, filtered, and finally separated from the remaining given. It is therefore necessary that the reduction control givenness, taking it back to its given (or noematic) core. In this way, under the strict condition that the reduction is accomplished correctly, it becomes "absurd"[25] to envisage that givenness does not give the given with certainty. And it follows that the given of givenness suffers no doubt.

---

[25] Edmund Husserl, *Logische Untersuchungen* II.I (Tübingen: Niemeyer, 1913), V, supplement to §11, 2, p. 425; *Recherches Logiques, 2: Recherches pour la phénoménologie et la théorie de la connaissance, 1re partie: Recherches I et II,* trans. Hubert Élie, Lothar Kelkel, and René Schérer (Paris: Presses Universitaires de France, 1961), p. 231; *Logical Investigations,* trans. J. N. Findlay, vol. 2 (London: Routledge and Kegan Paul, 1970), p. 595.

Is this a question of a repetition of the unconditional certitude of the *ego sum, ego existo* [I am, I exist]? Despite the habit of bringing them together, acquired since Husserl himself, I would insist first on that which distinguishes them. According to Descartes, the absolute certitude of this first truth only concerns precisely the domain of thought returning on itself, more exactly, its auto-affection. But, and the difficulty of then conquering other truths will affirm this, auto-affection remains essentially trapped in a real solipsism between the acquired thing (*res cogitans* [thinking thing]) and the other thing, inaccessible, or virtually inaccessible; for God and the world remain inaccessible perhaps in a certain sense, but the other person surely remains so. According to phenomenology, absolute certitude resides in the affectedness of consciousness by lived experiences from every origin, not only, or even entirely, by thought of self, on the express condition, nevertheless, that these lived experiences accomplish a givenness—that they give themselves completely and irremediably and, in certain cases, that they also engage intentional objects on each occasion involved. It is thus every lived experience (and possibly the intentional object) that, if it gives itself according to a reduction, is confirmed absolutely. In other words, phenomenology universalizes the Cartesian result: it does not support the *ego* alone and to itself, it certifies a whole world, because it no longer bases it on thought (thinking itself), but on the given as it gives itself (to consciousness). Certainly, this displacement would regress toward empiricism if the intentional given of the lived experience were the same as the sensible given (the *sens data*); but the given follows a scrupulous reduction, thus gives itself in an immanence that is itself reduced. In this way the given phenomenon includes, with the experience of its givenness, the experience of its certitude. One would not doubt a given, because either one considers it precisely insofar as given and, whatever its given mode (sensible intuition, imagination, vision of essences, categorical intuition and so on), it will be given, or else one will meet there with a deception, which simply attests that, by mistake (in fact, by a lack of reduction), one has taken as a given what has not given itself authentically—but which nevertheless was already given without any doubt, in another mode simply not yet distinguished in its specificity. There can and must be indefinite degrees of givenness, but no exception. In short, as Husserl would say: "Absolute givenness is an ultimate term."[26]

---

[26] "Absolute Gegebenheit ist ein Letztes." Husserl, Hua. II, p. 61; *L'idée de la phenomenologie,* p. 86 (corrected); *The Idea of Phenomenology,* p. 49.

From this certitude it therefore strangely follows that givenness, in-asmuch as certain, is also universalized. About what can we say that it does not appear as given? How would it appear—whatever it is, and in whatever manner it appears—if it did not give itself to any possible degree? To try to measure the unlimited fullness of the given, Husserl established a list (provisional, in my view) of what is given in diverse modes: thought, immediate memory (or retention), the unity of appear-ance in the flux of lived experiences of consciousness, their variations, the thing of so-called "external" perception, the diverse forms of imag-ination and memory (secondary), and other synthetic representations, but also logical givens (predicates, universals, states of things), es-sences, mathematical entities—or better: even nonsense and contradic-tions attest to a givenness. And as Husserl concluded: "*Everywhere givenness,* whether a mere representation or a true being is promised in it, real or ideal, possible or impossible, *is a givenness in the phenom-enon of knowledge,* in the phenomenon of thought in the most general sense of the word."[27] This indicates two decisive results. (i) Givenness is equivalent in fact to the phenomenon itself, the two sides of which, the appearing (from the side of consciousness) and that which appears (from the side of the thing), are articulated according to the principle of an "admirable correlation" only because the first is taken as a given, given by and according to the second, givenness itself. Without enter-ing further here into a demonstration conducted elsewhere, I take as understood that the fold of the phenomenon, such as it is unfolded in the appearing, would be equal to the fold of givenness, such that it harbors in it the given. This equivalence in fact follows directly from the identity between givenness and the reduction: the given reduced to the rank of full and radical phenomenon. Otherwise formulated by Husserl: that which is named ". . . effectively an absolute givenness *(eine absolute Gegebenheit)*" is not the psychological phenomenon but ". . . only the pure phenomenon, [the] reduced [phenomenon] *(das reine Phänomen, das reduzierte). . . .*"[28] (ii) Whence the other result: if everything appears as phenomenon—and as a phenomenon—then nothing would make an exception to givenness. Here again I cannot entirely set out the demonstration, but, on the model of the critique by Henri Bergson of the idea of nothingness (which always ends in an-

---

[27] Husserl, Hua. II, p. 74; *L'idée de la phenomenologie,* p. 100 (I have corrected it and emphasised my correction in the text); *The Idea of Phenomenology,* p. 59.

[28] Husserl, Hua. II, p. 74; *L'idée de la phenomenologie,* p. 100; *The Idea of Phenom-enology,* p. 59.

other given), one could confirm, rather than contradict, the most out-standing analyses of Heidegger. For even nothingness ends—or would like, at least, to end—in staging the phenomenon of being in distinction from beings as phenomena; even death still gives, since it allows *Dasein* to accede to its being-able-to-die, that is to say, to go beyond the ontically contradictory phenomenon of the factual demise of the other person, in order to reach its own phenomenality oriented toward the future. It is the same with the always possible description of absence (or for any privation that is possible), which always designates a specific absence and thus makes it appear as such for me.

A confirmation of the universality of givenness, at first unexpected but in fact very logical, can be recognized in the very theory of the object. If, with Alexius Meinong, one must admit the paradox that "... there are *(es gibt)* objects *à propos* of which one can affirm that they are not *(es gibt nicht)*" (like the square circle, the goat-stag and so on), it will be necessary to conclude from it that they are "... by nature outside being *(ausserseiend)*."[29] How, from that time on, can their mode of appearing be described—since they would nevertheless appear indubitably, would they not only be in order for us to exclude them from reality? There is only one response: this object, "... like every other object, is, in whatever manner, given first of all to our decision about its being or its non-being"; in effect, "... all that is knowable is given—precisely to the act of knowing. And to the extent to which all objects are knowable, givenness *(Gegebenheit)* can be at-tributed to them as a universal property, to all without exception, no matter that they are or are not."[30] Free of all judgment about existence, the theory of the object as such, precisely because it tries to free itself from metaphysical ontology, must take a step back outside being [*l'é-tant*]: that which cannot direct it toward givenness, just like phenome-nology, in the orbit of which it is doubtlessly inscribed.[31]

---

[29] Alexius Meinong, "Über Gegenstandstheorie," in the collection *Untersuchungen zur Gegenstandstheorie und Psychologie* (Leipzig: Barth, 1904), in *Gesamtausgabe,* ed. Rudolf Haller and Rudolf Kindlinger (Graz: Akademische Druck—u. Verlagsan-stalt, 1968–78), vol. 1; *Théorie de l'objet,* trans. Jean-François Courtine and Marc de Launay (Paris: J. Vrin, 1999), respectively §3, p. 73, and §4, p. 76.

[30] Meinong, "Über Gegenstandstheorie"; *Théorie de l'objet,* respectively §4, p. 74, and §6, p. 83 corrected: I am not translating *Gegebenheit* by *being-given,* since it is precisely a question of naming what is not; see §11, pp. 103, 104, and 107. There are excellent comments by Jean-François Courtine concerning *Gegebenheit* in his *Présenta-tion,* 30–36.

[31] Frédéric Nef, going back to the theory of *L'objet quelconque. Recherches sur l'ontologie de l'objet* (Paris: J. Vrin, 1998), believes to have seen there a vigorous

I thus conclude that no appearing is excepted from the fold of givenness, even if it does not always accomplish the phenomenal unfolding
in it entirely. Givenness is never suspended, even if and precisely because it admits an indefiniteness of degrees. Yet again, there can be
indefinite degrees of givenness but no exception from it. Givenness is
thus set up, by its certitude and its automatic universality, in principle
unconditioned. There could, therefore, be a "first philosophy" according to phenomenology.

5. GIVENNESS, LAST PRINCIPLE

Nevertheless, this hypothesis faces certain objections.[32] The main one
concerns the relation of the given to givenness. Here one can argue that
it reestablishes a gap between cause and effect, so opening the way to
a theological interpretation of this very cause: does God not intervene,
in revealed theology and the onto-theo-logical tradition (often confusedly assimilated),[33] as the cause of beings who have become his or her
effects, and possibly as the giver giving his or her givens? This unnu-
anced objection, nevertheless, does not bear up under examination.
First, because in revealed theology, causality is applied to God in such
a way that God nevertheless does not become comprehensible by
God's effects, but always remains known insofar as unknown; in effect,
causality can be exercised starting from God, without being exercised
on God (never an effect of anything) or designating the essence of God
(not *causa sui*). Next, because the givenness evoked here only belongs
to phenomenology and thus depends on the reduction in its very certitude, that is to say, that it puts in parenthesis all transcendence, includ-

---

opposition to the supposed "exaggerated" erring ways of phenomenology in general
and, in particular, of the one that is done here, founded on the last principle—"As
much reduction, as much givenness," p. 45. One thing is sure, at least: Meinong was
not thinking in this way, which assured to non-existent objects precisely the fold and
the ground of givenness.

[32] Point (c), introduced above, p. 15.

[33] The confusion between one and the other is frequent. Most often this is by impru-
dence or ignorance, sometimes by convenience (Jacques Derrida, see below, chapter
6, §1 and §§4–5), rarely by theoretical decision (Didier Franck, *Nietzsche et l'ombre
de Dieu* [Paris: Presses Universitaires de France, 1998], for example, p. 152). This
confusion nevertheless remains more than problematic; the theology of the God revealed in (and as) Jesus Christ has never been able to be developed so much, in fact
and rightfully, as *against* metaphysics and the "theology" that it induces as the one of
special metaphysics (see below, §6, pp. 27ff.).

ing that of God. Finally, because it would remain to be established conceptually that, according to revealed theology (of which we evidently do not have to treat here), God adheres only to transcendence, and not, more essentially, to radical immanence—under the figure of the *interior intimo meo* [within my innermost self].[34] In this last hypothesis, the putting in parentheses of ontic transcendence (the efficient cause) would not disqualify God in phenomenology any more than the putting in parentheses of intentional transcendence (of the object) threatens it.

But one can also contest more subtly the primacy of givenness and, instead of bringing it back to a metaphysical concept, make it a pure question of language. It will be asked if *Gegebenheit* must necessarily be translated—since the term dates back to Husserl—by *givenness* [*donation*], in such a way as to divide, illicitly, a single (certainly ambiguous) term between an act of givenness [*donation*] and a simple given fact, thus of creating a gap (if not theological, then at least transcendent) between the origin and the result of the givenness. Why not keep strictly to the translation by *given* [*donné*], or even, as some have, by *presence* [*présence*]? *Presence* will be excluded for the scarcely contestable reason that this term would bring givenness back to what it means exactly to go beyond—the persistent presence of substantiality, in short, the "metaphysics of presence." More attention will be paid to the term *given* [*donné*]—seductive, because apparently more neutral than the translation by *givenness*. But this appearance has nothing real about it. In effect, no given would appear without giving itself or finding itself given, thus without being articulated according to the fold of givenness. Consider the example—unquestionably neutral to the point of triviality—of the datum [*donnée*] of a problem; in that case why does one speak of a given, not of a fact or of a presence? Because it concerns a question, to which the response remains unknown or even the sense of which still remains unintelligible. In all cases (even if I immediately understand the question, if I instantly find the solution because I am very gifted), I have at least to resolve a datum, to which I must respond precisely because I have neither chosen it nor foreseen it nor straightaway constituted it. Now, this datum gives itself to me,

---

[34] Saint Augustine, *Confessions,* III, 6, 11, who, let us note, sees no difficulty in juxtaposing there ". . . et superior summo meo. . . ." *Œuvres de saint augustin,* Bibliothèque augustinienne, vol. 13 (Paris: Desclée de Brouwer/Études augustiniennes, 1962), ed. Fulbert Cayré and Georges Folliet, p. 382.

because it imposes itself on me, calls me, and determines me—in short, because I am not the author of it. The datum merits its name by its being a *fait accompli,* such that it happens to me, and in which it is distinguished from all foreseen, synthesized, and constituted objects, since it happens to me as an event. This unforeseen happening marks it as given and attests in it to givenness. Givenness does not indicate so much here the origin of the given as its phenomenological status. Better, most often, givenness characterizes the given as without cause, origin, and identifiable antecedent, far from assigning them to it. And it is sufficient that the given—the given phenomenon—gives itself starting from itself alone (and not from a foreseeing and constituting subject) in order that the fold of givenness is witnessed.[35] The objection turns in this way to the confirmation of my thesis: givenness does not submit the given to a transcendent condition, but rather frees it from that condition.

Finally, it then becomes possible to conceive how, according to givenness, phenomenology can take up again the question of a "first philosophy."[36] It authorizes it, in effect, but with precautions. For if one expects of a "first philosophy" that it determines what it brings to light in fixing to it *a priori* a principle or a group of principles, in particular, in imposing the transcendental anteriority of the *I* (or the equivalent), then phenomenology no longer reaches, nor especially claims, the status of a "first philosophy" understood in this way. For as I have just recalled, the determining originality of its enterprise consists in rendering to the phenomenon an incontestable priority: to let it appear no longer as it must (according to the supposed *a priori* conditions of experience and its objects), but as it gives itself (from itself and as such). To imagine that the reduction still imposes a prior condition to the appearing (in the mode of doubt or of critique in metaphysics) would be contradictory, since, to the contrary, it is limited to purifying the appearing of all that which, in it, in fact does not appear, because it is not yet given authentically (as a lived experience and as an intentional lived experience). The principle of phenomenology, "As much reduction, as much givenness," as fundamental as it remains, has nothing of the character of a foundation, or even of a first principle. Instead, it offers a *last* principle—the last, because there is not any other one

---

[35] See, on the question of this translation, *Étant donné* §6, in particular p. 97.

[36] This is, here, a revisiting of point (d), set out above, p. 15.

after it, the last, especially, because it does not precede the phenome-non, but follows and gives it priority. The last principle takes the initia-tive to give priority back to the phenomenon. It comments on the act by which what shows itself gives itself, and what gives itself shows itself, always starting from the irreducible and prime *self* of the appear-ing. The *I* is made the clerk, the recipient, or the patient of this process, but almost never the author or the producer. In this way, the metaphysi-cal and subjective figure of transcendentality here undergoes a reversal, definitive for the first time: like Nietzsche, Husserl speaks of *Umwer-tung*,[37] but, better than Nietzsche, Husserl accomplishes it.

But the principle "As much reduction, as much givenness," as much as it withdraws primacy from the *I,* does not reestablish that of οὐσία or of *causa,* since precisely the demand to appear and to give itself without remainder in phenomenality defines a criterion and opens a crisis. The essence, the substance, and the cause suffer from a constant deficit of appearing: as such, they remain at least in part confused, because always induced, reconstituted, supposed, and not given or seen face-to-face. Therefore they rely on the work, whether of the last indi-viduals (for essence), the accidents or attributes (for substance), or the effects (for the cause), and as a result appear by their intermediary. In phenomenology, οὐσία and cause alike lose their privileges, simply because they do not directly appear at all, or at best partially; they even yield their turn to the individual, the attribute, and the effect, which, for their part, only consist in their appearing and as a consequence affect us—that is to say, they happen to us, thus appear to us. In all cases, the formula "As much reduction, as much givenness" plays as last principle: not only the last one to be found, but above all the princi-ple stating that the last—the seeming, in its supposed metaphysical fragility—is finally always equal to the single and unique first—to the appearing, the unique screen open to receive all manifestations, all truths, all realities. The last becomes first, the principle is defined as

---

[37] Husserl, Hua. III, §31, p. 65; *Idées directrices,* I, p. 99 (translation modified and modification emphasised in the text); *Ideas,* I, p. 108–9: ". . . it is a matter, rather, by means of this expression [that is to say, put between parentheses, disconnected, and so on] like all parallel expressions, of characterising by this notation a determined and *specific mode of consciousness,* which is joined to the simple, primitive thesis . . . and *inverts the value (umwertet)* of it in a manner itself original. *This inversion of value* (Umwertung) *is the concern of our complete and entire freedom. . . .*" [Insertion in text by Marion—Trans.]

last principle, and thus phenomenology would only retake the title of "first philosophy" in inverting it—"last philosophy."

6. CONCERNING A USE OF GIVENNESS IN THEOLOGY

At the end of this redefinition of "first philosophy" starting from the phenomenological principle "As much reduction, as much givenness," one could not avoid the question of a possible use of givenness in theology.[38]

Some observations are in order. (a) The relation between theology and phenomenology is an object of debate, even a polemic: does the exclusion of all transcendence by the reduction not forbid in principle that one envisage even the mere possibility of an application to religion? But, apart from the fact that the question of God is played out as much in the dimension of immanence as in that of transcendence, the reduction does not imply any more an a-theological interpretation than the use by Husserl of the Augustinian theme "*Noli foras ire, in interiore homine habitat veritas* [Do not be angry, truth lives in the inner man],"[39] or the deployment of infinite teleology in the texts of the last period implies a theological choice. (b) If phenomenology could "turn" to theology (which remains to be established elsewhere), and this among indisputable phenomenologists, this turning itself would remain impossible without some phenomenological predisposition. It is not enough to denounce it (to suppose, first, that it is obvious that this turning implies a fall, although one could also just as legitimately recognize there a heightening); it would be first necessary to explain it. What would phenomenology thus harbor in its own right for it to be able to "turn" in this way—in the sense of Husserlian, Heideggerian, or even Wittgensteinian turnings? No turning of this importance would be able to take place without an anterior turn, hidden but real, waiting for it or preparing it. The accusation would only have weight if it were

---

[38] In fact, I have already sketched in advance a response in "Phänomenologie und Offenbarung," in Lois Halder, Klaus Kienzler, and Joseph Möller, eds., *Religionsphilosophie heute*, vol. 3 (Düsseldorf: Verlag, 1988), and in "Métaphysique et phénoménologie: Une relève pour la théologie," *Bulletin de literature ecclésiastique* 94, no. 3 (1993): 189–206; "Metaphysics and Phenomenology: A Relief for Theology," *Critical Inquiry* 20, no. 4 (1994): 572–91.

[39] Husserl, citing Augustine, *De vera religione*, XXXIX, 72, in the conclusion to Hua. I, §64, p. 183; *Cartesian Meditations*, p. 157.

to identify this turn, its figure and its origin. Since such is not the case, it remains an arbitrary and sterile suspicion. (c) Husserl himself posed a restrained rule to govern the relationship between the two cases: "My immediate intention does not concern theology, but phenomenology, even if under its mediate form the second [phenomenology] should be of great importance for the first [theology]."[40] This means that the distinction between the domains, objects, and methods remains absolute, but that the first can shed some light on the second without destroying it or being destroyed.

How is this equilibrium affirmed? Let us recall that it is necessary to distinguish strongly between two theologies that always confuse the polemics surrounding this question: metaphysical theology (in which we could include "first philosophy") and revealed theology. Concerning the theology of philosophy, that is to say, "first philosophy," comprising onto-theo-logy, no ambiguity remains: since it is based on real transcendence, causality, substantiality, and actuality, it cannot resist a phenomenological reduction. Phenomenology would not be able, in any manner, to admit speculative arguments that go beyond the given, ignoring the constraints of givenness and asserting a non-immanent foundation. It exercises here a purely and simply critical function, in a strictly Kantian posture. But it is not the same, paradoxically, with revealed theology. For revealed theology, by the very fact that it is based on given facts, which are given positively as figures, appearances, and manifestations (indeed, apparitions, miracles, revelations, and so on), takes place in the natural field of phenomenality and is therefore dependent on the competence of phenomenology. What is surprising here is that phenomenology should disqualify that theology called "natural" and rational, but it cannot deny further interest in revealed theology, precisely because no revelation would take place without a manner of phenomenality. It cannot thus avoid, as strict phenomenology, questions in the style of the following: are phenomena of revelation still rightfully phenomena? If yes, do they belong to objective or ontic phenomenality, or even to phenomenality of another

---

[40] Husserl, Hua. III, §51, p. 122; *Idées directrices,* I, p. 170; *Ideas,* I, p. 157. Or as Jean-Louis Chrétien notes: "It is not enough to set up customs at the supposedly sure border between philosophy and theology; it is first necessary, in philosophy, to ask oneself about the very plotting of this border. . . ." *L'appel et la réponse* (Paris: Éditions de Minuit, 1992), p. 11.

type—that of the event, the paradox, or the saturated phenomenon,[41] and so on? Should one enlarge the extent of phenomenality until now known or admitted? Should one admit unapparent phenomena, and in this case are they unapparent provisionally, partially, or definitively? All these questions, although they can only be formulated in the field of revealed theology, belong nevertheless also and rightfully to phenomenology, since revelation itself claims to deploy a particular figure of phenomenality.

This situation allows us to ask two questions. The first comes from phenomenology and is addressed to the theologians: why do the latter not undertake, or undertake so little (Hans Urs von Balthasar remains here insufficient and exceptional),[42] to read phenomenologically the events of revelation recorded in the Scriptures, in particular in the New Testament, instead of always privileging ontic, historic, or semiotic hermeneutics? The second question goes from theology to the phenomenologists: if appearing is always ordered to givenness according to the principle "As much reduction, as much givenness," if nothing is shown that is not given and nothing is given that is not shown, what does *to be given* ultimately signify? Why has phenomenology always practiced givenness as if it were self-evident and always studied the reduction as problematic, when it could be that givenness, being more essential, might also remain the most enigmatic?*

---

[41] The position sustained in my "Le phénomène saturé" should from now on be rectified following *Étant donné*, §§23–24: the phenomenon of revelation no longer enters into the series of four saturated phenomena (under the title of the icon), but, outside the series, picks up the four figures again in a paradox to the second degree, outside the norm, although accomplishing all of them (see p. xxii, note 3).

[42] See, on Hans Urs von Balthasar, the evocative essay of Jean Greisch, "Un tournant phénoménologique de la théologie," *Transversalité* 63 (Paris: Institut Catholique de Paris, 1997), pp. 75–97, and, more generally, Vincent Holzer, "Phénoménologie radicale et phénomène de revelation," *Transversalité* 70 (Paris: Institut Catholique de Paris, 1999), pp. 55–68.

* We acknowledge our debt in many parts of this chapter to the excellent translation by Jeffrey L. Kosky of Jean-Luc Marion, "The Other First Philosophy and the Question of Givenness," *Critical Inquiry* 25 (Summer 1990): 784–800—Trans.

2

The Event or the Happening Phenomenon

1. WHAT SHOWS ITSELF AND WHAT GIVES ITSELF

All phenomena appear, but only to the extent that they show themselves. Heidegger established and managed to have it admitted that the phenomenon is defined as what shows itself in itself and starting from itself: ". . . that which-is-shown-in-its-self."[1] But he left largely undetermined the means by which the *self* at work in what shows *itself* can be thought. In effect, how can a phenomenon claim to be deployed by itself and in itself if a transcendental *I* constitutes it as an object, placed at one's disposal for and by the thought that governs it exhaustively? In such a world—that of technical objects, ours for the most part—phenomena only attain the rank of objects; their phenomenality thus remains borrowed, as derived from the intentionality and from the intuition that we confer on them. To admit, to the contrary, that a phenomenon shows itself, we would have to be able to recognize in it a *self,* such that it takes the initiative of its manifestation. From that point on, the question becomes one of knowing if and how such an initiative of manifestation can fall to a phenomenon. I have proposed an answer: a phenomenon only shows *itself* to the extent that it first gives *itself*—all that which shows *itself* must, in order to reach that point, first give *itself.* Nevertheless, as we will see,[2] the reverse is not the same: all that which gives *itself* does not show *itself* necessarily—givenness is not always phenomenalized. But how do we identify what gives itself? Self-givenness cannot actually be seen directly, since only that which already shows *itself* is seen, or at least, in the case of objects, is shown. If manifestation perhaps results from givenness, givenness must precede it; it therefore remains anterior to it, in other words, not yet en-

---

[1] Heidegger, *Sein und Zeit,* §7, p. 31; GA II, p. 41; *Being and Time,* p. 54 [Macquarrie: "the showing-itself-in-itself"]; p. 27 [Stambaugh: "the self-showing in itself"].
[2] See below, §5, pp. 50ff.

gaged in the space of visibility and consequently, strictly speaking, unseen. We could not accordingly accede to givenness, to the movement by which the phenomenon gives *itself,* in bypassing the visibility of that which possibly shows *itself* there, supposing, of course, that a non-objective phenomenality could be attested in this way. There thus only remains a single way: to try to circle, in the space of manifestation, regions where phenomena show *themselves,* instead of letting them be shown simply as objects. Or again, to disengage the regions where the *self* of what shows *itself* attests indisputably to the thrust— the pressure and, so to speak, the impact of what gives *itself.* The *self* of what shows *itself* would indirectly manifest that it gives *itself* more essentially. The same *self* that one would identify in the phenomenon showing *itself* would proceed from the original *self* of what gives itself. More clearly, the *self* of the phenomenalization would manifest indirectly the *self* of givenness, because the latter would operate it and, in the end, would become one with it.

But can one detect such a positive transformation from the phenomenalizing *self* to the giving *self?* Which phenomena keep within them the trace of their givenness, to the point that their mode of phenomenalization will not only open such an access to their original *self* but render it incontestable? I propose the hypothesis that it is a question of phenomena of the type of the event. Actually, the event appears in effect as other phenomena, but it is distinguished from objective phenomena in that which, in it, does not result from a production, which would deliver it as a product, decided and foreseen, foreseeable according to its causes and as a consequence reproducible following the repetition of such causes. To the contrary, in happening, it attests to an unforeseeable origin, rising up from causes often unknown, even absent, at least not assignable, that one would not therefore any longer reproduce, because its constitution would not have any meaning. Nevertheless, it will be objected that such events remain rare, that their unforeseeability renders them precisely inappropriate to the analysis of manifestation, in short, that they do not offer any safe ground for the inquiry into givenness. Can this judgment—apparently evident—be put in question? I am going to try, at least, in taking the example of an indisputable factuality, that of this room—the lecture hall where this academic meeting is held today.

Even this hall appears, in effect, according to the mode of the event. I do not question the fact that it offers itself to be seen as an object—

four walls, a false ceiling hiding a veranda, a podium, a certain number of seats, available as permanent and subsistent beings, and which stay there, waiting for us to occupy them by using them or noticing their subsistence. But this "permanence in waiting" here signifies curiously the contrary to objective availability. (a) First, according to the past. For, inasmuch as always already there, available for our entry and our use, this hall imposes itself on us as preexisting us, being without us, although being there for us, which therefore rises into our sight like an unexpected fact, unforeseeable, coming from an uncontrollable past. This surprise does not only come in the rooms of such a Roman palace (often passed by during strolls outside by unknowing tourists or during the rushed walks of indifferent inhabitants of the Eternal City) into which sometimes we are exceptionally invited, discovering all of a sudden the unforeseeable—and remaining until then unseen— splendor. This surprise is triggered in fact as well in the case of the lecture hall—already there, rising from a past of which we are ignorant, restored many a time by forgotten initiatives, charged with a history exceeding memory (is it a converted ancient cloister?), it imposes itself on me in appearing to me. I enter it less than it happens by itself to me, takes me in and imposes itself on me. This "already" attests to the event. (b) Next, according to the present. Here the eventmental* nature of the phenomenon of this hall is indisputably proved correct. For we are no longer dealing with the lecture hall as such, in general, such that it would subsist, in its indifferent emptiness, between such and such an occasion of filling it with an undifferentiated public. It is a question of this hall, this evening, filled for this occasion, to hear these particular speakers, on such a theme. The lecture hall in this way becomes a "house"—in the theatrical sense of a "good house tonight" (or of a bad one); it provides a stage, which such or such an actor can first own, in order then to be the center of attention. It is a hall, finally, where what happens is neither walls nor stones nor audience nor speakers, but the impalpable event, which their word goes to capture, in order to make the event understood or to spoil it. And this is a moment that, accordingly, will be inserted in other occasions (other academic meetings, other conferences, other university ceremonies, and so on) but which will never be reproduced identically as such. Tonight, on *this* theme and no other, between us and no one else, an absolutely unique

---

* The neologism "eventmental" will be used to designate *événementiel*—Trans.

event is played out, unrepeatable and, for a large part, unforeseeable—for in this precise moment when I say "precise moment," neither you, nor the dean who presides, nor I, know yet if this will be a success or a failure. What appears in this given moment before our eyes in this way escapes all constitution: although it has been organized, following clear and amicable intellectual and social intentions, it shows *itself* from itself, starting from itself. And in the *itself* of its phenomenality is anticipated—better, is announced—the *self* of what gives *itself*. The "this time, once and for all" attests therefore also to the *self* of the phenomenon. (c) Finally, in the future, no witness, however educated, attentive, and informed he or she is, could, even after the fact, describe what is happening in the present instant. For the event of this speech accepted by a consenting public and a benevolent institution does not, evidently, mobilize only a material setting—itself impossible to describe exhaustively, stone by stone, epoch by epoch, onlooker by onlooker—but also an undefined intellectual setting. It would be necessary to explain what I say and what I mean, from what perspective I say it, starting from what presuppositions, from what readings, from what personal and spiritual problems. It would also be necessary to describe the motivations of each listener, his or her expectations, disappointments, silent and spoken agreements, or disagreements hidden by silence or exaggerated by polemics. Further, to describe what the actual hall of this lecture hall welcomes today as event, it would be necessary to be able—which happily remains impossible—to follow from it the consequences in the individual and collective evolution of all the participants, including the principal orator. Such a hermeneutic would have to be deployed without end and in an indefinite network.[3] No constitution of an object, exhaustive and repeatable, would be able to take place. Consequently, the "without end" attests that the event

---

[3] One sees already that even the banal interpretation of the phenomenon as given not only does not forbid hermeneutics but demands it. I would respond in this sense to the objections of Jean Grondin, in his review of *Sur le prisme métaphysique de Descartes* in *Laval philosophique et théologique* 43, no. 3 (1987), and "La tension de la donation ultime et de la pensée herméneutique de l'application chez Jean-Luc Marion," *Dialogue* 38 (1999), or of Jean Greisch, "L'herméneutique dans la 'phénoménologie comme telle': Trois questions à propos de *Réduction et donation*," *Revue de métaphysique et de morale* 96, no. 1 (1991). In the same way, for the saturated phenomenon of the face, a hermeneutic is required (see below, chapter 5, §5, pp. 123ff.). The debate does not concern the necessity of a hermeneutic, out of question at least since Heidegger and Hans-Georg Gadamer, but its phenomenological legitimacies, which assure some saturated phenomena better than others.

happened starting from itself, that its phenomenality rose up from the *self* of its givenness.

From this first analysis, precisely because it rests on a phenomenon that is, at first sight, simple and banal, it is evident that the fact of showing *itself* can open indirectly an access to the *self* of what gives *itself.* For the event of the "hall" of the lecture hall allows a phenomenon to rise up for us in full light that not only does not proceed from our initiative, or respond to our expectations, and could never be reproduced [*ni ne pourra jamais se reproduire*], but especially that gives *itself* to us starting from its *self,* to the point that it affects us, modifies us, almost produces us. We never put into play the event (nothing is more ridiculously contradictory than the would-be "organization of an event"), but, itself, at the initiative of its *self,* it produces us in *giving itself to us.* It produces us in the scene that opens its givenness.

2. The *Self* of the Phenomenon

This analysis, as rigorous as one would want it to be, nevertheless presents a difficulty, or at least a peculiarity: it makes us consider as an event that which, at first sight, evidently passes for an object—in the occurrence, this hall. On what basis can we interpret an object as an event in this way—a hall as a "hall"? In pursuing this logic, could every object not be described in the end as an event? Would it not be appropriate to keep a more reasonable distinction between the two concepts? And besides, what do we gain from such an interpretation, when the object certainly belongs to the domain of phenomenality, whereas it is not obvious that the event still relates to it?

Doubtlessly, we must respond to these commonsense objections in reversing the question and asking completely the opposite: how can the essentially and originally eventamental character of the phenomenon, and even of all phenomena (including the most banal, that I have just described), be dulled, attenuated, and disappear, to the point that it only appears to us as an object? This is no longer to ask: until what point can we legitimately think the phenomenon as an event, but why: can we miss its phenomenality in lowering it to objectivity? We can respond to this question, in turn, with inspiration from Kant. The first of four rubrics that organize the category of the understanding and thus impose on phenomena the quadruple seal of object-ness concerns quantity.

Kant indicates that in order to become an object, every phenomenon must possess a quantity, extensive size. According to this size, the totality of the phenomenon is equal to and results from the sum of its parts. Whence follows another, decisive characteristic: the object can and must be anticipated following the sum of the parts that compose it, in such a way that it is always ". . . intuitioned in advance [*schon angeschaut*] as an aggregate (the sum of parts given in advance [*vorher angeschaut*])."[4] This accordingly means that the size of a phenomenon can always be modeled in a quantity by rights finite, thus inscribed in a real space or transcribed (by models, parameters, and coding operations) in an imaginary space. This means especially that the phenomenon is inscribed in a space that we can always know in advance in performing the summation of its parts. This hall has a quantity, which results from the sum of its parts—its walls define its volume, whereas other, non-spacial parameters (its building and maintenance costs, its contents, and so on) define its budgetary weight and its pedagogical utility. There no longer remains in principle anything in it of the least surprise: what appears will always be inscribed in the sum of what its parameters allow always already to be anticipated. The hall is foreseen before even being seen—enclosed in its quantity, assigned to its parts, fixed, so to speak, by its measures, which precede it and await empirical effectivity (construction). This reduction of the room to its foreseeable quantity makes of it an object, before and in which we pass as if there were nothing more to see there—nothing, at least, that could be anticipated from the plan of its traced conception. It is the same for all technical objects: we no longer see them, we no longer have even the need to see them, because we foresee them for a long time. And we manage to use them even better for having anticipated them without being preoccupied with seeing them. We scarcely begin to have to see them when we can no longer or cannot yet anticipate them, that is to say, when we can no longer use them (breakdown) or cannot yet use them (apprenticeship). In the order of normal technical usage, we do not in this way have to see objects: it suffices for us to anticipate them. We reduce them to the rank of phenomena of the second order, of common phenomena, without according to them full, autonomous, and disinterested appearance. They appear to us transparently, in the neu-

---

[4] Kant, *Critique de la raison pure*, A 163/B204; *Œuvres philosophiques*, ed. Ferdinand Alquié, vol. 1 (Paris: Gallimard, 1980), p. 903.

tral light of objectivity, without holding up the gaze or overwhelming it.[5] What has been "removed" from the foreseen and not seen phenomenon that is the object? Since we qualify it as an anticipated phenomenon, would it not be this anticipation that disqualifies it as a full phenomenon? What does "anticipation" mean here? That in the object all remains foreseen in advance—that nothing unforeseen happens. The object remains a fallen [*déchu*] phenomenon, because it appears as always already *expired* [*échu*], nothing new can happen to it anymore, since, more radically, its-self seems, under the gaze that constitutes it, never to arrive. The object appears like a shadow of the event that we deny in it.

But, from there, we can invert the analysis and go back from the object, transparent phenomenon, fallen from all occurrence, to its original phenomenality, governed completely by eventmentality—conforming to the essential rule [*la règle d'essence*] that what shows *itself* truly must first give *itself*. We have in fact already accomplished this going back from the object to the event in describing a common phenomenon—this "hall," thus precisely *not* the lecture hall—as a triple event according to the "already" of its facticity, the "this time, once and for all" of its accomplishment and the "without end" of its hermeneutic. We still have to take another look at the description of the eventmental character of phenomenality in general, basing our thoughts, from now on, on phenomena indisputably thematizable as events. One qualifies as event, at first glance, collective phenomena ("historical": political revolution, war, natural disaster, sporting or cultural performances, and so on), such that they satisfy three features at a minimum. (a) They cannot be repeated identically and reveal themselves in this way precisely identical to themselves alone: unrepeatability, thus irreversibility. (b) They cannot be accorded [*se voir assigner*] a unique cause or an exhaustive explanation, but demand an indefinite number of them, constantly enlarged to the measure of the hermeneutic of historians, sociologists, economists, and so on, being able to develop for their purposes: surplus of effects and of *fait accompli* over every system of causes. (c) They cannot be foreseen, since their partial causes not only always remain insufficient but are only discovered once the fact of their effect has been accomplished. Whence it follows that their possibility, not being able to be anticipated, remains, strictly speaking,

---

[5] Contrary to the idol of the painting (see below, chapter 3, §§1–2, pp. 54–62).

an impossibility with regard to the system of anteriorly indexed causes. Now—a decisive point—these three features of the event do not concern only collective phenomena but also characterize certain private or intersubjective phenomena.

Let us analyze an exemplary—and in a sense, banal—case, the friendship of Michel de Montaigne and Étienne La Boétie. One recognizes in it canonical determinations of the phenomenon as event, such as I have thematized elsewhere.[6] Friendship with the other person first makes it my duty to cast a gaze on him,* which does not follow my intentionality toward him but submits me to the point of view that he takes of me, therefore places me at the exact point where his own line of sight waits for me to expose myself. Montaigne describes this *anamorphosis* precisely: "we are looking for each other before seeing each other"; to be looked for means that, as rivals eye one another and provoke each other, each tries to situate himself at the point where the look of the other could, consequently, settle on him. In other words: ". . . it is I do not know which quintessence of all this mix that, having seized my will, brought it to plunge itself and lose itself in his . . ."—I take for myself his point of view on me, without reducing it to my point of view on him; and thus he comes to me. Whence, secondly, the event of this friendship is accomplished all at once, without warning or anticipation, according to an *arrival* without expectation and without rhythm: "And at our first meeting . . . we found ourselves so taken, so known, so obliged between ourselves, that nothing from then on was as close as we were for one another." It is therefore a question of a fact always "already" accomplished, that its *facticity* ". . . by chance in a big party and with fine company" renders irremediable, far from making it fragile. Thirdly, the phenomenon that gives itself in this way gives nothing other than itself. Its ultimate meaning remains inaccessible, because it is reduced to its *fait accompli,* to its *occurrence* [*incidence*]. This sort of accident no longer refers to any substance; if it must signify more than itself, this surplus remains as unknowable as this ". . . heavenly command," which could alone inspire it. Whence the third trait, which, itself, characterizes most perfectly the eventmentality of the phenomenon: we cannot assign to it a single cause or

---

[6] Marion, *Étant donné,* II, respectively §§13–17 and 23, pp. 318ff.

* The description takes the masculine form throughout and, to keep the flow of the text, has not been forced into inclusive language—Trans.

any reason, or rather, none other than itself, in the pure energy of its unquestionable happening: "If one presses me to say why I loved him, I sense that this can only be expressed in replying: because it was him; because it was me."[7] The phenomenon of friendship only shows itself therefore inasmuch as, as pure and perfect event, its phenomenality imposes itself in the mode of the event such that it gives itself without contest or reserve.

In this way, the eventmentality that governs all phenomena, even the most objective in appearance, manifests without exception that what shows *itself* only manages to do so by virtue of a *self,* strictly and eidetically phenomenological, that assures to it the sole fact that it gives *itself* and which, in return, proves that its phenomenalization pre-supposes its givenness as such and starting from itself.

3. The Time of *Self*

Let us contemplate this result: the *self* of what shows itself, that is to say, the phenomenon, attests, by its universally and intrinsically event-mental character, that it accomplishes an originary givenness. Is it not necessary to conclude in a commonplace manner that all phenomena, even objects poor in intuition or common, are temporalized? In this case, would we not just rediscover a very classical position, that of Kant? Doubtlessly, if we were to admit two corollaries of its critique, rightfully inadmissible. (a) First, this one: temporality is consecrated entirely to allowing the synthesis of phenomena as objects and there-fore works to assure in them permanence in presence. Now, my analy-sis established the contrary: temporality brings about originally the arrival of the occurrence according to its *fait accompli,* without reason or cause, but in imposing anamorphosis. In short, it allows phenome-nality to be understood in the mode of event, against all objectivity, which, at its best, becomes in it a residual case, provisionally perma-nent, illusorily subsistent. Temporality no longer works here for the object but rather in favor of the event, which undoes and overdeter-mines the object. The object—again, simple illusion of an a-temporal event. (b) There remains its other corollary: temporality, as an internal

---

[7] Michel de Montaigne, *Essais,* I, 28, *Les Essais,* ed. Pierre Villey and Verdun-Louis Saulnier, vol. 1 (Paris, 1965), pp. 188ff.

sense, depends on sensitivity and is only exercised for subjectivity in orienting it toward the synthesis of known objects. But the transcendental *I*, worker of this synthesis (of syntheses), if it magisterially puts to work temporality, does not define itself, *at least strictly as such,* according to this temporality. If phenomena temporalized as objects keep, from this very fact, a trace of eventmentality (which could be discussed elsewhere), then the transcendental *I* itself, as temporalized as it is, is absolutely not phenomenalized as an event. And this is so for an absolutely obstructive reason: it is never itself phenomenalized, never appears among other phenomena, even excepts itself from the phenomenality that it is restricted to producing. That said, the Kantian objection will not be overcome with only negative arguments. To go beyond it in truth it will be necessary to establish eidetic phenomena temporalized as events and, further, temporalized in such a way that they provoke the *ego* to phenomenalize itself according to this unique eventmentality. Can we plead for such a thing?

A first case of such a phenomenon is asserted: death, a phenomenon that can only be phenomenalized in happening [*se passant*], because, save this passage, it cannot strictly be; it is not, therefore it only appears inasmuch as it happens [*se passe*]; if it were not happening [*s'il ne se passait pas*], it would pass immediately and would never be. Death only shows *itself,* therefore, in giving itself by way of event. It would never be made visible if it did not happen. Nevertheless, in happening [*se passant*] in this way, what does it show of itself? Does it not succumb to the classic aporia according to which, as long as I am, death is not, and, when it happens, I am no longer there to see it? Does it not then furnish only the illusion of an event, thus the illusion that a phenomenon gives *itself*? In order to respond, it is necessary to come back to its not quite precise description and to distinguish between the death of the other person and my own death. (a) The death of the other person appears in that it happens [*se passe*], since it consists precisely in a pure and simple passage—the passage, in itself not real, from the state of being alive to the state of being a cadaver. This passage is not seen directly, to the contrary of the two states that it traverses. As a phenomenon, the death of the other person only lasts, therefore, the instant of a passage (even if the affectation of the funeral ceremony tries to make it last and must try to, precisely because the passage has not lasted more than an instant). The death of the other person only shows *itself* in a flash and only gives *itself* in being withdrawn—in withdrawing from us the living other. Pure event without doubt, but too pure to show *itself* and thus to give *itself* as a perfect event. Especially since this flash of event does not implicate my *ego* directly, since, in enclosing me in my residual life, the death of the other person bars me all access to that *ego* and to that life. (b) My own death obviously involves me totally and it too only appears in happening, thus as an event such that it attests a phenomenal givenness. Nevertheless, such an evident aporia compromises its pertinence: if death passes in me (supposing, by the way, that a phenomenon were to appear in this passage), as I die with it, I can never see the event in it. Accordingly, this aporia only threatens the point of view of the one who has not yet tested this passage, who does not yet know if it will annihilate me or instead "change" me (1 Cor. 15:22); thus this aporia of my death is only valid for the one who, as all of us here, has not yet received the gift of death. What death gives (an event or a nothingness of phenomenality?), we do not know. In effect, the human condition is not characterized first by mortality (animals and civilizations die too) or even by the consciousness of having to end by dying, but in effect by the ignorance of the knowledge nevertheless owed and required of what happens [*se passe*] (or shows *itself*) for me at the instant when my death passes in me. My death does not place me thus before any effectivity, any passage, but before a simple possibility—the possibility of impossibility, not only impossibility of possibility. And this possibility of impossibility, which is necessarily going to give *itself,* also keeps until the end the possibility of not showing *itself,* of showing nothing. In this way, the event of my death, the closest, the least distant, from which a failed beating of the heart suffices to separate me, remains inaccessible to me by the excess in it, provisionally at least inevitable, of its pure givenness over phenomenality. There too, it is very likely a question of a pure event, but too pure to show *itself* and therefore also to give *itself* as a perfect event. This phenomenon, which perfectly merits the title of event and implicates me radically in it because it gives *itself,* nevertheless steals away as a phenomenon showing *itself.*

What way therefore remains accessible to us? We come back to the event itself: it gives *itself* as much as it shows *itself,* but only insofar as the manifestation happens in it in the mode of an arrival, which falls as a *fait accompli* upon my gaze, where it is accommodated (anamorphosis). These determinations evidently all refer to time, which the event radically presupposes. But does the event not only presuppose time as one of its constituents or conditions? In effect, no. For time itself happens first in the mode of an event. Husserl sees it; he defines time starting from an "original impression," which, as "origin-point ['source-point']," does not cease to rise up in and as the pure present and, precisely because it happens, also does not cease to pass in the already-more-present, a time retained by retention, even before foundering in the past.[8] The present rises up as first and the first happens as pure event—unforeseeable, irreversible, unrepeatable as such, immediately past and devoid of cause or of reason. It alone escapes objectivity, though it renders it possible, because it is absolutely excepted from all constitution: "The original impression is the absolute non-modifiable, the original source for all consciousness and being [être] to come."[9] Here the movement of what gives *itself* is also accomplished almost without allowing the opportunity of appearing to what shows *itself,* since the original impression changes immediately and, at once rising up, turns continually into retention. But, to the contrary of death, this excess of givenness does not prevent here an event's being accomplished effectively, perceptibly even, since the original impression does not cease to re-arise from the absolute unseen, from the area of uncertainty [*la bouche d'ombre*], whence it emerges. The original impression gives *itself to be seen* as the pure event without respite, coming about from an unconditional and indefinite birth. From the "origin-point," givenness always in action, what scarcely shows *itself* (any given moment) is *born* from each instant of what gives *itself* thoroughly (the original impression).

Birth—I am considering here the phenomenon that shows *itself* truly in the mode of what gives *itself,* the properly eventmental phenomenon. In effect, how am I to understand that my birth shows *itself* as a phenomenon, when, properly speaking, I have never seen it with my own eyes and I must rely on eyewitnesses or a birth certificate? Since it is

---

[8] Edmund Husserl, *Zur Phänomenologie des inneren Zeitbewusstseins,* Hua. X, ed. Rudolf Boehm (The Hague: Martinus Nijhoff, 1969), §11, p. 29; *Leçons sur la conscience intime du temps,* trans. Henri Dussort (Paris: Presses Universitaires de France, 1964), pp. 43ff.; *On the Phenomenology of the Consciousness of Internal Time,* trans. John B. Brough, *Edmund Husserl: Collected Works,* vol. 4 (Dordrecht/Boston, MA: Kluwer Academic, 1991), pp. 30ff.

[9] Husserl, Hua. X, §31, p. 67; *Leçons sur la conscience intime du temps,* p. 88; *On the Phenomenology of the Consciousness of Internal Time,* p. 70: "The primal impression is something absolutely unmodified, the primal source of all further consciousness and being."

accomplished without me and even, strictly speaking, before me, it should not be able to show *itself* (if it were to show itself) to anyone at all, except to me. Nevertheless, I consider it rightfully as a phenomenon, since I do not stop aiming at it intentionally (wanting to know who and from where I am, undertaking research into my identity, and so on) and filling this aim with quasi-intuitions (secondary memories, direct and indirect witnessings, and so on). My birth is even offered as a privileged phenomenon, since my whole life is solely occupied, for an essential part, with reconstituting it, attributing to it a meaning and responding to its silent appeal. Nevertheless, I cannot, as a matter of principle, see this irrefutable phenomenon directly. One can formalize this aporia by suggesting that my birth shows me precisely the fact that my origin does not show itself, or that it only shows itself in this very impossibility of appearing; in short, that only in this way is the ". . . *original non-originalleity of the origin*" attested.[10] This must be understood doubly. Either my birth happens before I am able to see it and receive it, thus I am not present to my own origin; or my birth, origin for me, has nothing original in itself but proceeds from an indefinite series of events and of happenings (". . . *sumque vel a parentibus productus . . .*") [and I have been produced by parents].[11] To describe this aporia does not, nevertheless, yet suffice to dissolve it. It remains to be understood how a phenomenon that does not show *itself* not only affects me as if it were showing *itself* (and in a sense it shows itself well and truly by numerous intermediaries) but affects me more radically than any other, since it alone determines me, defines my *ego,* even produces it. In other words, if an origin cannot in general show *itself,* still less could an origin dispossessed of its originality show itself. How, therefore, does this happen to me—because it happened to me, it happens to me, I come from it—this original non-originalleity, since it remains necessarily non-demonstrable? It happens to me precisely insofar as it happens, and it only happens insofar as it has precisely given to me a future. My birth is not qualified as a phenomenon (that of a non-original origin) because it would show *itself* but because, in the very absence of all direct monstration, it happens as a never-present event, always past, but never surpassed for all that—in fact,

---

[10] According to the excellent formula of Claude Romano, *L'événement et le monde* (Paris: Presses Universitaires de France, 1998), p. 96.

[11] Descartes, *Meditationes de prima philosophia,* III, AT VII, pp. 21ff.

always to come. My birth does phenomenalize itself, but as a pure event, unforeseeable, irrepeatable, exceeding all cause and rendering possible the impossible (that is to say, my life always new), surpassing all expectation, all promise, and all prediction. This phenomenon, which is accomplished in a perfect reduction of what shows *itself,* thus attests, in an exceptional and paradigmatic mode, that its phenomenality proceeds directly from the fact that it gives *itself.*

We therefore reach what we were looking for: all that which shows *itself* not only gives *itself* but it gives *itself* as an event according to a temporality itself eventmental, to the point that, in exceptional cases (birth), a phenomenon attains directly to *self*-giving without *self*-showing.

In fact, several characteristics justify the phenomenological privilege accorded in this way to birth. (a) The phenomenon of birth gives *itself* directly without showing *itself,* because it happens as an event *par excellence* (origin originally non-original), but this excellence comes to it from the fact that it *gives me to myself* when it gives *itself.* It is phenomenalized in affecting me, it affects me in giving me not only to myself, but (since without it I would not yet be there to be affected by it) in giving, so to speak, prior to me a *me,* a *myself,* who receives itself from what it receives.[12] (b) The phenomenon of birth carries directly to its limit the inclusion of the *ego* in eventmentality, in founding it exemplarily according to its status of being given over [or "gifted"] [*son statut d'adonné*]: the *ego* that is itself received from what it receives. The phenomenon of birth exemplifies the phenomenon in general—that which is only phenomenalized as far as it gives *itself*—but, at the same time, it institutes *l'adonné* [the given over, or gifted one], originarily *a posteriori,* since receiving itself from what it receives, as the first phenomenon (rendering possible the reception of all others). (c) The phenomenon of birth thus rightfully gives *itself* as a saturated phenomenon (or paradox). In effect, its event, first original impression and thus more original than any other instant, renders possible an indefinite, indescribable, and unforeseeable series of original impressions to come—those that are accumulating throughout my life and define me to my end. In this way birth opens the course of life to innumerable temporal intuitions, for which I will seek without end, but always too

---

[12] Be careful—I am saying: "in giving a *me,* a *myself,*" not "in giving it *to me,*" since at the moment when it gives it [to me], I am not precisely yet there to receive it.

late, meanings, concepts, and noeses inevitably missing. I will always try to find words to say (to myself) what will happen to me or, rather, what will already have happened to me without ever yet adequately explaining it, understanding it, or constituting it at the moment of this advent. The excess of intuition over intention bursts open irremediably from the point of my birth—and, moreover, I will speak not only by means of having [repeatedly] intuited in silence, but especially after having heard others speak. Language is first listened to, and only then is it uttered. The origin remains to me, indeed, originally inaccessible, not by default, nevertheless, but because the first phenomenon already saturates all intention with intuitions. The origin, which refuses itself, does not nevertheless give *itself* in penury (Derrida), but indeed in excess, determining in this way the regime of all givens to come. In other words, nothing shows *itself* that does not first give *itself.*

4. THE *EGO* IN THE REDUCTION TO THE GIVEN

Let us suppose it has been established that the phenomenon, considered according to its radical eventmentality, is reduced to the given. Such a given, especially if we think it starting from my birth, insofar as it manages to give *itself* without showing *itself* directly as a phenomenon to sight and of which I could proclaim myself a spectator (disinterested or not, it matters little here), is accomplished as a saturated phenomenon that strikes, as an event, an *ego* that becomes under this blow an *adonné.* Such an event gives *itself,* in effect, all at once: it leaves us without a voice to speak it; it leaves us also without any other way to avoid it; and it leaves us finally without a choice to refuse it or even to accept it voluntarily. Its *fait accompli* is not discussed, is not avoided, is not decided either. It is not even a question there of a violence, because violence implies an arbitrariness, therefore an arbitrator and already a space of freedom. It is a question of a pure phenomenological necessity: from the moment that the event always already gives *itself,* from a done deal [*une donne révolue*] and from a necessary contingence, as it happens with the phenomenon of birth or with the original impression, it renders manifest the *self* of what gives itself. It attests that it, and thus all other phenomena by derivation, can give itself in the strict sense because it proves, insofar as it is a pure event, that it has such a *self.* Not only does the event give itself in itself (annulling the withdrawal of a thing in itself), but it is given starting from self and thus as a *self.*

The stakes of this analysis cannot be underestimated: if the *self* returns to the phenomenon and proceeds from it, no *ego* can therefore any longer claim to assume, in the first place and in the first instance, ipseity, the *self.* Doesn't the *ego* of Descartes itself have access to its *self* in response to the *nescio quis* [I do not know who] that happens to it, as deceiver or instead as almighty?[13] Doesn't *Dasein* accomplish its ipseity only by an anticipatory resolution that renders possible the event of the nothing, such that it tears it from beingness?[14] I postulate that the attempts, as grandiose as they were, to assign the first *self* to the *ego*—in short, to elevate the *I* to transcendental dignity—only succeeded in underlining all the more the radical primacy of the *self* of an event, whatever it may be (a being of the world, outside the world, or being [*l'étant*] in totality) and however denied it is. It must be recognized, even if it is just to be disturbed by it, that if the phenomenon gives itself truly, it then obligatorily confiscates the function and the role of the *self,* and therefore can only concede to the ego a *me* of second rank, by derivation. And I explicitly draw this conclusion in challenging the pretension of any *I* to a transcendental function, or, what comes down to the same thing, the pretension of a possible transcendental *I* to the last foundation of the experience of phenomena. In other words, the *ego,* deprived of transcendentalizing dignity, must be admitted as it is received, as an *adonné:* the one who is itself received from what it receives, the one to whom what gives itself from a first *self*—any phenomenon—gives a second *me,* the one of reception and of response.* The *ego* keeps, indeed, all the privileges of subjectivity, save the transcendental claim to origin.

Let us admit that all *egos* are gifted [*adonné*], endowed with a *me* that is given, and given to receive what gives itself. Among the possible objections against such a *diminutio ipseitatis* [diminution of the self] of the *ego,*[15] one, more than any, must hold our attention, because it

---

[13] See Marion, *Questions cartésiennes II,* chapter I.

[14] Heidegger, *Sein und Zeit,* §64, pp. 316ff.; GA II, pp. 419ff.; *Being and Time,* pp. 364ff. (Macquarrie); 292ff. (Stambaugh).

* The sense of this sentence reads better as "the one to whom what gives itself from a self first—any phenomenon—gives a me, second," although this is not clear from the text—Trans.

[15] Claude Romano, "Remarques sur la méthode phénoménologique dans *Étant donné,*" *Annales de Philosophie* 21 (Beyrouth: Université Saint-Joseph, 2000).

questions the phenomenological claim of our enterprise. In effect, all phenomenology puts to work, explicitly (Husserl) or implicitly (Martin Heidegger, Emmanuel Levinas, Michel Henry, Derrida), a reduction as the non-negotiable touchstone, because it is neither a question of one concept among others nor of a doctrine to discuss, but of an operation—that which brings back the semblance of appearing to the appearing of phenomena such as they are. And all reduction demands an authority that operates it—a transcendental *I* or its equivalent (*Dasein,* the face of the other, flesh). Thus the reduction of the appearing to the given that I am trying to accomplish is distinguished dangerously from the two principal figures of the reduction that it tries to go beyond. (a) This is, first, because it no longer only brings back the phenomenon to its constituted object-ness (Husserl) or to its being-ness in being (Heidegger), but ultimately to the given, showing itself inasmuch as it gives itself—thus fixing the given in terms ultimate and irreducible by any other reduction. (b) But it is especially because this third reduction only brings us back to the given in also reducing the *I* to the derived rank of *adonné.* This would matter little if it were only a question of a new title and not of another function—the function of receiving oneself from what gives itself, without any longer exercising a transcendental role, in short, without any longer fixing the conditions of possibility of experience, in short [*sic*], of phenomenality. Nevertheless, the reduction has precisely as a task to modify the conditions of possibility of phenomenality; it demands therefore such an *a priori I* (or its transcendental equivalent) and seems not to be able to be content with an *adonné, a posteriori* by definition. In fine, the reduction of the phenomenon to the given such that it gives itself, in going as far as disqualifying the transcendental *I* in a pure and simple *adonné,* becomes a performative contradiction—it is deprived of the very operator of the givenness that it nevertheless claims to render manifest by reduction.

Such a difficulty cannot be resolved all at once, but an argument is nevertheless asserted: if all reduction demands an operator who brings back the semblance of the appearing to the full appearing of phenomena, this operator him- or herself is found modified—and essentially—by the reduction that he or she puts to work. For Husserl, the phenomenological reduction (without evoking others, who would doubtlessly allow the same result) does bring back the things of the world to their lived experiences of consciousness, in order to make of them intentional objects; but the *I* does not remain untouched there, or an outsider. It is itself reduced to its pure immanence ("region of consciousness") and brings back the totality of its empirical me to the transcendence of the "region of the world."[16] The *I* in this way becomes transcendental in the phenomenological sense, because it is reduced to itself and is extracted from the natural world in first renouncing for itself the natural attitude. For Heidegger, the still phenomenological reduction of objects of the world (subsistent or common) to their status of beings seen according to their diversified ways of being is only operated by *Dasein,* sole being in whom there is being. But it is still necessary that this *Dasein* is accomplished as such and therefore appropriates its unique manner of being and rids itself of an inappropriate way of being (that of the "They" who claim to understand themselves as if they were intra-worldly beings). *Dasein* must thus be itself reduced to itself—to its status of being [*étant*] transcending all the intra-worldly beings by virtue of Being* itself, that which the challenge of anxiety accomplishes in it. The disappearance of all anthropological determinations (flesh, sexuality, ideology, and so on), for which *Sein und Zeit* has been so naively reproached, attests precisely to this modification of "man" into a *Dasein,* which recoils the reduction on its agent. The reduction thus always first reduces the one who operates it—and it is by this recoiling on itself that the phenomenological validity of each attempt at reduction is measured.

Without claiming to compare what cannot be compared, I nevertheless suggest that it is the same for the third reduction. It is first a question of reducing all that which claims to appear—object, being [*étant*], semblance, and so on—to a given. For the formula "As much reduction, as much givenness" postulates, in effect, that what the natural attitude accepts without discussion as a given often does not yet give itself, or, inversely, that what it rejects as problematic is found, in fact, absolutely given. It is next a question of tracing the necessary bond by which all "that which shows *itself* must first give *itself*" and removes the weight of the *self,* whence only givenness validates the manifestation. But how are we to imagine that the one, whomever it is, who reduces to the given and who brings back the "*self*-showing" to the

---

[16] Husserl, Hua. III, §59, pp. 140ff.; *Idées directrices,* I, pp. 160ff.; *Ideas,* I, pp. 175ff.

* In contrast to most of his uses of *être,* Marion uses the capital in the text here—Trans.

"*self*-giving" in describing the phenomenon as pure event (thus also as anamorphosis, delivery, *fait accompli,* incident) could maintain its identity uninterrogated, perhaps even keeping the identities that correspond to the two preceding reductions? How could this one still claim to fix the conditions of possibility of experience of phenomena, of which it has just, precisely by the third reduction, recognized that they only show *themselves* by virtue of their *selves,* as it shows through in the event where they give *themselves* and it fixes itself its own conditions of manifestation? How would the *ego* alone except itself from the reduction to the given that it claims to let be accomplished? Save to contradict the result of the third reduction—the phenomenon gives *itself* from itself—the *ego* must get rid of all transcendental pretensions. This is not to say that the reduction is compromised, but, inversely, that it is accomplished even in the one who makes it possible, *l'adonné. L'adonné* does not compromise the reduction to the given but rather confirms it in transferring the *self* from itself to the phenomenon.

This first argument hints at a second one. *L'adonné,* in losing transcendental status and the spontaneity or the activity that this implies, does not amount, however, to passivity or to the empirical me. In fact, *l'adonné* goes as much beyond passivity as activity, because in being liberated from its royal transcendental status [*la pourpre transcendantalice*], it annuls the very distinction between the transcendental *I* and the empirical me. After that, what third term could be invented between activity and passivity, transcendentality and empiricity? Let us take again the definition of *l'adonné:* the one who *receives* itself from what it receives. *L'adonné* is therefore characterized by reception. Reception implies, indeed, passive receptivity, but it also demands active capacity, because capacity *(capacitas),* in order to increase to the measure of the given and to make sure it happens, must be put to work—work of the given to receive, work on itself in order to receive. Work, which the given asks from *l'adonné* every time and for as long as it gives itself, explains why *l'adonné* does not receive itself once and for all (at birth) but does not cease to receive itself anew in the event of each given. But reception will only really deliver *l'adonné* from the dichotomies that imprison metaphysical subjectivity if we understand its properly phenomenological function more clearly. In other words: if *l'adonné* no longer constitutes phenomena, if it is limited to receiving the pure given and even to being received from it, what act, which operation, and what role can it still assume in phenomenality itself? But we have, exactly, in posing this objection against *l'adonné* just noted an essential gap—between the given and phenomenality. We have just repeated what we have already often glimpsed: if all that which shows *itself* must first, in order to do this, give *itself,* it does not suffice, nevertheless, that the given give *itself* in order to show *itself,* since sometimes givenness almost shocks manifestation. *L'adonné* functions precisely to measure *in itself* the gap between the given—which never ceases to be imposed on it and to impose itself on it—and phenomenality—which is only accomplished as much and insofar as reception achieves phenomenalization or, rather, lets it be phenomenalized. This operation—to phenomenalize the given—by rights is owed to *l'adonné* by virtue of its difficult privilege of constituting the only given in which there is the visibility of all other givens. It therefore reveals the given as phenomenon.

5. RESISTANCE TO THE REVEALED

Now we have to understand how *l'adonné* reveals (phenomenalizes as event) the given—and to what extent it can.

Let us first examine the revealed according to a strictly phenomenological meaning. Consider the given obtained by the reduction: it can be described as what Husserl named the lived experience, or *Erlebnis.* The lived experience does not show itself as such but remains invisible by default (a capital point that is often misunderstood). It will be said, for the lack of a better expression, that it affects me, imposes itself on me, and weighs on what one dares name my consciousness (precisely because it does not yet have the clear and evident consciousness of anything when it receives the pure given). The given, as a lived experience, remains a *stimulus,* an excitation, scarcely a piece of information; *l'adonné* receives it, without its showing itself in any case. How does this given sometimes succeed in passing from the unseen [*l'invu**][17] to the seen? I in no way intend to enter into physiological or psychological considerations, both for want of data and also as a matter of principle: before explaining a process, it is first necessary to identify it, and

---

* Suggesting what remains unseen rather than what simply goes unnoticed—Trans.

[17] On the concept of the unseen, see Jean-Luc Marion, "Ce que cela donne," *La croisée du visible* (1991; rev. ed., Paris: Éditions de la Différence, 1996), §2, pp. 51ff.

the process of the rising up of the visible starting from the unseen is properly dependent on phenomenology. Along these lines, I will risk saying that the given, unseen but received, is projected on *l'adonné* (or consciousness, if one prefers) as on a screen; all the power of this given comes from crashing down on this screen, provoking all at once a double visibility. (a) First, that of the given, of course, the impact of which (until then invisible) bursts, explodes, and is broken up in its outlines, the first visibles. One could also imagine the model of a prism that stops white light, until then invisible, and breaks it up into a spectrum of elementary colors, colors that are finally visible. *L'adonné* phenomenalizes in receiving the given, precisely because it is an obstacle to it, stops it in blocking it and fixes it in centering it. If *l'adonné* therefore receives the given, it is in receiving it with all the vigor, even the violence, of a goalkeeper blocking a shot, of a defender marking, of a receiver sending back a winning return. Screen, prism, frame— *l'adonné* takes the impact of the pure, unseen given, holding back the *momentum* of it in order in this way to transform its longitudinal force into a slack, even, open surface. With this operation—precisely, reception—the given can begin to show *itself* starting from the outlines of visibility that it concedes to *l'adonné,* or rather that it receives from it. (b) But the visibility risen from the given provokes at the same time the visibility of *l'adonné*. In effect, *l'adonné* does not see itself before receiving the impact of the given. Relieved of its royal transcendental status, it no longer precedes the phenomenon, or even accompanies it any longer as a thought already in place. Since it is received from what it receives, it does not precede it, and especially not by a visibility prior to the unseen of the given. In fact, *l'adonné* does not show itself more than the given—its screen or its prism remains perfectly unseen as long as the impact, crushed against them, of a given does not illuminate them all at once. Or instead, since, properly speaking, *l'adonné* is not without this reception, the impact gives rise for the first time to the screen against which it is crushed, as it sets up the prism across which it breaks up. In short, *l'adonné* is phenomenalized by the very operation by which it phenomenalizes the given.

The given is therefore revealed to *l'adonné* in revealing *l'adonné* to itself. Each is phenomenalized in the mode of the *revealed,* which is characterized by this essential phenomenal reciprocity, where to see implies the modification of the seeing by the seen, as much as the modification of the seen by the viewer. *L'adonné* operates as the developer of the given, and the given as developer of *l'adonné*—developers understood in the photographic sense of the term. Perhaps one could risk saying that the philosophical paradox of quantum physics with regard to the interdependence of the object and the observer is valid, by analogy, for all phenomenality without exception. But could we still speak here of "phenomenality without exception"? Have we not conceded previously that, if all that which shows *itself* first gives *itself,* the reciprocal is not valid, because all that which gives *itself* does not manage thus to show *itself*? In fact, far from landing us in a new aporia, we have just found precisely the way to get out of it. For if the given only shows *itself* in being forced up against and spread out on the screen which, itself, becomes *l'adonné*, if *l'adonné* must and can alone in this way transform an impact into visibility, the extent of the phenomenalization depends on the resistance of *l'adonné* to the brutal shock of the given. Let us understand resistance in the sense, suggestive because trivial, of electricity: when, in a circuit, one establishes or provokes on purpose a restriction of the movement of free electrons, part of the energy is dissipated in heat or light. Resistance in this way transforms an unseen movement into phenomenalized light and heat. The greater the resistance to the impact of the given (therefore first of the lived experiences, intuitions), the more the phenomenological light shows *itself.* Resistance—a function proper to *l'adonné*—becomes the index of the transmutation from what gives *itself* into what shows *itself.* The more the intuitive given increases its pressure, the more a great resistance becomes necessary in order for *l'adonné* still to reveal a phenomenon there. Whence comes the inevitable and logical hypothesis of saturated phenomena—so saturated with given intuitions that significations and corresponding noeses are lacking. Before such phenomena, which are in fact partially non-visible (except in the mode of being dazzling), it solely depends on the resistance of *l'adonné* to manage to transmute, up to a certain point, the excess of givenness into a monstration to an equal extent, that is to say, unmeasured. This opens the way for a phenomenological theory of art: the painter renders visible as a phenomenon what no one had ever seen before, because he or she manages, being the first to do that every time, to resist the given enough to get it to show *itself*—and then in a phenomenon accessible to all. A great painter never invents anything, as if the given were missing; he or she suffers on the contrary a resistance to this excess, to the point of making it render its visibility (as one forcefully makes restitution). Mark Rothko resists what he has received as a violent given—too violent for anyone else than him—in phenomenalizing it on the screen of slack colors: "I have imprisoned the most absolute violence in each square centimeter of their [the paintings'] surfaces."[18] What is true about the arts is also true of literature and of all speculative thought: an immense effort of resistance to the given, in order to phenomenalize as far as *l'adonné* can bear it. Genius only consists in a great resistance to the impact of the given revealing itself. In all cases, the phenomenon, which happens as an event, takes the aspect of the revealed, that is to say, it phenomenalizes *l'adonné* in the same gesture where *l'adonné* forces what gives *itself* to show *itself* a little more.

The revealed does not thus define an extreme stratum or a particular region of phenomenality, but rather the universal mode of phenomenalization of what gives *itself* in what shows *itself*. It fixes all at once the originally eventmental character of every phenomenon insofar as first it gives *itself* before showing *itself*. It is therefore time to pose a final question. Does the universality of the meaning of the phenomenon as event, thus as given acceding to manifestation as revealed by and for an *adonné,* not abolish definitively, *de facto* if not *de jure,* the caesura that metaphysics has not ceased to hollow out between the world of objects, supposedly constituted, producible, and repeatable, thus exclusively rational, on the one hand, and the world of the revealed of Revelation, a world of events neither constitutable nor repeatable nor presently producible, thus supposedly irrational, on the other? This caesura is imposed at the very moment when the doctrine of the object has tried (and succeeded) to reduce the question and the field of phenomenality to only apparent phenomena, deprived of *self,* devalued as beings as well as certitudes. As soon as phenomenology was able to reopen the field of phenomenality, to include objects there as a simple, particular case of phenomena (poor and common) and to surround them with the immense region of saturated phenomena, this caesura is no longer justified. Or, rather, it becomes a denial of phenomenality, itself irrational and ideological. If we admit that this caesura no longer has a place to be, what consequence follows? This one: the data produced by Revelation—there the unique Jewish and Christian Revela-

---

[18] Mark Rothko, in James E. B. Breslin, *Mark Rothko: A Biography* (Chicago: University of Chicago Press, 1993), p. 358, cited by E. Michaud, "Rothko, la violence et l'histoire," in *Marc Rothko* (Paris: Musée d'Art moderne de la Ville de Paris, 1999), p. 80.

tion—must be read and be treated as rightfully phenomena, obeying the same operations as those that result from the givens of the world: reduction to the given, eventmentality, reception by *l'adonné*, resistance, saturated phenomena, progressiveness of the transmutation from the *self*-giving into *self*-showing, and so on. Without any doubt, the phenomenological place of theology will necessitate (and finds already) very particular protocols, conformed to the exceptional phenomena of which it is a question. For example, the event can take the figure of the miracle, the given becomes election and promise, the resistance of *l'adonné* is deepened into conversion of the witness, the transmutation from the *self*-giving into *self*-showing requires theological virtues, its progressiveness is prolonged in eschatological return of the eternal beginning, and so on. Philosophy has neither the authority nor the competence to say more, but it leaves at least the right to appeal about it to the theologians. They must stop wanting to reduce the extreme givens of Revelation to objectivizing models, more or less exactly repeated from human sciences. For the same phenomenality covers all givens, from the poorest (formalism, mathematics), to the common (physical sciences, technical objects), to saturated phenomena (event, idol, flesh, icon), up to the point of the possibility of phenomena combining the four types of saturation (phenomena of Revelation).

3

The Idol or the Radiance
of the Painting

1. To See or to Look at

The visible surrounds us. Wherever we turn, it is unveiled, ready, brilliant, ironic. When I open my eyes, I fall on it, unfolded from head to foot all across the horizon. Does it seep through the sides? But there is no place for anything "on the side" of the visible, since it faces me with the envisageable breadth of space. Would I escape from it in turning my back on it and fleeing? But if I turn around I always run into it, as it has preceded me and gets around me in advance. When I raise my head, it was already hanging over me. When I lower my eyes, it always still expects me. The visible obsesses us because it lays siege to us. Wherever I turn, it surrounds me.

Does blindness protect us from it? Only someone non-sighted from birth could try to respond without indecency. In any event, one can suppose that the understatement that advises us to define the blind person as a non-sighted one thinks blindness resolutely starting from sight, therefore from the visible. Must blindness, metaphysics asked, be understood as an absence of vision (a neutral determination, referring back only to itself, or even a positive one, in the sense of only having five senses and not a sixth) or, on the contrary, as a privation—the failure and the lack of a perfection intrinsically owed to our nature?[1] Usage responds, in fact, that blindness can only be tested as the privation of vision owed, required, or necessary. This is to such an extent that blindness does not cease to try to reconstitute, by other means, natural or technological, a quasi-vision, an insensible and intellectualized vision, perhaps finally, too, even more powerful than sensible and natural vision, because better exercised and deliberated. This admirable effort, never discouraged and so effective, to go back from blindness

---

[1] Spinoza, Letter XIX, in *Opera Omnia*.

to vision by analogy, attests of course that humanity always wants more than that of which its nature is capable. It attests also, to the contrary, that the visible exercises its empire over us when it is physically and ontically lacking. We remain obsessed with the visible, even when it no longer lays siege to us and is withdrawn from the plain, left empty and obscure as far as the eye can see. The blind person still wants to see, whatever happens to him or her. And the ancients even suggested that the greatest seers (sages, poets, or prophets) had given up the vision of the sensible visible in order to exercise better that of the insensible visible (intelligible or religious). As if visibility remained, there still, the unsurpassable horizon of blindness.

Unless, on the contrary, a certain blindness could alone open to us a breach in the visible that besieges us, and that in order to look at what must be visible [ce qui doit l'être], it would first be necessary to manage not to let oneself be dazzled by the ordinariness of the visible. For to be exposed unwillingly to all that which emerges that is visible does not yet allow us to see anything, but only to let us be affected by the extravagant rhapsody of the accident as it happens. To be convinced of this, it is enough to take the abandoned posture of a suddenly inattentive look: I only open my eyes on themselves, I let my attention be conformed to the simple movements of their spheres, without daring to venture beyond. I do not see further than my eyes. I no longer choose any contour in the flux of the visible, which from now on runs inorganically, without rupture or caesura, like a slow river of formless colors. The depths and the surfaces, the figures and the limits are merged like on the reverse side of a tapestry, like on the obverse of a finally limitless Pollock, become what he always tried to achieve, a universe—a unique account enveloping all things and deploying them. To see does not require any choice or decision; it is enough to be exposed to the wave always recommenced from the visible. In order to see, it is enough to have eyes. To look demands much more: one must discern the visible from itself, distinguishing surfaces there in depth and breadth, delimiting forms, little by little, marking changes, and pursuing[2] movements. In short, one must aim—in the indistinction of the

---

[2] "To pursue" must be understood here in the sense of a "spotlight of pursuit" ["followspot"]—which follows, as closely as possible, an actor (an artist, a singer, and so on) who changes place in a somber scene and whom the halo of light keeps under the gaze of the spectator, almost immobilizing him or her, despite the rapid changing of place.

ordinary visible always renewed—at objectives, pay particular attention to them, encircle them, underline them, even over-line them in
order finally to pick out shapes—this one rather than that one, this one
here taken as a single one that remains, although to apprehend it in this
way, the variations and the undulations that would make it almost flee
outside itself must be unceasingly brought together again, with a uni-
fication always to be recaptured, to be watched over, to be kept. To
keep watch over (*in-tueri, intuitus,* the Latin literally says) the flux of
the visible in its rest, always menaced by the almost immobile shape,
in fact never immobilized, but always immobilizing as much as it can
the mobility of the visible, its slipperiness. To look at [*regarder*]—to
keep watch over [*garder du regard*], to keep an eye on [*garder d'un
œil*], to keep in custody [*maintenir en garde à vue*]—comes back to
imposing ends on the visible, and, little by little, to making objects of
it.[3] The knowledge and the look do not always reach the clear and the
distinct, but all their objects are only extricated from the depth of the
visible in becoming arduously and tangentially distinct there, or rather,
distinguished from the flux, and from the wave of what does not cease
to give itself obstinately to be seen. The objects do not so much organize themselves in the field of the visible as they organize it; in being
posed in its middle, they impose a scene on it: right and left, before
and behind, center and periphery, near and far, big and small; they
crisscross it. They do not, nevertheless, crisscross it in fixing a frame
for it (because the horizon of the visible, strangely, ceaselessly displaces its limits and therefore contradicts the very notion of horizon),
in framing it in their objectivity, but in being centered—in sketching
in it frames that are almost fixed, maintained with much striving by the
care of an attentive look. They are conformed to the center of the visible in instituting limits there, in fixing references to it, as one founds
strongholds in the too vast, undefined plain, where everything would
otherwise be merged, in short, in taking a stand in order not to be lost
there. Doubtlessly, even well-tended objects will not cease to change,
to break loose, to fall. But limited as they are, the look will always be
able to hope, first to recapture them, then to bring then back within
their limits (possibly displaced, widened, but never broken), and to
reassign them to their respective ends. The objects remain respective—
relative to the look, of course, but in this way also respected in them-

---

[3] See below, chapter 5, §3, pp. 115ff.

selves, because inspected by the *inspectio mentis* [consideration of the mind], under the inspection of the look of the mind, *intuitus mentis*. The object learns how to behave itself, how not to cede to the indistinct flux of the visible. In this way it mimes a stability that each visible left to itself nevertheless denies to it. The look limits the visible in order to distinguish there the object that it is not yet.

"To look at" therefore means to resist the flux of the visible, the rising of *l'invu,* which, in tight battalion, does not cease, volcanically, to make its new redness shine on the submerged surface of the world. "To look at" means to avoid the irrepressible discharge of *l'invu* aspiring to be made visible. "To avoid it" means in turn to remove one part of the visible from the silent flow of the unseen showing itself, in assigning it to a limit ideally but not effectively fixed, this effort always recaptured by the look, guarding the visible. I am looking at the visible by subtraction from a frame outside its endless tide, without beginning or limit. "To look at," that is to say, "to manage the excess of the visible," means to frame it in the frame, the *templum* [temple, sacred space] that the inspection of my look traces.

2. The Admiration of Art

Pascal scrutinized the question with which we are occupied here, in a text to be delicately interpreted: "What vanity art has that draws admiration by the resemblance to things that one scarcely admires as originals!"[4] It is with difficulty that one avoids, on a first reading, only seeing in Pascal's comment a mimetic and therefore superficial under-

---

[4] Blaise Pascal, *Pensées,* ed. Louis Lafuma (Paris: Éditions du Seuil, 1963), §40, p. 508. Emmanuel Martineau recently joined ("pasted") this fragment to §647 (The vanity of the louts and the burglars) into a vaster whole (under title XIII "Of glory") and opposes also his current mimetic interpretation, in suggesting that here vanity ". . . 'draws towards *the painter* the admiration which is not even attached to limited objects'; Pascal would aim thus less at the painting in itself as social prestige, the 'sacred' of the artist as subject" (in *Pascal, "Discours sur la Religion et sur quelques autres sujets,"* ed. and resituated by Emmanuel Martineau [Paris: Fayard, 1992], pp. 120, 248). Without failing to appreciate the elegance of his reading, or the arguments in favor of this juxtaposition, I will not, nevertheless, follow the interpretation of Martineau, in my view uselessly subjectivist (and thus metaphysical); it ends by lacking the properly phenomenological status of the joining together of the visibility of the "original" and that of the "[res-]semblance," a joining together that alone justifies the concurrence of two admirations, that is to say, of two intentional looks.

standing of painting. One would be surprised to wonder rather at the reproduction, without wondering at the original, since, after Plato, metaphysics has taught us to focus our attention not on the painted thing (the bed, in this instance), but first on the material thing (the first model for the painter), and next and especially on the immovable, true idea that upholds the one and the other (the true model for the sage).[5] It could be, nevertheless, that this metaphysical interpretation does not do justice to the quote from Pascal. For he is not interested here in the resemblance, elsewhere so often analyzed beginning from the habitual opposition of an "illustration"[6] to a "pattern" (or "model," to the "truth," to the "nature"),[7] but very precisely in the "original." In art, the original evokes less admiration than its "resemblance." The "resemblance" indicates here how the painted "things" differ from their "original"; it does not designate a relation (between model and reproduction, thing and image, and so on) but rather one of the terms of the relation—the "resemblance," which differs from the "original."

How, then, in painting, does the "resemblance" differ from the "original"? It is distinguished from it in stealing admiration from it. Thus, since to admire indicates a manner of seeing, we must conclude that the "resemblance" provokes more vision and summons the look more than the "original" does. It does not double the original, as a reproduction comes to double, after the event and more weakly, the radiance of the first visible that remains the ultimate reference, but confiscates from it this original radiance and reduces it to a disqualified beginning, obscure, even forgettable. Or, rather, the resemblance shines from a radiance so intense that it goes beyond the original, that it doubles it, just like in a race a rival overtakes the one whom he or she catches up with and steals from that person the attention of all the spectators. The resemblance appears so much more than the original that it forces it out of sight. Admiration is therefore concentrated on the resemblance, precisely because it no longer resembles anything, but, drawing onto itself all the glory and confiscating it from everything else, it enters alone into pure semblance. The resemblance alone "seems"—appears, shines, sparkles. Phenomenologically, it becomes the original, and the ontic original has no more status than a sketch, an

---

[5] Plato, *Republic*, X, 597a–e.

[6] For example, Pascal, *Pensées*, §826, p. 606.

[7] As in other fragments, such as §§248, 573, 826, 585, 652, respectively pp. 532, 581, 605, 582ff., 588.

outline, or even a reproduction by anticipation. Not only do we forget the ontic original in the face of the phenomenal original, because it becomes useless for us, even distracting us from the perfect semblance, but the semblance that makes the painting glorious itself forgets its anecdotal origin, so as not to refer to anything but itself alone, sole source of its light, matrix sufficient to its proper form. This reversal of the center of gravity of visibility—of the point where glory weighs—from the fallen original toward the rising semblance, affects the look, here described as admiration. In effect, admiration must here be understood as the most powerful exercise possible of the look, such that it is fixed permanently, quasi-fascinated, on what it meets, or rather on what happens to it, instead of wandering about in the manner of simple sight, which roams from one visible to the other without being delayed there. "Admiration is an unexpected surprise of the soul, making the latter consider with attention the objects that seem to it rare and extraordinary"—Descartes, who is here still followed by Pascal, clearly assigns admiration to the service of what "appears" the most intensely phenomenologically; admiration is obedient to the sole attraction of pure semblance, its "happening" [*arrivement*].[8] Consequently, it is only fixed on what can stop it by its deployment of visibility; it therefore notes the phenomenal reversal and now concentrates the attention of the look on the semblance, inevitably abandoning the original, offended forever. The painting has shown its power: not only has it displaced admiration (in other words, the look) from the physical world to a new and other spectacle, but it has especially provoked the appearance of a pure semblance, which confiscates, at a given moment, almost all the available phenomenality in the opening of the world. The painting has not repeated or adjusted phenomenality; rather, it has mastered it (to the detriment of nature, of the "original"), produced it (in instituting the privilege of the "resemblance"), and finally consecrated it in displacing the center of gravity of the pure semblance.

Before asking ourselves *how* art arrives in this way to take possession of phenomenality to the point perhaps even of mastering it, let us consider for a moment *what* is understood to be accomplished here. It is the raising of the semblance to the rank of original of originals, in

---

[8] René Descartes, *Passions de l'âme*, §§70 and 71, AT XI, 380 and 381. On this term and the concept of *arrivage* [arrival] that it confirms, see above, chapter 2, §2, p. 37.

fact to nothing less than the imperial origin of phenomenality, to the place and position of the thing of the world. Things already available in nature and therefore already set out by it no longer govern phenomenality: phenomena that nature and the world do not know now appear—and it is to them that the last excellence of all radiance comes back. Later we will have to try to meditate on this unequaled reversal. For the moment, we consider its effect: painting can provoke visibles of a semblance so powerful that they confiscate all the admiration that a look has in a given time. The look cannot refrain from consecrating all its admiration and all its available power to these visibles that the painting imposes on it. Why can't the look be kept from fixing—at least spontaneously, in the usual course of vision, from day to day, in the daily regime of sight—on the painted visible? Doubtlessly and simply because this visible exercises a greater visibility than that of the natural world and thus unconditionally fascinates. The painter does not have, besides, any other end than this—to dazzle us, to offer to our usually vagabond and aesthetically unfaithful sight (in short, a free child who passes from one spectacle to another without ever stopping there) a visible such that it cannot,* for once, perhaps even for the first time, turn away from it and go to the next thing, but finds itself fascinated with it, a prisoner, and dependent on it for quite a long time. The painter aims to capture sight in fascinating its attention. He or she therefore gives rise to a semblance that resembles nothing already seen before his or her intervention, not in nature, not in other paintings. This is in order that, all at once, a sum and an organization of the visible is imposed such that it overwhelms and blocks the errant view, making the look dedicated to what it keeps watch over. Instead of the common gaze passing from one visible to another, because none holds it (it "sees through" each), the look comes up against the painted semblance, being swallowed up and engulfed there. It no longer traverses it, but is crushed there. Satisfied, it can no longer go to see any other thing elsewhere but is exhausted in going over it, in recognizing it and assimilating it. It is, to the contrary, the painted semblance that envelops it, draws it in, and captivates it. Sight captivated becomes an assigned look. In this way the *idol* is accomplished: the first visible that sight cannot pierce and abandon, because it saturates it for the first time

---

* For *un visible tel qu'elle en puisse plus* we have read *un visible tel qu'elle n'en puisse plus*—Trans.

and hoards up all admiration in it. The first insurmountable visible, the idol says to the look what capacity it has hidden right from the start, because it gives to it for the first time too much to see—thus just enough. It follows that the idol, from its semblance *par excellence* and by excess, also returns to the look its proper measure, of which it was not aware, until then not having had enough of what is visible. It shows it not only or first what it gives to look at, but especially the measure of this look itself. Name your idol, and you will know who you are. The first visible of a look is thus also equivalent to an invisible mirror. The semblance that the painting puts to work therefore essentially [*par essence*] goes beyond the field of what is called—to banalize it—the aesthetic. Right away and originally it concerns my inscription in pure phenomenality, as also the truth of my ipseity. My idol defines what I can bear of phenomenality—the maximum of intuitive intensity that I can endure while keeping my look on a distinctly visible spectacle, all in transforming an intuition into a distinct and constituted visible, without weakening into confusion or blindness. In this way my idol exposes the span of all my aims—what I set my heart on seeing, and thus also want to see and do. In short, it denudes my desire and my hope. What I look at that is visible decides who I am. I am what I can look at. What I admire judges me.[9]

There is therefore no reason to oppose aesthetics too sharply to ethical responsibility. For art can never (even if it wants to) avoid radically ethical choices, since it has very often desired to phenomenalize thoroughly ethical situations. But its inevitable pretension to satisfy and fascinate the look of the spectator implicates it especially in an irremediably ethical intrigue, where it plays with the other person as such—as "looker." Art bears the responsibility of what it gives to see and, even further, the responsibility of its power to make us look. In all cases, the painting, because it diverts admiration from the "original" to the "resemblance," annuls the prestige of the visibility of the world and, in this sense, dismisses the physical from all primacy, even epistemological. It therefore liberates the look from all inscription in the world, from all cosmic imprisonment. Art tears the look from the attraction of the earth, from the fascination of its single landscape. This liberation does not yet evidently accomplish, as such, an ethical act (and will

---

[9] On the idol, see *Dieu sans l'être* (Paris: Arthème Fayard, 1982; Quadrige/Presses Universitaires de France, 1991), chapter I; *God Without Being*, trans. Thomas A. Carlson (Chicago: University of Chicago Press, 1991), taken over by *Étant donné*, §23, pp. 319ff.

perhaps forbid it), but it displaces us already outside physical necessity and places us in a posture where an ethics of the look could become at least possible.

3. THE FRAME OF THE PAINTING

We can now ask *how* the painting takes hold of phenomenality. In fact, we are not stripped of all elements of a response, since we have already received two indications of one. The first says that we are looking, by cutting up and deletion, at an isolated frame outside the [*sa*] tide of the endless visible, without beginning or limit. To look—in other words, to be protected from the excess of the visible—requires centering it in a frame. The second indication says that the look is fixed on its idol, this first visible that sight cannot pierce and abandon, because it saturates it for the first time and hoards all the admiration. The idol and the frame would in this way allow painting to master phenomenality. But would this pair of responses not raise more difficulties than they bring to light? Does the idol not imply an excess of visibility, while the frame implies the limiting of it and the immobilization of the flux? Unless the excess does not contradict here the obligation of the frame, but increases with it; unless the centering of the frame only puts an end to a *failure* to appear of the "original," which would prevent the semblance from being accomplished as an idol.

In effect, the physical thing must cede to the painted idol, because the natural experience enjoins it, by an essential law [*par une loi d'essence*], to appear less than the painting is authorized to. To take a visible [thing] of the world, any visible whatever, for example the book that I open and read—does it appear to me? Of course, since I read from this page, then the next, and since, in order to read them, they must be readable to me, that is to say, visible. Certainly, but apart from all its pages being able to appear to me simultaneously (short of pulling apart the binding, but it would still be necessary to photocopy all the *verso* to place them adjacent to the *recto* originals), the book, taken as a thing of the world, thus as an approximate rectangular parallelepiped, can never present to me its six sides all at once and at the same time. I only ever see three sides together, the other three remaining invisible to me. Certainly, I know that there are three other sides, that I can either assume as given or, to verify it (does one ever know?), check, in turning the book on its three other sides; but, at that moment, the three new visible sides will make the three preceding sides disappear. It will be enough for me, of course, to come back with a simple gesture to the three first sides, but this gesture will necessarily make the three last disappear anew. Therefore, at any moment, I will not see the six sides at once. This impossibility does not unsettle me beyond measure—I well know that it results directly from my situation in space and from the *a priori* condition of experience of objects of the world. Nevertheless, physical objects (the "originals") can never appear fully; the book is only presented in part, even if this part varies. Reciprocally, as bright as the light is, a part always remains in the shadow; better, the more the light increases, the more the thing will give itself a shadow (a shadow rightly called "shadow side") in sending away outside immediate presence an essential part of itself. One will say of this shadow part, which can never be presented, that it can only be appresented. All appearance in the world consists of presentation and of appresentation, obliging presentation to come to terms with appresentation, presence with absence.[10]

Within the frame of the painting, it does not happen like this: the contrary becomes true. Here and here alone, the appresented tends to disappear and leave the way entirely free for the presented. Certainly, the painting can offer to the look presented aspects of a physical thing, but it will always strive to present precisely those aspects that shine with a greater radiance, to the point that they will often succeed in sparing us from trying to reconstitute indirectly the appresented aspects, which, in natural experience, would be lacking. Why? Precisely because in the painting they are no longer lacking. The painting no longer represents certain presentable aspects of an object (of the world) that would remain, for its other aspects, only appresentable; it reduces the object to the presentable in it, in excluding the appresentable. In short, it pulls apart the object in order to reduce it to the visible in it, to the pure visible that is without remainder. In the painting, only the visible remains entirely presented, without further promising anything else to see save what is offered already. This reduced visible, presented in the pure state without any remainder of appresentation, reaches such an intensity that it often saturates the capacity of my look, even exceeds

---

[10] See the celebrated analyses of Husserl, in particular Hua. I, §50, pp. 138ff.; *Cartesian Meditations,* V, §64, pp. 108ff.; see below, chapter 5, §1, pp. 104ff.

it. In front of *La Sainte-Victoire au grand pin,* I do not try to bypass
the mountain in thought in order to imagine the other side, nor to reconstitute the complete trunk of the pine tree, nor to sketch the elevation
of the house of the middle ground to the left. I have enough to look at
with what is presented to my look with such a brutal force—the telluric
architecture of the mountain so strangely sheltered by the oscillation
of the plants and so embedded in it that the stone and the branch exchange their attributes—the first vibrates from heat, whereas the second is immobilized by calm.[11] In front of *The Conversion of Saint Paul,*
knocked down, lowered from his warlike posture of a horseman, or
rather, paralyzed in free fall, eyes closed by an anonymous light that
seems to come from the exterior of the painting and is reflected on the
flesh of his horse, I am not wondering about the largely hidden anat-
omy of the animal, or about the silhouette of the manservant, almost
vanished, moreover, in the shadow. I am not even inquiring about the
identity of the light (or of the voice) that calls him: I am overwhelmed,
the luminous lake flooding all at once the side opposed to the flash of
lightning, which seems to have struck in front of the painting, thus
behind my back. This is to the extent that I should even have the reflex
to turn around, in order to understand what has happened in front of
the painting. Here the visible does not only crush the painted spectacle
but also encloses the spectator, seen by the light more than he or she
sees it.[12] Moreover, if by chance the painter decides really to make
visible, under my amazed look, not only what is presented but also
what in the world would only be appresented, he or she will not hesitate
to distort the laws of natural vision in order, according to the audacity
of the first cubism, to crush on the canvas the appresented (supposed)
beside the presented, as if it could be presented to him or her as well,
in contempt of all the *a priori* conditions of physical experience in
space—the top of the guitar beside its bottom, the feet of the pedestal
table beside its shelf, two or three sides of the jug side by side, the
inside of the glass adjacent to its exterior—and still attributing to each
nuance of each color its own surface, in the measure of its role in
the entirety, replaced tone on tone with the most appropriate, without

---

[11] Paul Cézanne, *La Sainte-Victoire au grand pin,* 1886–88, Courtauld Institute,
London, Venturi 454 = *Catalogue de l'Exposition Cézanne 1996* (Paris/London/Phila-
delphia), no. 92, Paris, RMN, 1995, pp. 208–9 and 258.

[12] Carravagio, *The Conversion of Saint Paul,* 1601, Rome, Santa Maria del Popolo
church.

consideration for natural form, to the point of recomposing according to the pure harmony of the visible what perspective or natural disposition had, in the physical space, arbitrarily dissociated or confronted.[13] There is no need to turn to cubism in order to get rid of the appresented in this way from the painting, before bringing it back to presentation, pure and simple: religious art does not refrain from making appear, on the same canvas, successive episodes of a Nativity or of a Way of the Cross, or putting in perfect light "what the eye has never seen" (I Cor. 2:9 = Isa. 64:3)—the angel, the Holy Spirit, and first the Resurrected One himself.[14]

But couldn't it still be objected that each of the figures presented in this way nevertheless offers objectively appresented faces, not directly given in intuition? Precisely not in the painting. First, because here the possibility of effectively avoiding the object becomes impracticable, not because space is lacking for a turning around of the visible face, but because objects are simply lacking. We see directly the vision of the painter, no longer physical objects of his or her intention; the painting would appear neither as a subsistent object nor as an object, because it has nothing to do with object-ness, or even with being-ness.[15] Next, because—and the mastery of the painter consists first in this—nothing of what must be seen according to this now accomplished in-

---

[13] Among many others, on this last aspect, [see] for example Georges Braque, *Man at the Guitar,* 1911, New York, Museum of Modern Art. This recomposition can even sometimes better be accomplished in a simple sketch, black and white: so J. Gris, *The Pedestal Table,* collection of the musée de Céret. Other processes end at the same disappearance of appresentation: collage, the direct reemployment in the painting of raw materials (Tapiès), even of organic materials (Barcelo)—what, in natural space, would remain an object (thus presented and appresented), turning to the pure visible, reduced to the presented without remainder. Can it go the same way when one remains in physical space (sculpture)? The *ready-made* would allow us to suppose so—that which, inasmuch as a utilizable object in the world, would be withdrawn essentially into the appresented of its opposed sides, rises immediately in the present as soon as it accedes to *exhibition* [exposition] (of which installation only offers a weak variant).

[14] For example, F. Buoneri (Cecco di Caravaggio), *Resurrection* (1619–20), Art Institute, Chicago. More stupefying yet is the visibility in the background of the Risen One (less powerful than in the *Retable* of Mathieu Grünewald at Colmar or such a Flemish artist), imposed here on the whiteness of the clothes of the angel in the foreground: it appears so to speak more than visible, as in the Transfiguration the clothes of Christ became ". . . resplendent with an excessive white, such that no fuller in the world would be able to whiten them" (Mark 9:3). One cannot escape the feeling that *this* white no longer belongs to the physical world and that the artist makes another world visible—as sentient as it remains.

[15] See the analyses in *Étant donné,* I, §4, pp. 60–84.

tention is lacking, nothing is still to be seen that is not already presented here. The painter manages to fill the frame only with visible elements, without leaving the least space to the only appresentable non-visible. What gives itself is seen, what is seen gives itself. No given that would be seen is dissipated in vain; in art—in great art—nothing is lost when something does not make itself seen. Protected in the frame of the painting, the visible gives up all its reticences to vision. Here, the painted given would be equal without remainder to the given visible. Pascal claims that a ". . . portrait bears absence and presence, pleasure and displeasure. Reality excludes absence and displeasure,"[16] but, in fact and rightfully, the painting proves the contrary: it excludes absence and deception from the look. All is there to see, nothing is kept in absence or sheltered by appresentation. The painting carries presence, to the point of bearing even absence (appresentation) to direct visibility. The painting *adds* presence to presence, where nature preserves space and thus absence.

Few painters have shown this better than Paul Klee. All his paintings privilege the frame, and the narrowness first of the material frame (the small size being the rule). But this narrowness could nevertheless still perfectly leave the visible to float in the emptiness of the unseen or of the less visible. Now, even the sketches—the last angels *(Ange oublieux, Angelus militans, Essai d'[un Christ aux] outrages),* especially the *Sans titre* of 1940, interlaced tightly like a weave of monocellular quasi-faces—impose, moreover, the feeling of an oppression, of a suffocation. Certainly, as *Le Timbalier* or *Enlacement (Umgriff)* proves without contest, it is a question there first of a disposition of spirit become, in the end, fundamental *(Grundstimmung),* according to the rising of exterior and intimate perils, and this fundamental disposition can only be understood in reference, among others and at least, to the analytic of *Dasein.* But it still had to be able to be seen, to become "painting-matter"—although his painting, his art, and his style allow Klee to make this oppression and suffocation appear, he had to make them seen as of the visible and among the visible, although they remained of themselves feelings that were invisible through and through.

---

[16] Pascal, *Pensées,* §260, p. 253. It would be better to say that ". . . those who add still more once they have done the painting are producing a picture instead of a portrait" (§578, p. 582 [trans. taken from A. J. Krailsheimer (London: Penguin, 1995), p. 197]). The painting, in effect, *adds;* that it turns [into] a portrait or not is of little importance.

His painting only manages to do this—for it managed to do this at a precise moment, in the 1930s—in transposing them into an obsession of the visible, become too dense, too pressing, even overpopulated by itself, to the point that it crushes against the frame that was supposed to welcome it. The push of the visible not only confers on it a density that almost solidifies it but also constrains the frame so much that it ends up playing the role of a confining fence—as in a nuclear reactor the first hydraulic circuit must remain absolutely watertight from the second, to avoid atomic contamination, while getting rid of its heat in inoffensive, usable energy. This rising of the visible, heavy with a literally formidable luminous density, to the edge of the chain reaction, to the extent of getting close to the explosion of the frame, is doubtlessly never marked as much as in *Ad Marginem*.[17]

It is a well-named painting: the red sun, which, a little raised from the center, would have to crush with its dense, nodal mass and its dark, explosive heat the greenish marshland which, spread out, surrounds it—crush it to the point of draining it, even fade it to the point of whitening it—this quasi-atomic sun seems imperceptibly, but indisputably, to be narrowed under the pressure of the green that lays siege to it, turning to yellow and digesting, so to speak, its redness, as if asphyxiated by the exponential growth of the quasi-plants that push on the margins of the painting. They buttress themselves there all the more visibly as the painting is narrowing in on itself in sketching an ocher frame, already woody, on the inside of its physical, material frame. This redoubling of the frame (to dimensions already abnormally restrained, 46.4 x 35.9 cm) renders visible, almost foreseeable, even inevitable, that the clash of the elementary forces of the sun and of the magma, both in fusion, ends in the implosion of enormous energy—the same energy of the visible struggling in the rarified space to rise, in spite of it all, to the day. The painting imposes itself like a double-armored casket, which tries to hold back the explosion of the immense visible, which will end inevitably by taking it apart and dispersing it. The painting attains the highest saturation possible of the visible in such a restrained frame. The saturation of the visible becomes, to the one who knows how to look at it as it gives itself, really unbearable.

---

[17] Kunstmuseum, Bâle, 1930; see the reproduction and commentary of Alain Bonfand (*Paul Klee, l'oeil en trop*, vol. 1 [Paris: Éd. de la difference, 1988], pp. 108ff.), on which I rely here.

The visible, too dense, reaches the margin of what the frame can endure—and our look with it. What the *Carré blanc sur fond blanc* had sketched programmatically—density making the fire of the visible white hot in "a unanimous and white struggle" (for once literal and filled with excessive reality)—Klee, more than Malévitch and no doubt more than any other, shows, imposes, and accomplishes here.

Here is the painting: the non-physical space where the visible alone reigns abolishes *l'invu* (the invisible by default) and reduces the phenomenon to pure visibility. The painting is the concern of the most classic and most strict phenomenology, because it reduces entirely the phenomenal to the visible. And this is what the transcendental reduction of Husserl can never attain, because it remains in the realm of nature, despite all his inversion of the natural attitude, because it remains essentially (if not, perhaps, uniquely) preoccupied with the objects of the world-region and obsessed with their constitution. The painting does not offer an example, interesting, but possibly optional, of phenomenological method of the reduction—it accomplishes it radically according to the quality (the intensity or the "intense grandeur") of the appearing. In reducing the visible to its atomic quintessence, in containing in its frame the mad energy of the visible, the painting reduces what gives itself to what shows itself—under the regime of the idol. Phrased otherwise by Plato: ". . . in fact, only the beautiful has received, in terms of being [the phenomenon], the most apparent, the ἐκφανέστατον (*ekhphanestaton*), and the most desirable."[18]

4. THE MOST VISIBLE

The excellence of the ἐκφανέστατον, the visible brought to a density such that its incandescence no longer leaves a place for anything invisible, in short, the visible elevated to the rank of idol, brings paradoxical consequences. All of them come from a phenomenologically indisputable fact: the painting, such that in its frame it operates a reduction of the given to pure visibility, produces (as a producer produces a show, putting forward an actor, a singer, in short, an "idol") a visible that has never previously been seen by anyone. Some *invus*, until then dissimulated in a pre-phenomenal obscurity, not even invisible or foresee-

---

[18] Plato, *Phèdre*, 250d.

able because we had no suspicion of them, arise and pass without even stopping for the natural visibility of the objects of the world (combinations of presentation and of appresentation), for visibility, the limits of which they abolish. *L'invu* at once appears as the most appearing possible [*le plus apparaissant possible*], even the unbearable appearing [*l'apparaissant insupportable*] of radiance. The abrupt metamorphosis from the unseen into the idol, which the painting in its frame accomplishes in its own right, reproduces nothing already seen and resembles nothing visible in the world. It adds to the visible of the world a visible that no longer belongs to it, transcending it and annulling it. The painter does not reproduce it, he or she produces, copying nothing, making seen—these are banalities. But these banalities signify more: the painter adds to the visible new visibles, because he or she alone, advancing imprudently to the extreme edge of the area of uncertainty [*la bouche d'ombre*], looks out for and provokes the rising up of *invus*, the violent novelty of which no look before had been able to or had dared approach. Hunter of unsuspected *invus*, the painter seeks in obscurity for something to add to the visibility already available. The painter tries to receive, in his or her frame, a newcomer, a new seen, and to hold it there in reducing it without remainder to its pure visibility. In this aesthetic transmutation, the phenomenological reduction is entirely applicable, and especially, the non-physical universe of the pure visible is constructed. The history of art must be understood as the emergence of a flux that is sometimes interrupted but always renascent until this point, of visibles so intense and dense that they irremediably submerge what the world gives to see. The visibles of the world cede it without hope of restoration to the always growing sum of the visibles that the painting tears from *l'invu*—visibles at once more archaic and more elaborated than the spectacles of the world. Humanity dominates and governs nature—but not only in managing it technologically and in populating it with a human lineage, or rather, the two dominations culminate (less than they originate) in the irrepressible provocation by the artist of new visibles, metamorphoses of *invus* absolutely inaccessible without the artist. With each painting, a new visible comes to dwell among us, definitive resident of our phenomenality. The painter produces absolutely new phenomena, and what phenomena—idols! It is the idols that, in each era, reign over the natural visibles, over the appearance of constituted objects, and that oblige us to see everything starting from the paradigms their fascination imposes.

The painter is king, as much and certainly more immediately than any philosopher, and none of our kings ignored it. The painting offers us a saturated phenomenon—but it saturates as well all the natural visibles that our look imagines it sees by itself, although in fact it only sees something there starting from a painting and in the frame of an idol. The painting records in the idol a new *invu* in the visible, *nouveau riche* of phenomenological glory.

It follows that we cannot see a painting once and for all. Unlike the objects of the world that—as long as one knows enough about their structure, their purpose, and their use—it suffices to see once in order to be able to use them daily and no longer have to come back there *to see* (it is precisely in this capacity that one measures the adaptation of an individual to technological society), the painting is distinguished by a clear criterion: we can never see it once and for all, but we must, at regular intervals, come to re-see it. All that which is seen but does not require us to re-see remains a simple object, a natural visible, of second rank; what must, on the contrary, be re-seen in order to be seen a little is a concern of paintings. The painting cannot be seen in a single instance; it must be reseen in order to appear, because it appears according to the phenomenality of the saturated phenomenon. The museum, decried a little thoughtlessly as a tomb of art's dead, offers perhaps also a social structure appropriate to this necessary return to the image, this free looking back on vision that the painting silently demands. And, since one must re-see it, one must therefore *go to see it*. It is there, and I am here: it is necessary—and I consent to it—that it is I who goes there, and not it that comes here (even the exhibition confirms it). Since our times seem to have lost the aesthetic means to build churches and even to construct palaces, let's not joke too much about the museum, this unavowed avatar of the sanctuary of pilgrimage. First, because a remnant of veneration, even without assurance or lucidity, is worth more than blind barbarism. Next, because the reverse tactic, that of the collector who forces the painting to come to give him or her homage, here, and who is dispensed from going to it, there, inspires an invincible mistrust, however discrete. Does the collector have the right to make him- or herself the center of the paintings, in rendering them slaves under the quite common pretext that they are affordable? Does the collector have the right to deprive other looks from contemplating these paintings? But most especially, does the collector have the right to deprive the paintings from innumerable other looks, which would make them live for what they are, pure appearances—in short, the right to imprison them under his or her look alone, when no single look, even exceptionally powerful and educated (quite a rare case, one imagines), could ever receive the immense excess of visibility that each of these idols diffuses? The frequent, final transformation of private collections into public foundations attests to this moral restraint before the aesthetic injunction.

The excellence of phenomenality of the painting (idol) therefore always surpasses a particular moment of contemplation, a particular empirical look borne on it. The intensity it deploys would demand an almost indefinite succession of looks, of which each would do justice to any radiance of the painting and would receive the effect (rather than the emotion) that results from it. The radiance of a color or chromatic harmony suffices to fill a given look (a *mens momentanea* [quick thought]), the appearing [*jaillissement*] of a line or the power of a form, the network of several points also linked by rays of light. On each occasion it is appropriate that a new, irrepeatable, and unsubstitutable meeting takes place. The computation of my visits to the same museum for years or months sketches less my own physical history than the temporal deployment of the visibility of paintings that on each occasion I put in a new light. My own look, always different on each visit, therefore postponed and deferred from visit to visit, makes the painting differ from itself, before advancing the deployment of it—and noting that it will never be a closed object, exhaustively seen. As much as my look demands the multiplication of visits in order to do justice to the immense visible of the painting, the painting itself demands that the origins of the look are multiplied: mine, but still those of all the other possible spectators. It would be better to consider groups, certainly often little suited to look at what they come to see, and who transform great exhibitions into huge waiting rooms. It would be appropriate to take into just consideration there the unimaginable sum of fragmented, confused, allusive—but on each occasion nevertheless enlightened—looks, which bounce over the paintings and are modified in sometimes distinguishing a splendor that no other look, even more educated, had until then yet glimpsed. At the back of the most conventional (and vulgar) commentaries, who will name the visual effects received? To what extent can the painting educate certain looks? To what extent will the apprehension of its glory have progressed under the effort of their vigil? Phenomenologically—that is to say, to consider only what appears as a given—each authentic painting consists, much more than in a fragment of canvas supporting diverse pigments assembled in a certain order, in the sum of all its potential visibles, that the sum, equally innumerable, of all the momentary looks that have fixed it in a point until then cheated of the visible to which it was aspiring, can alone deploy. The painting opens infinitely more than its frontal spectacle—that pictorial and museographical science can almost reduce to a finite object. It opens an arena of space and time to all the contemplations that it gives rise to. It exposes itself as the potential sum of all that which all have seen, see, and will see there. The life of the painting is deployed as the regulatory idea of looks that it attracts to itself, as a given definitively visible and never actually seen.[19] It is always to be reseen and to come to be seen, precisely because it raises to a quasi-unbearable intensity the incandescence of the exploding frame. There is an eventmentality of the painting.

Inaccessible to a solitary look, the painting is reduced to the pure visible—there is no contradiction here, but the same tension, the ἐκφανέστατον. The pure seen, reduced phenomenologically to its visibility without remainder, must be confronted as exposed, put in a monstrance [*ostensoir*] (the frame), ostentatious to the extreme, fully exposed [*ostenté*] if I dare say. To describe the evidence of it, without filter or gloss—which is, by definition, impossible, otherwise we would be dispensed from seeing it again and from confronting it—let us follow a sure guide, Mark Rothko. Consider several canvases and their evolution. To begin with, the *Subway Scene*.[20] Here the tonality of the ensemble of purple roses hollows out again the empty spaces between the silhouettes, the ones half swallowed by the staircase, the others kept in the background: the look can still dream of embedding itself in a perspective, therefore of playing the "full" visibles against the quasi-"empty" spaces. Some ten years later, almost in the same chromatic tonalities, *Aquatic Drama*[21] dissolves all perspective distinctions and

---

[19] Mark Rothko: "A picture lives by companionship, expanding and quickening in the eyes of the sensitive observer. It dies by the same token. It is therefore a risky and unfeeling act to send it out into the world. How often it must be permanently impaired by the eyes of the vulgar and the cruelty of the impotent who would extend their affliction universally!" (in *Tiger's Eye*, no. 2, 1947, quoted from Nicholas Serota et al., *Mark Rothko: 1903–1970* [New York: Stewart, Tabori and Chang, 1987], p. 83).

[20] *Subway Scene*, 1938, no. 7, Estate of Mark Rothko, in Serota, p. 96.

[21] *Aquatic Drama*, 1946, no. 23, National Gallery of Art, Washington, D.C., in Serota, p. 112.

all division between the "empty" and the "full"; the brown, whitish, red, and yellow stains start to fluctuate in a closed, but light, atmosphere. The visible takes hold univocally of all the canvas, without leaving anything to the background or in a lesser intensity. Nevertheless, as in the canvases that follow over some time yet, some forms remain still legible there which accordingly no longer coincide with the islands of homogeneous color but nevertheless disperse the look in search of residual hierarchies, of probable organizations. Won't Rothko then title certain canvases *Multiforms*?[22] But this last hypothetical will be finally raised with the glorious series of paintings in horizontal stripes of almost homogeneous colors. To take *Number 7:* from now on no form will contradict colors or otherwise structure them, since the three stripes are not modeled in lines that would separate them. The clear purple of the summit eats into the top of the central yellow stripe and harmonizes furtively with it in a dark orange *coulis,* while the base of the same series of yellow allows itself to be separated from the inferior orange stripe by a scarcely perceptible whitish *stratus,* along its whole length, but without overflowing all the way to the edge of the canvas. Each color in this way supports its own form freely, as if it were spontaneously delimiting its respective area following its intimate forces of expansion, without encroachment, contact, or rivalry with the other colors. None of the stripes claims anymore to touch the physical limit of the frame. A narrow but continuous contour dissuades them from it or protects them from it, with a strange color, by the way, which varies under the influence of what it adjoins (successively pink, yellow, and orange), all the while remaining faithful to its original anonymity (ocher, red, brown). This fragile peace, where the frontiers are sketched less by a common accord than by a miraculous and simultaneous exhaustion of their rival tides, presents a miraculous equilibrium, so supple that it seems at the same time almost indestructible. The canvas distends itself and breathes from the free commerce—nevertheless sterile, without exchange or mixture—of colored stripes, which remain docile enough to go on their own, without nevertheless being separated. This breathing or this calm fluctuation of color-stripes persists because they have nothing to defend, no form, no line, no movement. The canvas no longer rests on a material foundation, but is detached from it. It undulates on itself alone, not even on any water (like the

---

[22] So, *Multiform,* 1948, no. 26, Estate of Mark Rothko, in Serota, p. 115.

Nymphéas), or on the least support-surface—glued on nothingness.[23]
The canvas rests without depth on the pacified coexistence of color-
bands, on their slow-paced brushing together, stopped just at the moment of contact always denied, without nevertheless avoiding it.
Forms—if there really are any—become ". . . organisms with the will
and a passion to assert themselves": they ". . . move themselves with
an internal liberty." The canvas is auto-affirmed and auto-positioned,
because it has annulled all the constraints and interventions that would
have been able to build it from the outside. The painter becomes again
a useless player, an "outsider," and therefore the spectator is going to
be able in return to enter into the canvas. "I paint very large canvases.
. . . To paint a small canvas, is to place oneself outside one's experience, to look from above at an experience with a stereoscopic vision or
with a reducing glass.* But, in whatever way you paint a large canvas,
you are within it. It is not something you command." Not only is the
painting no longer placed as an object posed facing us, but we are not
even called before it anymore—it is henceforth way too small, because
we are absorbed in it. A similar reversal of mastery characterizes in its
own right the painting as the saturated phenomenon: the ". . . *Action
painting* is the antithetical opposite of the very appearance and of the
spirit of my work. The work must be the final arbiter." It has stopped
presenting itself to our look as an object that we would produce, however one understands it. It holds itself erect opposite us; better, the
visible that saturates it and without which it could not rise up from
itself overflows on us—or rather draws us as a great mass draws a
smaller one. ". . . [T]he canvases are intimate and intense, quite the
opposite of what is decorative. . . . In *saturating* the room with the
feeling of the work, the walls are overcome and the poignant impact of
each work becomes for me more visible." This autonomy of the seen
reduced to its pure visibility is precisely what Rothko attains in deliver-
ing the proper life of the canvas, its breathing and its floating. All rest
on an absolute principle: "Paintings have their own inner light."[24] The
idol rises up before us, silent, irresistible, adorable.

---

[23] If it was necessarily a reference to the tradition (and it evidently was one, see
Robert Rosenblum, "Notes on Rothko and Tradition," in Serota, 21–31) it would instead be Matisse, *Homage to Matisse* (New York, 1954) coll. "McCrory Corp." (in
Diane Waldman, *Mark Rothko, 1903–1970: A Retrospective* [New York: Abrams,
1978], no. 107).

* Parts of these quotes are in English in the text—Trans.

[24] Rothko, respectively in *Possibilities* 1 (Winter 1947/1948), *Interiors,* May 10,
1951, then *Letter to Art News* 56, no. 8 (1957), *Letter to Katharine Kuh* (Archives of

5. WHAT THE IDOL MASKS

The idol accomplishes the phenomenological reduction of the given visible to the pure seen. It takes back this given to the surface, without withdrawal, emptiness, or depth. The visible finds itself again without subterfuge, crushed on the plane, whence it will never leave, except in full visibility.

We must be very conscious here that the simple surface and the naked plane have the duty of operating a drastic reduction to nothing less than the truth: "We come to opt for simple expression of complex thought. We are in favor of great form, because it exerts the impact of the non-equivocal. We want to re-establish the picture plane strongly. We are in favor of flat forms, because they destroy illusion and reveal truth."[25] It is a question of a choice, almost of method, taken in perfect knowledge: "There are certain artists who want to say everything to us, but I think that it is more judicious to say little. My paintings are sometimes described [that is, by the critics] as facades, and indeed, they are facades." This declaration, which radicalizes the pictorial tool (image plane, flat form) in assigning to it its only possible result (the facade), does not go without saying, even and especially for Rothko. He only reached it as constrained and forced, because he had to renounce reaching another result, once envisaged, precisely to envisage the face, to paint the figure—the human figure: "I belong to a generation that was interested in the human figure and I studied it. It is only unwillingly that I perceived that it was not responding to my needs. Whoever makes use of it, mutilates it. No one can paint the human figure as it is, in having the feeling of producing something that expresses the world. I refuse to mutilate and I have had to find another mode of expression. . . . My current paintings are concerned with the *scale* of human emotions, with the human drama, as much as I am capable of expressing it."[26] A decisive text: the painting cannot give

the Art Institute, Chicago), and *Notes prises au Musée d'art moderne,* New York; cited from pp. 84, 85, 86, 59 that I emphasize (cited also by M. Compton, "Rothko, the Subject of the Artist"; see Katharine Kuh, "Mark Rothko," *Institute of Chicago Quarterly* 48, no. 4 [November 1954]) and p. 88. The quite loose translations of these fragments in French are available in J. Stewart, "Chronologie," in *Mark Rothko* (Paris: Musée d'Art moderne de la Ville de Paris, 1999), pp. 251–72.

[25] Rothko and A. Gottlieb, Letter to the *New York Times,* June 13, 1943 (cited in Serota, p. 79).

[26] Extract from a conference at the Pratt Institute, October 27, 1958, in Breslin, pp. 394–95.

the human figure to be seen, still less its face. This automatic impossibility has been in fact verified by the unaccomplishment, either of the first figurative attempts (such as *Self Portrait* and the yellow nude *Untitled* of 1936)[27] or of the tentative mythologies of the 1940s (*Antigone, The Omen of the Eagle, Syrian Bull,* and so on)—"This was not satisfying."[28] What aporia did Rothko encounter? Evidently not a technical difficulty—that of the animated human silhouette, or even that of the portrait (Rothko sometimes tried it); the tradition had the means of confronting them, that Rothko knew perfectly. It was therefore a question of an automatic difficulty: if painting exercises the phenomenological function of reducing what gives itself to what shows itself, the potential visible to the pure seen, if it operates this reduction in bringing back all the visible to the pure and simple plane-ness of the surface, it must end inevitably in the facade. An aesthetic consequence is imposed here. But it does not yet allow us to understand why the facade would forbid the "painting of the figure such as it is," save by "mutilating" it. What automatic incompatibility does Rothko find here that so many others have not perceived? Why did he not want, or no doubt *was not able,* to follow the way so easily and violently opened by Pablo Picasso and trampled on by so many others after him? I can see only one response: it is that it was necessary to renounce putting "humans" into a facade in order not to make himself complicit with their disfigurement, to not have to mutilate without respite the flesh and the faces of people in order to make them enter by force into a flat visibility (the only one available). Even the uneasy pretext of denouncing the violence of *Guernica* can't help it: one does not surmount the mutilation of the human in accomplishing it. And we really must understand this response: it is not about either a technical aporia or a retreat from goodwill—or even about a reverential fear before the obscurity of evil. No, it comes from a truly ethical decision.

In order to show it, I return to the initial argument: the painting, inasmuch as reduction and as frame, brings back to the flat plane, to the facade. The facade cancels all depth. This cancellation does not

---

[27] In Serota, nn. 3, 4 and 5, pp. 92–94. But it only ends in forming a ". . . *tableau vivant* [in French in the text] of human incommunicability" (p. 84).

[28] In Serota, nn. 8 and 10, pp. 97 and 99; the text cited exactly: ". . . I used mythology for a while substituting various creatures who were able to make intense gestures without embarrassment. I began to use morphological forms in order to paint gestures that I could not make people do. But this was unsatisfactory." Text in Breslin, p. 395.

result in any damage to the things of the world: objects lose perspective, granted, but their disorganized figures become again just as free for other apparitions, otherwise more "miraculous."[29] The cancellation of depth by the facade therefore only wrongs the figure of the human and primarily the face. In order to understand this very thing that Marcus Rothkowitz understood so intensely that he consented to reform entirely his whole enterprise of painting, we must bring him together with another émigré, his contemporary, coming not like him from Russia to Portland, Oregon, but from Lithuania to Strasbourg, France, Emmanuel Levinas. For Levinas established the absolute incompatibility between the facade and the face [side]. By "facade" he understands, as if echoing Rothko (the flat surface entirely visible, without depth), ". . . the thing that keeps its secret—exposes itself closed in its monumental essence and in its myth where it shines as a splendor, but does not deliver itself . . . subjugated by its grace as by magic, but not revealing itself."[30] The facade confronts [fait face], but it closes itself all the more, for if everything is visible there, the seen must necessarily be seen on the plane, reduced to flatness [platitude], and therefore the facade closes off access to the intimate.[31] What intimate? Isn't that a question of spiritualist and subjectivist illusion? It is not, but is instead a radical interrogation of two modes of appearing without common measure: "Can things take a face? Isn't art an activity that lends faces to things?" Now, things rightly only show a facade, even and especially in art (painting), but never a face: "The facade of a house, isn't it a house that is looking at us?"[32] Evidently the facade does not look at us: only a face can do so, because it alone comes to expose itself in the mode of encounter. For to appear, for the human figure, does not exactly mean to force some visible in reserve (and without doubt very hypothetical) to spread itself out on the flat surface of the painting. This bewildered research would bring us back precisely to a frenetic

---

[29] "Paintings must be miraculous." *Possibilities* 1 (Winter 1947/1948).

[30] Levinas, *Totalité et infini*, p. 166 (Librarie Générale Française edition, p. 210); *Totality and Infinity*, p. 193.

[31] Levinas, *Totalité et infini*, p. 87.

[32] Emmanuel Levinas, "L'ontologie est-elle fondamentale?," a text published in the *Revue de métaphysique et de morale* in 1951 (reprinted in *Entre-nous: Essais sur le penserà-l'autre* [Paris: Grasset et Fasquelle, 1991], pp. 13–24, 23; *Entre Nous: Thinking-of-the-Other*, trans. Michael B. Smith and Barbara Harshav [New York: Columbia University Press, 1998], p. 10), almost contemporaneously with that of Rothko and where the allusions to painting merit the greatest attention.

objectivation of the other person, and so to the massacre of the innocent (in the way of expressionism, of Picasso, even of Soutine and of Bacon). To appear as such for the human figure comes back, on the contrary, to imposing oneself as the other person [*autrui*], no more as the other [*l'autre*], the neutral visible without retreat. How would the other person thus impose him- or herself? If, on the one hand, I impose myself on the world in exercising my intentionality on it (by which, among other things, I open to myself the painting as saturated idol), and if, on the other hand, the other person must, in order to take the status of a me other than me, receive my ultimate privilege in order to submit him- or herself to me no longer as one seen among others, it is necessary, in order to appear to me as such, that the other manifests me in exercising on me an intentionality as original as mine. In this way the face arises—a counter-intentionality that does not manifest itself in becoming visible but in addressing its look to me. "Responsibility for the Other [*Autrui*]—against the grain of intentionality and of the will that intentionality does not manage to dissimulate—means scarcely the unveiling of a given and its reception or its perception, but the exposing of me to the other person, prior to all decision."[33] From that point on, one understands that the side [*face*] or face [*visage*] neither can nor must enter into the visibility of the painting, into the frame of the seen. It holds itself back from it, because it can only manifest itself, "neither seen, nor known,"[34] according to an epiphany irreducible to vision, the silent statement of the imperative "Thou shalt not kill (me)!" The face does not appear; it manifests itself by the responsibility that it inspires in me. Rothko, then, had perfectly foreshadowed what Levinas means: the facade forbids us to paint the face, and therefore it is necessary to choose between either killing the face in enframing it in the flatness [*platitude*] of the painting and putting it to death in the idol, or "mutilating" oneself as a painter and giving up producing the face directly in visibility. Rothko chose to mutilate himself in order not to kill the face, which he named the "human drama."

With this decision, he accomplished a great deal. First, he marked what masks the idol without any ambiguity—the [sur]face, the face [*visage*], the other person in his or her epiphany. Pictorially, he con-

---

[33] Emmanuel Levinas, *Autrement qu'être ou au-delà de l'essence* (La Haye: Martinus Nijhoff, 1974), p. 180.

[34] Levinas, *Totalité et infini*, p. 168.

firms what Levinas establishes in phenomenology, or rather, he puts to work phenomenologically what the phenomenologist shows in concepts. Next, he lays down in painting, in any case in the art of the time of the "death of God" and of the "end of art," a properly ethical prohibition, the same one that philosophy enunciates. No idol can claim to accede to the face of another person, and until proven otherwise, modern painting does not provide other ways than that—royal, it is true—of the idolatry of the visible.[35] For the face of another person there must be another way, that of the icon, but it does not depend on the painter as such to follow it as it is. And if the painter transgresses this prohibition—as the majority of them have not ceased authorizing themselves to do without regard—he or she not only puts in peril the painting itself in its legitimate domain (the frame of the painting, the idol saturated with the visible), but, besides this aesthetic danger, exposes it to being rendered an accomplice to the murder of the human (in ways that this century has practiced unimaginably and incomparably to any other era). And in fact, painting has played its role in the putting to death of the human: whether only in taking pleasure in rendering it visible, thus foreseeable, or even in assuming as a matter of principle that one could no more paint the human than death, as a corpse or prostituted. But Rothko knew how to accomplish more still. He did not give up, in spite of his ethical mutilation, on making himself be ". . . very intimate and human" in the "human drama," that is to say, among other things, on keeping "a clear preoccupation with death. All art has to do with the intimations of mortality"—thus also with "sensuality, the foundation for being concretely aware of the world," "tension," "irony," "spirit and humor," "an amount of the ephemeral, a stroke of luck," and even "around ten percent hope. . . . If you need this type of thing: the Greeks never mentioned it."[36] But how does one keep the closeness with this depth of "human drama" if one wants to remain an artist assigned to flat forms, to the flat screen of the painting and the enframing of the idol? The ten percent hope with which the Greeks could perhaps dispense, because they doubtlessly did not have

---

[35] Setting aside the way of Rouault and perhaps of Giacometti. Who has assumed it from them?

[36] Respectively, *Interiors,* May 1951, and *Conference* at the Pratt Institute, New York, October 27, 1958 (cited in Serota, pp. 85, 87, and Breslin, p. 390). Here, as elsewhere, the French translation (p. 267) is more than approximative—inventive, rather (perhaps one is reading another text?).

any great need of it, at a time of life for art and for the human—is that ten percent sufficient to preserve the equilibrium Rothko imposes on himself: simultaneously, visibility reduced to the pure seen on the plane and attention to what intimates death, sensuality, and tension, in short, the face of the other person?

Evidently not. And in this way the intimidating secret of the *Chapel* of Houston could be clarified. The canvases of the 1960s already manifest the contradiction: the frame and the flat figures had to meet with what the death and the life of the other person (of the human as such) intimate, but the necessary and decided absence of all visibility from its face cannot do it justice directly. All the sufferings, all the desires, and all the tensions can only rise to presence indirectly, always by the play, floating and aerial, of the color-bands. It will then be their chromatic variation that will become the unique resource left to the idol, in order to receive (as one receives a blow) and to endure the haunting and impossible claim of the other person and of his or her death to be manifested—a manifestation that the idol should renounce promising, since it would have to be an icon, but a manifestation that it does not have the right to dismiss, since it alone remains practicable, as access to the icon is closed up. Then it remains for the red to brush the brown, then the brown the brown, then the brown the blue and the black. Sometimes, the pink tries to save the appearances with the evanescent gray, even the dirty white with itself. When, at the end, two reds frame an orange a little too much,[37] they seem to show the last instant before the conflagration of an ultimate red, overwhelming all the frame, like an explosion of a tension that nothing can contain any longer.[38] The *Chapel,* the elaboration of which occupies almost all of the last decade, only deploys the crushing and magisterial symphony of its browns, purples, and blacks in order to exemplify the tension, or even the freely assumed contraction, between the facade and the face, the idol and the icon. It delays the ineluctable implosion in multiplying the paintings, depending on whether the architectural space accords to them, for once, ironically or as surety of hope, depth.

A depth that no look of the other person, especially not that of the Christ, can reassure in occupying it. The temple is empty of a look

---

[37] *Untitled,* 1969, Washington, D.C., National Gallery of Art, no. 92, in Serota, p. 181.

[38] *Untitled,* 1969, Washington, D.C., National Gallery of Art, no. 93, in Serota, p. 182. Both are gifts from the Rothko Foundation.

that it desires to death. It is no accident that, foreseen to be initially Catholic—which means destined to receive the eucharistic presence of the risen Face—the *Chapel* today remains "non-denominational," indicating less a vague (and urgent) ecumenism than its lack of a proper name, of a divine name. The lack of the Name that would open a look and would make an icon appear. From then on, with this last effort, the painting can explode.

4

Flesh or the Givenness of the Self

1. THE FEELING BODY

Daily life scarcely gives me access to myself; actually, it dispenses me from having the desire and even the need of it. For I have passed a tacit accord with myself [*moi*]: I will pretend I have access to myself, but I will exempt myself from verifying it too often so as to be able to deal with my worldly business with a free spirit. Since I am here (or rather, there), why burden myself with confirming it? I assume myself sufficiently assured of the faithfulness of myself to myself not to go at each moment to verify it. The course of things slips away like this: too certain of myself ever to go to see if I am there, I only concern myself with the rest of the beings. Since I am well looked after by another me [*moi-même*], I can forget myself. In this way I traverse my life in a state of separation of body and of thought from myself. I am not without me—without self. But, in fact, am I really assured of being able at will to have access to myself? And besides, how can I experience myself as such—myself by myself? Where and when could I (if I could) not remain a stranger to myself, undefined, even absent? To the disquieting simplicity of the question, the false evidence of the response echoes: I come back to myself in experiencing myself, and I experience myself in taking flesh. It remains to be understood what "to take flesh" means.

To try to do so, I will begin with the one who seems to have ignored it and forbidden it, Descartes. Nevertheless, I will not draw out an argument from the too famous and so fragile reproach of dualism. Let us consider, earlier than that, one of the moments of the demonstration of the existence of the *ego,* still badly in need of its own *cogitatio:* "Nunquid ergo saltem ego aliquid esse? Sed jam negavi me habere ullos sensus et ullum corpus. Haero tamen; nam quid inde? Sumne ita corpori sensibusque alligatus, ut sine illis esse non possim?" The Duke of Luynes translated this as follows: "Myself at least, then, am I not something? But I have already denied that I had any sense or any body; I hesitate, nevertheless, because what follows from that? Am I so dependent on the body and on the senses that I cannot be without them?"[1]

I reconstitute the reasoning of Descartes in this way: I already admit the hypothesis that an *x* (God, an evil genie, or whomever you like) deceives me in sending me false ideas. But in this case, am I not therefore already necessarily something, since this "aliquis" [someone][2] needs an "aliquid"—something like me—in order to be deceived about it? I must nevertheless deny it, because which "aliquid" could I be, what is left for it to be, from the moment that I convinced myself that I had neither sense nor, therefore, body? This refusal itself nevertheless presupposes that to be, for me, is uniquely equivalent to being a body gifted with feeling—". . . sensus et . . . corpus [sense and body]." It follows that I hesitate with reason to deny that I am an "aliquid" under the simple pretext that I am not—which I admit—a body gifted with feeling. In effect, I am there not perhaps so bound (*alligatus,* stronger than *dependent*) that I could not be something else, and, in fact, I will define myself instead as something different, a *res cogitans* [thinking thing].

The question is expressed from now on in this way: Descartes excluded, in any case at least outwardly and according to almost all the interpretations of this text, [the idea] that I am an *x* linked indissolubly to a body gifted with feeling (". . . ullos sensus, et ullum corpus . . . / . . . corpori sensibusque . . . [. . . any senses, and any body . . . / . . . and the perceptions of the body . . .]"). Therefore, if I must be something, it will not thus be spatial extension (a point already established), but thought (a point still to be established here). And, in fact, my body is found disproved by its assimilation to what is found extended, the world: ". . . nihil plane esse in mundo, nullum coelum, nullam terram, nullas mentes, nulla corpora . . . [. . . nothing plainly being in the world, not sky, not earth, not rational souls, not bodies . . .]."[3] But this argument presupposes the evidence that my body *gifted with sense*—me and in me—could undergo the same disqualification as what is in the world, thus that it could be inscribed within the sky, the earth, and so on, that is to say, outside me. It could also presuppose

---

[1] Respectively, AT VII, pp. 24, 25–26, 2, and AT IX-1, pp. 18, 23–30.
[2] AT VII, p. 24, 2.
[3] AT VII, p. 25, 4.

that the sentient body, in the sense of what feels, the feeler, falls under the same refutation as the sentient bodies, in the sense of what is felt, of the feel-able.[4] This assimilation appears immediately untenable.

This is first because the *bodies* of the world (sky, earth, and so on) are absolutely not identified with *my body gifted with sense*. The difference is not obvious here: the bodies of the world are objects of sense (sentient as feel-able) but themselves feel nothing (insentient as non-feeling), whereas my body, even if it is inscribed in the world and can, as such, be found there felt like an object, has as its proper characteristic—according to the same text of Descartes—to feel itself and to be able to let itself be affected by the sensible, precisely because indissolubly gifted with sense. In short, as a feeler, my body is radically distinguished from the bodies of the world, only felt, but never sentient as feeling. Then the argument that I would not be a *feeling* body, because I can doubt the existence of *felt and non-feeling* bodies, collapses. Descartes must himself, in any case, suspect it, he even tacitly avows it, since he reinforces his argument in surreptitiously adding to the enumeration of the beings of the world (sky, earth, bodies) another term: ". . . nullas mentes—no minds [feelings, spirits, rational souls]. . . ."[5] The motive of this addition goes without saying—if I admit, moreover, that there is no mind in the world, then my body *gifted with sense* will also find itself disqualified. But his arbitrariness equally follows—Descartes has never exactly established previously that doubt, even hyperbolic (by recourse to the divine omnipotence), puts minds in question, which alone feel. The conclusion of the *Meditatio I,* here cited by *Meditatio II,* only actually puts in doubt ". . . coelum, aërem, colores, figures, sonos *cunctaque externa* . . . [. . . the sky, the air, the earth, colors, figures, sounds and *all other exterior things* . . .]," never the "minds, *mentes.*"[6] It is therefore without reason that Descartes in-

---

[4] This neologism seems to me admissible along the lines of "visible, audible, touchable, perceptible," and so on.

[5] AT VII, p. 25, 4. On this addition, as on the difficulty that he raises (and which has kept the attention of critics very little), see *Questions cartésiennes II,* pp. 31ff.

[6] AT VII, p. 22, 26–28 (AT IX-1, p. 17; my emphasis). In the same way, the list of objects submitted to the hypothesis of the divine omnipotence: ". . . nulla plane sit terra, nullum coelum, nulla res extensa, nulla figure, nulla magnitudo, nulkus locus . . ." (VII, p. 21, 4–6). In the same way too, and more precisely: ". . . Qualia ergo ista fuere? Nempe terra, coelum, sidera et *omnia quae sensibus usurpebam*" (VII, p. 35, 18–19). It is quite uniquely a question of all that which remains external to me, ". . . foris vero . . ." (VII, p. 74, 27–28).

troduces, in *Meditatio II,* the "mentes" never put in doubt by *Meditatio I* as objects of the physical world, alone submitted to hyperbolic doubt (with simple, material natures, their conditions of intelligibility).

This illegitimate addition introduces, evidently, a grave difficulty in the order of reason—since, strictly speaking, the existence of me as feeler, that is to say as *mens* ". . . dubitans . . . et sentiens [doubting and sensing],"[7] having never been questioned, should therefore never have had to be reestablished as a certitude, either. The *ego,* at least as a *mens* who feels without being felt as a body, does not need anyone to prove its existence, because doubt has only ever, as hyperbolic as it is, questioned the felt sentient and the extension that makes it able to be conceived. How can we explain this logical fault? Either we do not see directly that the *mens,* outside the world, is an exception to the objects of doubt, all external, and in the world precisely constitutes an effect of confusion where doubt immerses the philosopher. Or it would be a question of an excessive prudence on the part of Descartes. Concerned to end with defining the unconditioned existence of the *ego* at the sole level of the *cogitatio,* but fearing that, if he were to establish it from sensation linked to the body, certain readers would only wish to conclude that the body itself thinks (one imagines Thomas Hobbes and Pierre Gassendi), and on misunderstanding that in sensation it is the soul that feels, and not the body,[8] he would have radicalized pedagogically his argument—the *ego* would sink in doubt if it became identified with the sentient, feeler as well as felt—without making an essential distinction, but too subtle for the average reader, between the extended sentient and the thinking act of feeling (which will nevertheless be validated in the *res cogitans* as early as its first definition).[9] Unless a third explanation were to reconnect the two preceding ones: Descartes himself would not have been able to raise to the level of the concept the distinction between the sentient in the sentient feeler (mind) and the sentient felt (feel-able body), of which, nevertheless, this very process was already obliged to make use. The phenomenon to describe would require more than those concepts which the philosopher had at his disposal could demonstrate. The hermeneutic would suffer from a phenomenological deficit and would remain in this way in the back-

---

[7] AT VII, p. 28, 21–22.

[8] An essential point, acquired from the *Dioptrique* IV, AT VI, p. 109, 6–7.

[9] AT VII, p. 28, 22.

ground of what it was wanting, nevertheless, to put forward. He would still have to deliver the phenomenon as given in *itself*.

Nevertheless, this addition acknowledges a decisive point. For what does this cheap addition mean to put into doubt, of the argument from hyperbolic doubt? How can we not see that it intends after the event what, precisely, the *corpora* [bodies] did not include—in other words, nevertheless still a body, but an exceptional body: *my own* body *insofar as gifted with sense*. In this way Descartes recognizes almost in spite of himself the exception of this *feeling* body that I am and which does not count among the bodies of the world, since it is necessary, in order to challenge it, to add to the objects of doubt a term that is distinguished from it radically—the *mens,* internal, able to feel and in this way already perfectly thinking, which does not belong more to the world than to extended felt bodies. In other words, it would be necessary to recognize not only, as Michel Henry has definitively established, that the *res cogitans* is deployed starting from an original act of feeling,[10] but also that the *feeling* essence of the *ego,* which thinks insofar as it feels (itself), appears, more than implicitly, right *before* its existence is proved—in a flaw in argumentation that claims precisely to prove it.

In short, before the *cogito* exists, the *ego* would be well and truly already established in its unconditioned existence as *corpus et sensus.* The feeling body would be anterior and not posterior to the *cogitatio.* The definition of the *res cogitans* includes there admittedly the feeling thought, but at the lowest rank: "Res cogitans. Quid est hoc? Nempe dubitans, intelligens, affirmans, negans, volens, nolens, imaginans quoque et *sentiens*— . . . a thing that also *feels* a lot, as by the intervention of the organs of the body."[11] According to the exigencies of the phenomenological description, the correct hermeneutic would have required that, immediately after the modality of doubt, the *res cogitans* deviated according to the modality of the original act of feeling, before and not after all the others. In this way, and despite the fact that he had some doubt, even for Descartes I am first and definitively bound—

---

[10] Michel Henry, *Généalogie de la psychoanalyse: Le commencement perdu* (Paris: Presses Universitaires de France, 1985), 35ff., "5" (see above, "Philosophy and Phenomenology"), confirmed in "Le *cogito* s'affecte-t-il?" *Questions cartésiennes I,* chapter V, pp. 153ff.; *Cartesian Questions,* pp. 96ff.

[11] AT VII, p. 28, 21ff. (AT IX-1, p. 22). My emphasis.

alligatus—to my feeling body. The *ego* gives itself as flesh, even if one wants to hide it.

2. "THE MOST ORIGINALLY MINE"

What Descartes half missed, because he only thought it at this stage by hendiadys *(corpus et sensus)*, it is up to Husserl (evidently after Aristotle)[12] to expose in its phenomenological unity, articulated as flesh subdued by strict opposition to the body (always physical, of the world). "Among the bodies truly seized by this *nature*, I find my flesh *(Leib)* with a characteristic trait, in other words [being] the only one to not be simply a physical body *(Körper)*, but precisely a flesh *(Leib)*, the sole object in my abstract layer of the world on account of which I feel." My flesh is distinguished from every object of the world, therefore from every body, in such a way that before even being able to perceive itself as a possible external object in the world, it perceives; before even making itself be felt, it allows one to feel; in short, before making itself be seen and appearing, it makes me feel (myself) and appear. In effect: "If I reduce other humans to their peculiarities, I specifically reach physical bodies *(Körper)*; but if I reduce myself as human, I reach my flesh *(Leib)* and *(thus) my soul or psychosomatic unity*, I reach my personal *I*, who acts in this flesh and through its intermediary in the outside world, *and I suffer from it.*"[13] The essential property of my flesh has to do with its suffering, its passivity, and its receptivity, which are not of the world, but without which nothing of the world would ever appear. To become flesh does not only consist in perceiving—when I stretch out my hand toward a thing to touch it, I do not stretch out there a physical thing, which would then be enriched

---

[12] These analyses find their origin, of course, with Aristotle, *De l'âme*, II, 11, in particular 423 *b* 23: "By which it is also evident that feeling [the organ of the act of feeling] is on the inside of the tangible"—and that, consequently, one can only feel the tangible in feeling as well the organ of touch itself "at the same time" (423 *b* 16ff.). Hence Lucretius, "Tangere enim et tangi, nisi corpus, nulla potest res" (*De Natura Rerum*, I, v. 304).

[13] Husserl, Hua. I, §44, p. 128; *Méditations cartésiennes*, V, pp. 146ff. (corrected); *Cartesian Meditations*, p. 97 ["If I reduce *other* men to what is included in my own-ness, I get *bodies* included therein; if I reduce *myself* as a man, I get '*my animate organism*' and '*my psyche*,' or myself as a *psychphysical unity—in the latter, my personal Ego*, who operates in this animate organism and, 'by means of' it, in the '*external world*,' who is affected by this world . . ."].

with a supplementary ownership, but ". . . it becomes flesh, it feels *(empfindet)*."[14] One does not pass from the body to flesh by addition, but by opposition, contrast, and, for continuity's sake, from the only felt to the lone feeler. To the feeler, oneself indissolubly felt by self as a feeler, or even feeling that one feels at the same time that one feels oneself felt.

The translation of *Leib* by "proper body," in spite of its reasonable appearance, or because of it, therefore invites the expression of the opposite. It suggests in effect that one should begin by having a body, thus a physical body in the space of the external world, in order then to make it one's own closely enough to finally appropriate it. Well, not only would it be a question there of a patent dualism on principle surmountable with difficulty, but especially, if one begins with a body of the world, felt but not feeling, it becomes by an essential law [*une loi d'essence*] impossible then to reach its opposite—a feeling flesh, never felt otherwise than as originally feeling. Only flesh, admitted absolutely straight off, can possibly attach me to a body of the world, because first it will feel it, therefore it will be able to feel it like its own, indeed appropriate it as its own. One can only envisage defining a body of the world as proper because, of itself, it remains always improper, neutral, unassigned, ordinary, and non-individuated. Only a flesh, properly itself because indissolubly feeling and felt, will be able to appropriate anything, even sometimes a body of the world. Flesh can take body [appear]; body can never take flesh. There is more: flesh and body are phenomenologically opposed all the more radically that one has for its function to make appear in feeling, to the point that it remains invisible as such, while the other, having for its definition to appear as visible, is never in a position to make appear, or feel, or intend. The body appears, but flesh remains invisible, precisely because it makes appear (one thinks here inevitably of the phenomenological

14 Edmund Husserl, *Ideen zu einer reinen Phänomenologie und phänomenologischen Philosophie. Zweites Buch: Di Phänomenologie und die Fundamente der Wissenschaften*, in Hua. IV, ed. Marly Biemel (The Hague: Martinus Nijhoff, 1952), §36, p. 145 (see §37, p. 151); *Idées directrices pour une phénoménologie, Deuxième Livre: Recherches phénoménologiques pour la constitution*, trans. Elaine Escoubas (Paris: Presses Universitaires de France, 1992), p. 207 (modified); *Ideas Pertaining to a Pure Phenomenology and a Phenomenological Philosophy*, Second Book, trans. Richard Rojcewicz and André Schuwer, vol. 4 of *Edmund Husserl: Collected Works* (Dordrecht, Boston, London: Kluwer Academic, 1989), p. 152 (pp. 158–59) ["it becomes Body, it senses"].

relationship Heidegger established between being [*l'être*] and being [*l'étant*]).

Husserl extended in this way, with an unequaled virtuosity, the thesis of Aristotle that touch has its privilege over the other senses from the fact that in its case alone the *milieu* of perception is one with the perceiver in such a way that this feeler could never feel without first feeling him- or herself. These analyses remain so famous that I do not have to go over them again now. A single, slightly different point is actually of consequence to us here: all phenomenalization of the world for me passes through my flesh. Without it, the world would disappear for me: "First of all, it is flesh that is the *means* [*Mittel*, therefore also the *milieu*] of all perception. . . . It is in this way that everything that appears has *eo ipso* [by itself] a relationship of orientation to flesh."[15] Flesh has nothing optional about it—it alone converts the world into an apparition, in other words, the given into a phenomenon. Outside my flesh, there is no phenomenon for me. Not only must one speak of "spiritual flesh" (Baudelaire),[16] but one must also understand that only flesh spiritualizes—in other words, renders visible the bodies of the world that would remain, without it, in the night of the unseen. My flesh opens to me the only area of uncertainty.

Now, this exceptional phenomenological function implies another consequence: I cannot separate myself from my flesh. Husserl underlines it: "Flesh cannot be suppressed." Whatever happens to me, this will appear to me by the intermediary of my flesh or will not appear to me at all. Thus, to the contrary of the physical body, for which there is always an "*over-there*" in the world in order to replace a perhaps unbearable *here*, my flesh fixes me definitely to its *here*, which becomes my *here*, the only one possible for me, because the sole means of all phenomenalization. In short, I never have ". . . the possibility of distancing myself *(entfernen)* from my flesh or of distancing my flesh

[15] Husserl, Hua. IV, §18 a), p. 56; *Idées directrices II*, p. 92 (modified); *Ideas II*, p. 61. See ". . . *mittels*": Hua. I, V, §44, pp. 124ff.; *Cartesian Meditations*, pp. 92ff.; Hua. IV, §36, p. 144; *Idées directrices II*, p. 206; *Ideas II*, p. 152 etc.

[16] Charles Baudelaire, *Les Fleurs du mal*, "Spleen et ideal," XLII, ed. Y.-G. Le Dantec and Claude Pichois (Paris: Gallimard/La Pléiade, 1966), p. 41. In other words: "Flesh is the condition of possibility of the thing, better, the constitution of flesh is presupposed by all constitution of thing[s], that is to say, by all constitution of worldly transcendence in general." Didier Franck, *Chair et corps: Sur la phénoménologie de Husserl* (Paris: Éditions de Minuit, 1981), p. 95.

from me."[17] My flesh assigns me to myself because it assigns me to
myself in fixing me to ". . . the most originally mine *(das Ursprüng-
lichst Meine)*." And to specify: "My flesh is, among all things, the
nearest to my feeling and my will." Nothing is more original to me
than it, because it gives me my sole possible origin as *I*, phenomeno-
logizing the world: "My *flesh*, that is to say, this thing originally given
(original gegebene Ding), that I originally move, that I originally modify, which in all these 'movements' and its own changes subsists as the
existent original unity for me *(original für mich daseinde Einheit)* and
has for me the character of a self-givenness in person *(Selbstgegeben-
heit)*. . . ." And if a thing can be here for me in my own sphere,
this will be precisely always ". . . by the medium of my flesh and
its originality."[18] Similar concepts of "distancing" *(entfernen)* and of
"existent unity" *(daseinde Einheit)* very likely already go beyond the
transcendental thematic of the *ego* as pure and simple representative
thought, in order to join, no doubt, instead those who had shortly before proposed the analytic of *Dasein*. I do not have to emphasize it
here, because what is essential for my inquiry is still to be found elsewhere.

The *ego* of the *cogito* is assured of itself, in principle, less by identity
to itself (even for Descartes)[19] than by an immediate and thus irrefutable access to itself. Now, the *cogitatio* in the mode of understanding
does not open this access, since it maintains the distance of a representation. The fact that this gap plays between the *ego* and itself does not
reabsorb it but hollows it out all the more. It has also been proposed
(by Michel Henry in particular) to conceive the *cogitatio*, alone able to
accomplish there a *cogitatio sui* [thought of his], along the lines of an
original act of feeling of self by itself. Descartes did not succeed in
eliminating (or even try to eliminate) this act of feeling, since it removes any doubt about the *corpus et sensus*—the feeling body, already
qualified as *mens*. If a *cogito* can therefore ever perform itself, this

---

[17] Husserl, Hua. IV, §21, p. 94 (see p. 95), and §41, p. 159; *Idées directrices II*, pp.
142ff. (see p. 224); *Ideas II*, pp. 99ff. (see p. 167).

[18] Respectively, Edmund Husserl, *Zur Phänomenologie der Intersubjektivität. Texte
aus dem Nachlaß. Zweiter Teil: 1921–1928*, in Hua. XIV, ed. Iso Kern (The Hague:
Martinus Nijhoff, 1973), p. 58, and Edmund Husserl, *Zur Phänomenologie der Intersubjektivität. Texte aus dem Nachlaß. Dritter Teil: 1929–1935*, in Hua. V, ed. Iso Kern
(The Hague: Martinus Nijhoff, 1973), p. 567.

[19] I will take this point as granted, at least plausible to the point of refutation of my
analysis on "L'altérité de l'*ego*," *Questions cartésiennes II*, chapter I.

would have to be in the mode of the act of feeling, conceived as the affection of self by self, anterior to any representative or intentional gap. It seems either that Husserl ended up with the same result by a more direct and radical path—in assigning the *ego* to flesh, or instead, in allowing it to be finally joined itself by the irreducible givenness of a phenomenological original act of feeling—phenomena of the world, certainly, but first of the self. The *cogito* accomplishes itself in flesh or does not accomplish itself—because, no more than the eye sees itself (or the ear hears itself), the understanding does not test itself. The self only attains itself in feeling itself. Whence the unavoidable paradox—formulated in the still too metaphysical language of Husserl—that ". . . an animate subject can certainly be thought without material flesh [that is to say, a phantom], but not without flesh at all *(keineswegs ohne Leib überhaupt).*"[20] A *mens* without original *sensus* would no longer be one.

One such displacement of the *cogito* also involves—and for us especially—another result: if the act of feeling acquires such a privilege, it is because it finally assigns the *ego* to itself. But it can do so only because flesh always remains original to it, because it can never distance itself from it; in short, because it is taken there. The taking of flesh *by* the *ego* thus has a price: the taking of the *ego in* its flesh. The *ego* takes, when it takes its flesh, like cement or plaster takes once the water has left it—in fixing itself. It does not fix itself to its flesh; it fixes itself to itself as flesh. As one "cast in plaster" the face of someone recently deceased in order to freeze it and then to draw a portrait of it, the *ego* casts itself in flesh in order to fix, if not freeze, itself, and in this way take its first *self.*

3. SUFFERING, PLEASURE, AGING

The *ego* only fixes itself when it takes flesh. It only takes when it takes flesh—when it takes in and as its flesh. And straight away definitively, because as soon as its flesh takes it, it no longer releases it.

How can I describe this situation? It does not actually suffice to affirm that the (second) reduction in the literal sense delivers flesh as the authority that is the most originally mine. It is still necessary to

---

[20] Husserl, Hua. IV, §21, p. 95 (see p. 96 and §20, p. 93); *Idées directrices II*, p. 143 (see pp. 144 and 140); *Ideas II*, p. 101 (see pp. 101–2 and 98–99).

show how it leaves me to myself, without loophole or possible evasion. As soon as the *ego* takes flesh, it finds itself stuck to itself as to its ground, to its phenomenological earth (the one that does not move): as earthed, the taking of flesh assigns the *ego* definitively to itself and itself alone. Or rather, in assigning it to a place that it can neither deny nor shake nor flee, flesh and its earthing identify it finally as an it*self,* as an *ipse.* We would have to be able to confirm it by a manner of experience crucial to flesh. In order to establish its inseparability from myself, I must calculate if I can withdraw myself from it, that is to say, appear—even if only to myself—without it. Now I must verify, by three arguments at least, that I can take neither leave nor distance from my flesh, because I do not have it, but I am it. I am it and I am in the trace, because it alone inscribes the trace of my ipseity.

Let us first consider suffering. As soon as I suffer, I suffer myself. I do not suffer from fire or iron, as I see the sword or the flame before me, their form, their colors, their dimensions, and so on—in short, from a distance, in being able to describe them as objects. I do not even suffer insomuch as I can hear my groanings or howls, creakings and shocks, still as resonant objects. For just as it is not the body that feels, but the soul (Descartes), as soon as I suffer it is in, by, and from myself that I suffer. The iron and the fire inasmuch as suffered no longer appear to the world, but appear in myself; they take flesh in the *milieu* of my flesh; I am the *milieu* of manifestation. Thus I only suffer them in suffering from their phenomenality. I do not suffer from the fire and from the iron—but, because immediately they hurt *me,* they only hurt me. I suffer *myself* by them. Between the iron and the fire and me who suffers them, the gap disappears. I can no longer make a retreat into a more withdrawn tower: once the enclosure has been invested, I am definitively invaded, taken, done. Suffering rivets me to myself as one rivets something to the ground—by earthing. Suffering does not only hurt me, it assigns me especially to myself as flesh. It could not hurt me if it did not reach me in my vital organs, thus if it did not stick me to my flesh—did not take me by the flesh, as one takes by the throat. Levinas perfectly analyzed it: ". . . physical suffering, in all its degrees, is an impossibility of detaching oneself from the moment of existence. It is the very irremissibility of being [*l'être*]. The content of suffering is blended with the impossibility of detaching oneself from suffering. . . . [T]here is in suffering an absence of any refuge. It is the fact of being directly exposed to being [*l'être*]. It is made of the impossibility of fleeing and recoiling. All the acuity of suffering is in this impossibility of recoil. It is the fact of being driven back against life and against being [*l'être*]."[21] Am I as a consequence driven back to being [*l'être*]? No, only to being [*être*]—to be suffering, in the impossibility of delaying the release onto me of this suffering, I must deliver myself to it without condition or delay or distance; suffering assigns me to myself as what I can never "put on hold." In any case, even when Pascal wants to analyze suffering as a temporary spiritual test, he reads it first as the test of my flesh: "It is well assured that one can never detach oneself without pain. One does not feel one's bond when one voluntarily follows the one who leads, as Saint Augustine says. But when one begins to resist and to walk away, one really suffers; the bond extends and endures all the violence; and this bond is our own body which only breaks off in death."[22] One can certainly debate here—theologically—whether what separates me from the divine will identifies itself with my own body, but one can only consent—phenomenologically—to "pain" being assigned without circumlocution to "our own body," that is to say, not only to our body as such, but well and truly to our flesh.

Pascal then introduces us to the second argument, which no longer involves suffering, but pleasure. On the first reading, the approach opposes suffering (involuntary) to pleasure (voluntary)—desired servitude, thus not absolutely passive.

> It is not shameful for man [*sic*] to succumb to pain, and it is shameful to him to succumb to pleasure. This does not come from the fact that pain comes from elsewhere, and that we are looking for pleasure. For one can look for pain and succumb to it on purpose without this type of baseness. Whence comes the fact that it is glorious to reason to succumb under the effort of pain, and that it is shameful for it to succumb under the effort of pleasure? It is because it is not the pain that tries us and draws us, but we ourselves who voluntarily choose it and want to make it dominate us, in such a way that we are masters of the thing, and in this it is man who succumbs to himself. But in pleasure it is man who succumbs to pleasure. Now, only mastery and empire are glorious, and servitude is shameful.[23]

---

[21] Emmanuel Levinas, *Le temps et l'autre* (Paris: Presses Universitaires de France, 1948, 1983), pp. 55–56; *Time and the Other,* trans. Richard Cohen (Pittsburgh: Duquesne University Press, 1987), p. 69.

[22] Blaise Pascal, *Seconde lettre aux Roannez,* II, September 24, 1656, p. 266.

[23] Pascal, *Pensées,* §795, p. 601. Pascal was evidently thinking of John 10:18 (and perhaps 13:37ff.), where the Christ voluntarily exposes himself to suffering [and] even to death.

But this argument can immediately be considered apart from Pascal's moral intention and be reversed. For if pain here spares reason from all shame, it is because one can voluntarily confront the other, or at least voluntarily not withdraw from it. And if it is ". . . voluntarily that we choose it . . . ," if we remain ". . . masters of the thing . . ." and if we only succumb finally to ourselves, it is necessary to conclude of it logically that pain still leaves a place for a will, a power to withdraw or to advance, in short, for an activity. In pain, even if I succumb to it, I have chosen it, thus it remains one of those ". . . sole actions that depend on free will, for which we are able with reason to be praised or blamed."[24] Pain, according to Pascal's definition, remains compatible with self-satisfaction according to Descartes, and therefore with the activity of reason. From then on, it appears that, to the contrary of pleasure, only pain goes to the end of passivity. For pleasure still imposes itself by an "incentive" (Nicolas de Malebranche),[25] since it disturbs not only my physical body but even my will, the soul of my body—my flesh. My flesh (at least in its present condition, in the disorder of sin) can neither scorn nor even delay pleasure. From that point on, the "servitude" of pleasure brings "shame" well and truly to reason, because it strips it of all independence toward flesh and drives it back there without rest or sparing it. Flesh escapes reason and will, as the indication of an obscure *self,* more original than the clear ecstasy of the mind [*esprit*] available to itself. Pascal's analysis therefore ends phenomenologically in reinforcing what it denounces theologically— the exemplary accomplishment of flesh in pleasure. Not that pleasure substitutes itself for pain, annuls it, or even stabilizes it, but because, strangely, it goes to the end of what it announces without accomplishing it: with it, even the will "succumbs" (with reason) to the taking of flesh. Flesh and ultimate passivity (thus pain) manifest themselves in this way for the first time without restriction, or exception, in pleasure. But is it perhaps also for this reason that pain and pleasure can sometimes scarcely be distinguished?

There remains a third argument in favor of the inseparability of flesh. But in order to formulate it, we must from now on cease to pursue the

---

[24] Descartes, *Passions de l'âme,* §152, AT XI, p. 445, 18–20.

[25] Nicolas de Malebranche, *Réponse générale auz Lettres du R. P. Lamy:* "Pleasure taken in general, that is to say sensitive or reasonable, actual or hoped for, is thus the unique incentive of all our loves," in *Œuvres completes,* ed. André Robinet, vol. 14 (Paris: J. Vrin, 1963), p. 164.

hermeneutic, first negative (Descartes), then positive (Pascal), of the *self,* in order to go to the second operation of the showing [*monstration*] in phenomenological style: direct access to the givenness of *self.* Is it possible to give oneself the given in process? Certainly, if we consider its temporalization, that is to say, the phenomenon of age, or rather of aging (and in this sense, sickness). Its force comes from the fact that it involves this very principle of finitude, temporality (Kant, Heidegger). One can, in any case, wonder that the analytic of *Dasein* describes the ecstasies of time, in particular the "That-before-which" of dereliction *(Geworfenheit),* without noting the essential trait by which it accomplishes exactly my most proper finitude. In other words, *time,* especially according to the having-been, *does not pass,* but, so to speak, accumulates. For it is a question there of a decisive paradox: phenomenologically, time does not pass; if it were passing, it would not leave any trace and thus would destroy nothing. The past is instead accumulated in the flesh of my members, muscles and bones, which, under what is appropriately named its weight, bend, harden, and lose their anterior performance. Above all, the weight of time is accumulated there where my flesh is the most openly visible—on my face. Actually, it is on my face that time prefers to leave traces, its traces. Better, these are the traces of time that mark it *par excellence,* lay it out and alter it without ceasing, changing it in so many insensibly altered sketches, each almost resembling those that surround it, but, once compared at a distance, almost completely unrecognizable. One never sees the same face twice, because time, in being accumulated, deforms it as much as it shapes it. Only time can draw the portrait of a face, since it alone sketches it. Time distinguishes the face, because it marks it—in the taking of flesh, in archive. But there is more: time, as the past accomplished, should never be able to appear if it were limited to passing. Like death, as soon as the moment has come, time is no longer it for me. If it were passing, by definition, time would die of itself and would be the first to do so. Time appears, nevertheless, since we rightly claim to see it pass. It therefore appears in the accumulation of its marks, which leave their traces to ruin the physical body (whence "the beauty of ruins"), but especially living flesh and, more than any other flesh, the flesh of my face. Completed time manifests itself in what it removes, destroys, and undoes—the phenomenality of ruins of stone, but especially of ruins of flesh. In this way, accomplished time only manifests itself in taking flesh in mine, which it defeats, affects, marks. It takes flesh in me.[26]

In this way, three arguments allow the crucial experience of the taking flesh of the *ego*—in other words, that the *ego* never phenomenalizes itself as a being in the world, but only when it is affected by itself, that is to say, when it takes flesh and lets itself be taken. The taking of flesh, as passive, involuntary, and factual as it remains, does not therefore indicate any downfall or alienation of the *ego,* but accomplishes its first taking of self, makes it enter into possession of self—the self is posed (and reposed) in itself in taking flesh. Flesh assigns me to myself without any possible return—this is what designates phenomenological time: flesh insomuch as definitively given, without remorse or return (not refundable, without deposit, disposable). In the taking of flesh, I am given without return to myself, according to a pure given— given utterly to myself in order to spend my time there. One can therefore in this way access a nevertheless surprising remark of Descartes, identifying joy as the first of the passions that renders possible the union of the soul and the body (this other name for the taking of flesh): ". . . it is not believable that the soul has been placed in the body, unless the body was well disposed and that, when it is in this way well disposed, this naturally gives us joy."[27] One would have to imagine that the taking of flesh is fortunate: I am finally (given to) myself.

4. INDIVIDUATING FACTICITY

We have in this way reached the original given of the taking of flesh. Our analysis can thus proceed further forward, following the direct demands of the thing itself, reduced and brought back to what it puts in play: to the putting in play itself, mine, which accomplishes my taking flesh *par excellence.* For once again, the taking of flesh is where I am taken. I am as taken—not so much a prisoner or under house arrest, as I am caught in the act, recaptured by and as my *self.* For I am only taken because, as flesh, I take; I am not where I am, but *that* which, thus *who* I am for the first time. The taking of flesh accomplishes facticity, in a way probably more radical, and certainly more

---

[26] See above, chapter 2, §3, and below, chapter 5, §§4–5.
[27] René Descartes, *À Chanut,* February 1, 1647, AT IV, pp. 604ff.

economical, than the way in which existence allows it to *Dasein,* since no resolution is found required here and no irresolution delays or disguises it. But with facticity is also accomplished—this is a positive lesson from the analytic of *Dasein*—individuation; the taking of flesh would thus have to assure, with facticity, individuation.

One can establish this in posing as a rule that understanding never individualizes—only taking flesh can do it. For, to the contrary of flesh, not only can another understanding also think what my understanding thinks, but rational commerce demands that any understanding can do it. Demonstrating reason as well as the scientific city imply, in order to function, that each of the arguers understands univocally, without "noise" (as much as it is possible), what each of the others means, therefore what each of the others thinks; the impersonality of the argument is its only constraining force. The political ideal of a perfectly democratic society implies a perfectly communicating and communicative reason (Jürgen Habermas), such that rational thoughts can and must be shared among all, therefore between no matter who; tangential unanimity demands a strict anonymity of the thoughts of the understanding. This non-individuation is not true in any case only of the *public square,** but also and especially of private conversation, which supposes a community of understanding in terms of the not-said, the implication, and nonverbal conversation. The secret of this sport, so exquisite but so dangerous (Marcel Proust), so well named "the world," comes from this impersonality of mind, that it is a question of mastering even in the finest words. The spirit of subtlety does not diverge from the spirit of geometry by the universality of meanings and of thoughts, but only by their modes of conceptuality (oblique) and their evidence (indirect). We find again here, in an entirely different register, the hypothesis of the unicity and thus of the universality of the agent intellect of Aristotle, such that, in the interpretation of Averroës, it involves the multiplicity of potential intellects, only registered in individuals. We find again also quite exact a contemporary echo of it in the myth of a universal computer, common to all regions and connecting all files, that would operate in all terminals, alone individuals, but inessential and nonthinking as such.

The individuation of the *ego* is thus made neither by form (the too universal understanding) nor by matter (the too undifferentiated physi-

---

* In English in the original—Trans.

cal body), but by the "unanimous white conflict" of the one with the other—precisely by the taking of flesh. For flesh indeed has, exactly in its own right, the only authentic individual property, that is to say, the appropriation of the individual to itself. Two *ipse* are never the same flesh, neither do they have the same flesh. The injunction that "they will become one flesh" would remain a pious vow, unceasingly contradicted, if it could not be understood from the flesh of the child at birth, effectively common.[28] But what one sometimes still names the "carnal union" is characterized precisely by the fact that it provides us with the most unquestionable proof that the flesh of the other remains absolutely inaccessible to me, like mine to him or her. Pleasure is not divided, especially if two pleasures stimulate each other and are accomplished simultaneously. As long as it is a question of my flesh, only me [*moi*] is taken—and it is mine. As soon as I am not taken into it, then the flesh of another *ipse* begins. Monad is always carnal. And it is why, to the contrary of Gottfried Leibniz, we understand that monads can die.

Individuation by facticity depends finally on flesh by a last trait. According to my facticity, I attain my individuality: in this flesh it is up to me and me alone and it is only up to me in this flesh and it alone. But this ipseity only finally individualizes me by an always already accomplished mineness. Now, it is up to the flesh to take me before I choose it, or before I decide to do so. This carnal *ipse* is true for me, precisely because it is not I who have chosen it although I have never been without it. There is admittedly a mineness *(Jemeinigkeit),* nevertheless not because I would have decided it, but because it happens to me, affects me, and determines me, in short because flesh, of itself and always already, takes me. I do not give myself my flesh, it is it that gives me to myself. In receiving my flesh, I receive me myself—I am in this way gifted [*adonné,* given over] to it.

Human specificity does not consist in having the *logos* but in taking flesh. Unless, of course, the *logos,* inasmuch as relation and relation to self, is only originally accomplished according to flesh. Birth, original taking flesh, does not therefore have a biological status but rather a phenomenological one. And if there must be an eternity, it will only be a resurrection of the body.

---

[28] We find here, besides, a common rabbinic interpretation, as the knowledge of S. Moses showed us.

5. Absolved of All Relation

Therefore, I do not give myself flesh; it gives me to myself in giving itself to me—I am given over [adonné] to it.[29]

How can one define the phenomenality of such flesh that gives me to myself? Evidently one cannot do it if one relies on a common definition of the phenomenon—adequation between appearing/appearance [l'apparaître] and what appears [l'apparaissant], intuition and signification, noesis and noema, and so on. For in flesh one cannot find this distinction precisely. Since in this sole case the perceived is one with the perceiver, the intentional aim is accomplished necessarily in an essential immanence, where what I could intend is blended with the possible fulfillment. A signification will never have capacity here for intuition, because this intuition precedes and renders possible all intentionality, therefore all signification intentionally aimed at. It is therefore necessary to think the taking of flesh starting from givenness, as the basic determination of every phenomenon. For even if all that which gives itself does not phenomenalize itself, all that which phenomenalizes itself must first give itself—unfolding according to the fold of givenness, by which its advent always bears the meaning of its facticity and its contingency. Thus, in the hypothesis of a phenomenality of the given, flesh becomes immediately the most simple and constraining case of what I name elsewhere a saturated phenomenon or paradox. Carnally, I am affected by an intuition—for example, pain—which invades me without ceasing even before I know its meaning: does it proceed from a bad disposition of my psychism (somatization), from my physical body (sickness), or from an object of the world (shock), or even from another subjectivity (a random, unfortunate meeting with a declared enemy)? Doubtlessly, it may become possible—but not always—to decide between the hypotheses, and to know if I suffer from a depression, from an infection, from a shock, or from an act of aggression. But I will never be able to precede the intuition of fulfillment of my fleshly pain with an intentional aim able to foresee, to choose, and to organize it. I will never manage to have a look at my pain: not only because my intention will be always to avoid it and not to run toward it, but especially because it will keep the initiative to

---

[29] See Étant donné, §26, pp. 361–66.

warn me and to surprise me like an accident, the happening of which imposes itself on me like a destiny—undergone, managed, but never probably wanted for itself.

This paradox or saturated phenomenon excepts itself from the definition of the common phenomenon, because it is freed from one of the essential characteristics of phenomenality according to Kant: relation. Whereas all common phenomena must, according to Kantian principles, be fitted into the rules of experience, therefore of time, in admitting in advance a relation with precedents (whether of substantial inheritance, causality, or community between substances), flesh only ever refers back to itself, in the indissoluble unity of the felt and of the feeling. Flesh is referred to itself as it auto-affects itself. In consequence, it eludes all relation—my pain, my pleasure, remain unique, incommunicable, unable to be substituted—in an absoluteness without compromise, without anything like it or equal to it. Moreover, this absoluteness, pure of all relation, constitutes precisely the privilege that renders it fit to lock me into my individuality. If flesh did not manage to absolve itself of all relation, it would not manage to accomplish what it alone can accomplish—to render me to myself, to assign me to myself—in the double sense of assigning me my proper place and of making me feel its power.

But there is more. It is not only a question of one of the saturated phenomena or paradoxes among others, which numbers with them— the event, which gives the world in its unpredictable quantity (chapter 2); the idol, which gives the seen in its unbearable intensity (chapter 3); or the icon, which gives the other person with an alterity that cannot be looked upon (chapter 5). With flesh, indeed, a phenomenon gives me to myself in my absoluteness: alone and first in the world, which is phenomenalized for that matter only by me, this phenomenon gives me to myself [*moi*]. With flesh, it is a matter of the first and of the only saturated phenomenon, which delivers the *ego* to itself—which delivers *l'adonné* to itself in putting it "under house arrest" within itself alone. It thus benefits from an incomparable privilege over all other paradoxes. Those other ones designate each time what the *ego* cannot constitute as its object, as a consequence of the excess in the phenomena of donating intuition over all anterior intentional signification, over all sense or noema already available. Flesh gives, to the contrary, nothing other than the *ego* itself, at the same time that every given gives itself to it. It fixes it in it as an *adonné*—that which receives itself from this very thing that it receives, according to the simultaneity characteristic of flesh since Aristotle. If a subjectivity must surmount the destruction of the metaphysical subject, it can only come from flesh, where hetero- and auto-affection are mixed.

Descartes may have, nevertheless, understood it first, despite appearances and the canonical interpretation, for at least two reasons. (a) At least once explicitly, he establishes the certitude of the existence of the *ego* directly starting from the pure act of feeling, without going back from this act of feeling to the *cogitatio* as its most derived mode: "Falsa haec sunt [light, sound, heat], dormio enim. At certe videre videor, audire, calascere. Hoc falsum esse non potest; hoc est proprie quod in me sentire appellatur; atque hoc praecise sic sumptum nihil aliud est quam cogitare." "But one will say to me that these appearances are false and that I am asleep. Let it be so; nevertheless, at the very least, it is most certain that it seems to me that I see, that I hear and that I become warm; and it is specifically what in me is called feeling, and this, taken in this way precisely, is nothing other than thinking."[30] A radical affirmation, and perfectly phenomenological: the act of feeling not reduced from an object in the natural attitude remains essentially doubtful, but it can always be reduced to a pure act of feeling—I feel at least that I feel—which assures it as the originary mode of the *cogitatio*. The *ego* therefore receives itself from its taking flesh and never from the reflection that would make it equal to itself. (b) When, at the end of his itinerary, Descartes wants to note the irreducibility of ". . . the union between the soul and the body," not only does he grant it the rank of "primitive notion" as he does for the soul alone and extension alone, but he also accords to it a specific mode of knowledge. Whereas the soul considered on its own is conceived by the understanding alone, and extension as such is conceived by ". . . the understanding aided by the imagination," ". . . things which belong to the union of the soul and of the body are only known obscurely by the understanding alone, and even by the understanding aided by the imagination, but they are known very clearly by the senses."[31] This implies several uncommon results. First, it implies that the act of feeling becomes the original mode of the *cogitatio* and no longer its last,

---

[30] Respectively, AT VII, p. 29, 14–18, and AT IX-1, p. 23.
[31] René Descartes, *À Elisabeth,* June 28, 1643, AT III, respectively, p. 691, 4; p. 691, 26; and p. 692, 3.

as in the definitions of the *res cogitans*.[32] Next, it implies that the union of the soul and the body, which I here understand as the taking of flesh, has the rank of a primitive notion, that is to say of a simple nature (like thought and extension), irreducible and never obtained by a combination of the two first, but as original as them, or even more original, since it came to crown them and reassemble them. Finally, it implies that this ultimate primitive notion cannot be attained, like ". . . metaphysical thoughts," by the pure thinking of trained philosophers, but first by ". . . those who never philosophize," or at least never according to the metaphysical mode of thought, predicative demonstration. It indeed remains, if taking flesh cannot be thought in the metaphysical way of the *cogitatio* reduced to pure understanding, to leave it to give itself in the mode (I risk myself here in qualifying it as phenomenological) that is followed by those who ". . . do not doubt that the soul moves the body and that the body acts on the soul."[33] In this way, Descartes, far from getting tied up in "dualism" where current interpretation persists in keeping him, would himself bring back the *ego* to the point of its ultimate factual and individualized self, that of taking flesh. And with this renewal he accomplishes the last reduction possible—that of the phenomenon to the given, what, in the case of the phenomenon of the *ego,* signifies the taking flesh of *l'adonné.*

This result remains provisional. Multiple questions remain in suspense, or rather, open themselves starting right from this acquired knowledge. First, concerning the taking of flesh, it will be successively asked: (a) if individuation, facticity, and the *self,* supposing that one agrees that they are found really attained by following the guiding thread of flesh, can be attained by other ways. In other words, would the transcendental reduction and the existential analytic allow, or do they exclude, as a matter of principle, ending with the same results as the phenomenology of givenness that I privilege here? (b) If the taking of flesh alone assures to the *ego* a self *(ipse, self, Selbst),* is it necessary to conclude that it alone can open what comes after the subject, whatever name it bears, and extracts it in this way definitively from the impasses of metaphysical subjectivity, that is to say, from an *I* that claims transcendental pretensions? (c) Can one describe more exactly, following the categorical decision of Husserl, the impossibility for

---

[32] AT VII, p. 28, 20–22, and p. 34, 18–21; see above, p. 86.

[33] Descartes, *À Elisabeth,* June 28, 1643, AT III, p. 692, respectively 10, 4, and 5–6.

every *ego* of tearing itself from flesh? In particular, what phenomenological status can one admit to the strangely intimate exteriority of
flesh and to the depth/superficiality of skin? (d) Especially, what perspectives does that taking of flesh open on the already ancient aporia
of what one should perhaps precisely from now on no longer name
intersubjectivity? (e) Finally, does the taking of flesh, understood as
the last phenomenological posture of the *ego,* open onto, at the very
least, a *possibility* of thinking in reason the theological Incarnation?

5

The Icon or the Endless Hermeneutic

1. THE VISIBLE IN DEFAULT

The object appears—it transmutes its reduced givenness into visible phenomenality. Consider the most simple case, where we cannot reasonably doubt that it is a complete appearance, or that it delivers an effective object, since we do manage to constitute a given in giving to it a complete and coherent sense. Consider (being inspired by the cube, the favorite example of Husserl himself) this simple box of tobacco (say, Capstan) that I take out of my pocket, perhaps in order to fill my Peterson at the end of this conference. I see it, just the same as it was at the shop of the retailer who sold it to me, and similar to many other ones that are found in many tobacco shops (even on Harvard Square) and no doubt will be for some time to come, if legislation is only toughened up slowly. It is nothing but a rectangular, metallic parallelepiped, blue and gilded, of about sixty grams, measuring ten centimeters by five, and about two centimeters high. I know this, and there would be nothing to add, if, indeed, I ever perceived it truly in this way. But what I perceive of it as lived experiences of consciousness will only ever be three of the six sides. If I want to see the three others, which at the moment I do not in fact see, I would have to turn it over with a movement of my hand, but when I see the three other sides (of course!), the first three will become invisible to me. Therefore I can never, in truth, see this box entirely; I only know it. I constitute it, but always in adding other, non-effective sketches to those that I actually perceive. I associate the apprehension of what presents itself with the apprehension of what does not present itself—I associate effectively given lived experiences with those not effectively given (that have been or will be given, but are not presented at this moment). Therefore, even for a physical body *(Körper)*, and not only for another flesh *(Leib)*, I must have recourse to what Husserl names ". . . a sort of *appresenta-*

tion (Appräsentation). There is already such an appresentation in external experience as long as the front face of a thing, which is properly seen, always and necessarily appresents a rear face of the thing, prescribing it a contents more or less determined." Appresentation, then, intervenes as soon as the knowledge of the object occurs, before and independently from access to the other person. Without doubt, in the case of an object of the world, I can always confirm the appresentation of three sides by that of three others a moment later. I can always "think it through" regarding this object (even though I could never do the same with another person), but I would, precisely, have to do it, and I would only manage it in abandoning in turn to appresentation the three sides already presented, in order to present to myself the sides previously appresented. Appresentation can be displaced, but it is never eliminated. Now, as appresentation ". . . represents a *there-with (ein Mit-da vorstellig macht),* which is nevertheless not itself there and can never become a self [*un lui-même*] there *(ein Selbst-da),*"[1] we have to admit, then, that all constitution encounters a weakness of the *Selbst-da.* I do not intend to look again here at the question of the failure of "presence" in Husserlian phenomenology—a decisive debate, but complex and overdetermined. I only underline an obvious point: even the visibility of a common object, the constitution of which does not offer in principle almost any difficulty since its reduction to its given is so obvious, already conceals and reveals an invisibility. We can identify it with reference to another trait of constitution. A unity, rendered visible in what it is pictured in the lived experiences of consciousness, must be reconstructed, but by recourse to often appresented sketches, not all present. The lived experiences essentially lack every given before showing themselves, because an essential law [*une loi d'essence*] makes simultaneous manifestations of all their sketches incompatible. Space imposes this law. In rendering impossibly incompatible the appearances of lived experiences, it imposes having recourse to appresentation in order to constitute the least object. The visible only breaks forth into day constrained to finitude—crowned with an invisible by default, *l'invu.*

It will be objected that space, if it makes the thing, composes together with temporality, such that it allows us, at least in the case of a

---

[1] Husserl, Hua. I, V, §50, p. 139; *Méditations cartésiennes,* p. 158; *Cartesian Meditations,* p. 109.

worldly object, to bypass the absence for a moment of certain lived experiences in producing them, after the first are brought into visibility and go out of it. In response: not only does the temporal delay not abolish the impossible incompatibility between the lived experiences inflicted by space, but it consecrates it instead, in forcing the phenomenological look to pass always from one lived experience to the other. This is in such a way that the temporalization of constitution reproduces and even aggravates the burden of *invu* that accompanies the rising of the phenomenon to visibility. It occurs in at least three ways. (a) First, it occurs in the fact that all constitution must admit the undefined character of its object. To see all sides of an object takes some time, which means [both] that it is necessary to learn to see the object as such and that this apprenticeship would be sufficient, even if one supposed it to happen by impossible instantaneousness for the visibility of the object to be necessarily temporalized. (b) But every object that shows itself also temporalizes itself. Directly, this is because this object itself changes. This is evidently true for all natural living things (which rise up, ripen, and come undone); for every produced object (technical, or industrial), which also deploys a history: the time of its conception, its fabrication, its commercial exploitation (the time of fashion, of need, demand and so on), finally that of its functioning (its "lifespan"), and then, in the end, of its destruction (in being recycled or deteriorating). The object therefore only ever gives itself in evolutionary lived experiences and cannot, strictly speaking, ever affect me twice in the same way. So, my look can never be drowned twice in the same lived experience of an object. The ineluctable temporality of its bringing into visibility endlessly surrounds past sketches (and all become so) in *l'invu.* (c) Every object that shows itself also temporalizes itself, indirectly, because all constitution depends on the original impression. First, in the sense that the first lived experience assigned to a constitutable object wells up from the original impression, whence rises up its first present, as a worldly fact as well as a visible sketch. In repeating itself endlessly, the original impression assures the continuity of an object identical to itself, which disappears as soon as it ceases to give it. But what the original impression assures to the constitutable object it also accords to the constituent parts, since consciousness does not cease to originate at each first moment, the present fact of which also provokes the present attention to presence. Husserl, in any case, established explicitly that the two sides of constitution take root equally in the original impression, in deducing from the temporal flux not one but two intentionalities—that of the temporal object ("transverse") and that of intentional consciousness ("longitudinal").[2] Well (it seems useless to insist on it),[3] this original impression of temporality, by definition, escapes constitution radically, which it alone renders possible in return. From that point on, we can debate another characteristic of constitution: the constitutable object does not always offer a permanent end to the intentional aim, since its temporalization always makes it possible that no identical kernel remains. If, even in its temporal course, the object is maintained identical to itself for a moment, this will only be in reducing its lived experiences, its sketches, and therefore its visibility to a smaller common denominator. It will be impoverished, therefore, in crowning itself with *invus*, sunken in a past more rich than its present. The visible phenomenon only appears in piercing the fog of its *invus*.

The central determination of constitution remains—that is, that it operates on an object. Must we consider it indisputable, or distinguish a new reserve of invisibility there? In order to answer, it is advisable to go back from the object to what its object-ness presupposes, that is to say, the intentional aim, and therefore the look. Now, no object can truly appear as such if just any aim whatever is exercised on it. In order to appear as such it requires a particular aim, privileged and adapted, whether to its finality and its usefulness—in the case of a technical object or tool, a common object (an object ready-to-hand, *zuhanden*)—or simply to its definition and its essence, as in the case of a subsistent object (an object present-at-hand, *vorhanden*). Even an object as simple as the box that we were analyzing requires it already. It only appears as the object that it is and demands to be if a precise intentionality is applied to it—the one that aims precisely not at what one could see (a simple parallelepiped, closed and probably empty, given that it is quite light), but what one can do with it, which is not seen at first (a box to open and close again, because it is destined to contain a fragile material). An aim, which would be restricted to pick-

---

[2] Husserl, Hua. X, §39, pp. 80ff.; *Leçons pour une phénoménologie de la conscience intime du temps*, pp. 107ff.; *On the Phenomenology of the Consciousness of Internal Time*, pp. 84ff.

[3] Especially after the works of Klaus Held, *Lebendige Gegenwart: Die Frage der Seinweise des transzendentalen Ich bei Edmund Husserl* (The Hague: Martinus Nijhoff, 1966), and Didier Franck, *Chair et corps: Sur la phénoménologie de Husserl.*

ing up what the sketches leave to be perceived, would, indeed, not see this object as such. In order to constitute it in its proper phenomenality, it is not a matter of what is perceived but of what is perceived insomuch as ordered to definition, to essence, or in short, to the sense of the object. Constitution, too, consists ultimately in a gift of sense *(Sinngebung)*. In this way the object only phenomenalizes itself in imposing, among all the intentionalities that can aim at it, the one that assigns to it the most appropriate sense. Thus it chooses an intentionality or, rather, fixes a target to it, failing which it does not rise to its proper visibility (anamorphosis). But in addition to this object intentionality (which the object imposes in order to be able to appear) there are nonetheless others, which, concerned as we are to constitute an object, we most often do not follow, but which nonetheless remain accessible. What do they or would they leave to appear, if we followed them? Consider again the same box that serves us as an example. Admittedly, one anamorphosis gives access to it as a usable object (as a container, a receptacle, snuffbox, and so on). But we can also aim at it either with the intentionality of another object (as a metallurgical product equipped with certain properties, such as resistance to pressure, watertightness, and so on); or without object intentionality at all (in terms of the decorative motif of the cover, the combination of the two colors, and so on); or even, finally, in aiming very precisely at its transformation from object to non-object, as a pure aesthetic visible (following the process of the *ready-made*). From that point on, the same lived experiences according to the same sketches are able either to be constituted according to an object intentionality or to escape all sense, therefore not being constituted in such an object. Now, the two attitudes of the look in front of the same visible given cannot be accomplished at the same time by the same intention. Therefore all constitution of the given in a phenomenon of the object type (to suppose that it can be accomplished without remainder) hides from view, by the very visibility that it conquers, other possible epiphanies, according to other intentionalities, without concept—like aesthetic, ethical, or other visibles. In this way, all constitution shocks, by the type of sense that it confers on phenomenality (most often that of the object), all the other visibilities that the same lived experiences and the same sketches had tolerated, or even demanded. Here again, the phenomenon constituted in the end only occupies the visible in repressing in *l'invu* the phantoms of other flashes.

I have thus clarified three ways in which the visible that constitution elaborates into a phenomenon obscurely gives rise to *l'invu:* according to space (the impossible incompatibility of sketches), temporality (the undefined nature of lived experiences given by the original impression), and constitution (the irreconcilable plurality of aims). From now on, it becomes clear that not all that which gives itself can nevertheless, by an essential law [*une loi d'essence*], show itself. In other words, it becomes clear that in phenomenology *l'invu* increases at the same rate as the constitution of seen phenomena.

2. THE VISIBLE IN EXCESS

I have thus removed what does not enter into the visible and have identified these three failures of the visible as clues of *l'invu.* By *invu* I understand purely and simply what, as a matter of fact, cannot reach or yet reach visibility, even though I could in fact experiment with it as a possible visible. In effect, the phenomenality accomplished by constitution gives rise, negatively, to a halo of *invu* around every phenomenon, in proportion to which it renders the phenomenon visible. For when concentrated on the object, constitution must "stick to it." It can only accede to the lived experiences of consciousness as much as the object manages to assimilate them. Now, the object always imposes two unbreakable limits on phenomenality. First, it imposes the limit of its own finitude, which necessarily excludes the infinity of all the lived experiences, sketches, and points aimed at that consciousness does not nevertheless cease to receive concerning it. Next, it imposes the limit of the finitude of intuition in it, which either stays in the background concerning meaning or, more rarely, equals it (it is then a question of the facts), without our ever envisaging that it can go beyond it and in this way be liberated from the horizon of the object.[4] At the end of these analyses, I will therefore conclude that all phenomenological constitution only produces a visible in showing as much *invu.*

Having reached this point, we cannot avoid the question of a "phenomenology of the unapparent *(des Unscheinbaren)."* What relation can be established between the *invu,* as I have just uncovered it, and

---

[4] On the penury of intuition for Kant and Husserl, see *Étant donné,* IV, §20, pp. 265ff.

the enigmatic formula that Heidegger introduced in 1973, at the time of the *Zähringen Seminar*?[5] In order to avoid any hypostasis of the invisible, certain distinctions are asserted. On the one hand, the text of 1973 seems to signal toward a phenomenology perfectly liberated from metaphysics and even from the Husserlian operations of phenomenology, since it designates nothing less than the *Ereignis:* "The *Ereignis ist das Unschienbarste des Unscheinbaren*—the least apparent of the unapparent."[6] Thus, in a radical sense, it signals a thought still to come, which would go back on this side of time and of being and only admit ". . . *unum necessarium* [the one thing necessary]: to bring thought and his thought into the clearing of the appearing [*paraître,* seeming] of the unapparent—*in die Lichtung des Scheinens des Unscheinbaren.*"[7] According to this line, a "phenomenology of the unapparent" would imply a transcending of phenomenology itself, beyond the gaps between subject and object, noesis and noema, intentionality and constitution, even beyond the reduction. Evidently I neither acknowledge this ambition as Heidegger's own nor take this risk. The "phenomenology of the unapparent" therefore cannot serve us here as a model. We could, in return, come back to another luminous definition of phenomenology advanced as early as 1927: "And it is precisely because phenomena are, at first sight and most of the time, *not* given (*nicht gegeben sind*), that there is a need for a phenomenology."[8] Phenomenology is not first required where phenomena are already given and constituted, but only where they remain dissimulated or still invisible. In this way it is in disengaging *Dasein* (and its existentials, anxiety and care), the manner of being of this being and the *Sinn des Seins* as phenomena by rights (until then remaining perfectly hidden and unthought), that

[5] Martin Heidegger, *Seminar in Zähringen* (1973), GA: I *Abteilung: Veröffentlichte Schriften 1910–1976, Band 15: Seminare 1951–73,* ed. Curd Ochwadt (Frankfurt am Main: Vittorio Klosterman, 1986), p. 399; *Questions IV,* trans. Jean Beaufret et al. (Paris: Gallimard, 1976), p. 339.

[6] Martin Heidegger, *Der Weg Zur Sprache* (1959), GA: I *Abteilung: Veröffentlichte Schriften 1910–1976, Band 12: Unterwegs zur Sprache,* ed. Friedrich-Wilhelm von Heffmann (Frankfurt am Main: Vittorio Klosterman, 1985), p. 247; French translation: ". . . is, among the unapparent, that which is the most unapparent" (*Acheminement vers la parole,* trans. Jean Beaufret et al. [Paris: Gallimard, 1976], p. 246).

[7] Martin Heidegger, Lettre à Roger Munier, February 22, 1974, in *Heidegger: Cahiers de l'Herne* (Paris: L'Herne, 1983), pp. 114 (translation) and 115 (text).

[8] Heidegger, *Sein und Zeit,* §7, p. 36; GA II, p. 48; *Être et temps,* trans. and ed. Emmanuel Martineau (Paris: Authentica, 1985), p. 47; *Being and Time,* p. 60 (Macquarrie); p. 31 (Stambaugh).

phenomenology, taken as the method of the *Seinsfrage,* works on what remains invisible to metaphysics. It therefore really earns the rank, if not the title, of a phenomenology of the unapparent, or at least of the not yet visible. But another difficulty comes to light here, the inverse of the preceding one. Does not such a conversion (of the not yet visible into a visible phenomenon) define all phenomenology worthy of the name? From Husserl disengaging categorial intuition to Derrida establishing *différance,* from Maurice Merleau-Ponty manifesting the flesh of the world to Michel Henry assigning auto-affection, which phenomenology is not attached to the invisible, in order to bring it into full light? From that point on, Heidegger's formula becomes enigmatic to the second degree: either it announces a post-phenomenological thought, about which we yet know almost nothing, or it characterizes, almost trivially, all phenomenology coherent with itself. In any case, it does not clarify the questioning that we have reached, which asks: what invisible—which mode of invisibility—renders possible the assignment of *l'invu* to the visible and, thereby, the visible itself?

It is therefore a question of acceding to an invisible that does not reduce itself to *l'invu,* distinguishing itself from it and preserving it. Well, *l'invu* results from the fact that the intentionality of the object cannot (and, without doubt, must not) give meaning to all the lived experiences and all the sketches nevertheless given to it. The object forces constitution to discern, choose, and exclude a considerable part of the intuition that concerns it. In effect, poverty in intuition, far from making the constitution of the object fragile, assures it, to the contrary, of certitude and permanence. The less the object calls for lived experiences, the more easily intention can find its confirmation, and the more continuously it can repeat its aim in an object which from that point is quasi-subsistent. That is why sciences (that is to say, the metaphysics that made them possible) have always privileged phenomena lacking in intuition, whether poor phenomena like logical statements and mathematical idealities (only formal intuition of space) or common phenomena like physical objects (mechanical, dynamic, and so on, adding to space the formal intuition of time). Moreover, metaphysics has first shown the way in looking for its undoubted point of departure in a subjectivity not seeking any intuition, except, perhaps, intellectual.[9]

---

[9] With the formidable ambiguities of this concept, underlined by Xavier Tilliette, *Recherches sur l'intuition intellectuelle de Kant à Hegel* (Paris: J. Vrin, 1995).

The Cartesian *ego* rises up from the questioning of all intuition (mathematical and sensory); the transcendental *I* disengages itself in opposition to the empirical me; *Dasein* appears by transgression of all being [*étant*] and by its resolution without object; and so on. It is the same for common phenomena, objects constituted in the sensible world: in the majority of cases, intuition remains within intention; and if, in some occurrences, it equals it provisionally and attains the facts [*à l'évidence*] in this way, the concept always controls the given and limits it to its measure.[10] Therefore, the visibility of objects, and thus the privilege of their principles, increases with the measure of *l'invu* that they leave behind them. And no recourse remains open to the invisible.

I am therefore proposing to follow another way to accede to such an invisible and to justify it phenomenologically: to consider phenomena where the duality between intention (signification) and intuition (fulfillment) certainly remains, as well as the noetic-noematic correlation, but where, to the contrary of poor and common phenomena, intuition gives (itself) in exceeding what the concept (signification, intentionality, aim, and so on) can foresee of it and show. I call these saturated phenomena, or paradoxes. They are saturated phenomena in that constitution encounters there an intuitive givenness that cannot be granted a univocal sense in return. It must be allowed, then, to overflow with many meanings, or an infinity of meanings, each equally legitimate and rigorous, without managing either to unify them or to organize them. If we follow the guiding thread of the Kantian categories, we locate, according to quantity, invisible phenomena of the type of the event (collective or individual); according to quality, phenomena the look cannot bear (the idol and the painting); according to relation, absolute phenomena, because defying any analogy, like flesh *(Leib);* finally, according to modality, phenomena that cannot be looked at, that escape all relation with thought in general, but which are imposed on it, like the icon of the other person *par excellence.* It is also appropriate to name them paradoxes, because they do not give themselves in a univocal display, available and mastered, according to a *doxa.* In effect, before the event, I cannot assign a single meaning to the immensity of lived experiences that happen to me. I can only pursue them by unceasingly multiplied and modified significations, in a hermeneutic without

---

[10] On this subject of phenomena, see *Étant donné,* IV, §23, pp. 309ff., which integrates the last case, here yet to come, of the saturated phenomenon.

end (chapter 2). Before the idol, where my aim cannot bear the intensity (qualitative), I can only slip away, and this very evasion will remain my only access to what crushes me (chapter 3). Before flesh, which feels and feels itself feeling without distinction, I cannot exactly locate myself outside in order to be in front of it, since it admits no "outside" and since I am irremediably in it and am it. I do not see it as a display, but I experience myself in and as it (chapter 4). There now remains the icon of the face to be considered. I cannot have vision of these phenomena, because I cannot constitute them starting from a univocal meaning, and even less produce them as objects. What I see of them, if I see anything of them that *is,* does not result from the constitution I would assign to them in the visible, but from the effect they produce on me. And, in fact, this happens in reverse so that my look is submerged, in a counter-intentional manner. Then I am no longer the transcendental *I* but rather the witness, constituted by what happens to him or her. Hence the para-dox, inverted *doxa.* In this way, the phenomenon that befalls and happens to us reverses the order of visibility in that it no longer results from my intention but from its own counter-intentionality. Consequently, doesn't the saturated paradox open an access to the invisible—to an invisible by saturation of the given, without common measure with *l'invu,* by constitutional default?

3. THE PARADOX OF THE FACE

Phenomenology might be able to accede to this invisible without losing its rigor or sinking into confusion if it attains it in view of authentic phenomena and not in their obscuration. It is the same with the saturated phenomena of the event, the idol, or flesh, to which one will contest neither the status of the phenomenon nor a certain invisibility by excess of intuition. In order to establish it, I will concentrate my attention on the last type of saturated phenomenon, the face.

The face shares the privilege of flesh: in the same way that the latter only feels in feeling itself feeling, the former only gives itself to be seen in seeing itself. But like flesh, the face becomes problematic when it is a question of recognizing it as the other person. For flesh, Husserl has already formalized the aporia: I can infer unknown flesh *(Leib)* from the other person, starting from his or her known physical body *(Körper),* following the analogy that their relationship forms with the relationship comparing my known flesh and my known body. But even recognized in this way, the flesh of the other person remains unknown as such, since by definition it would be merged with mine if it became immediately intuitable and would therefore disappear in it as other. The analogy, as also the imaginary transposition of points of view (the *over there* of the other person being inverted with my *here,* which in return would pass into his or her *over there*), does not correct this indirect recognition of the flesh of the other person, but underlines it. It is that which definitively stigmatizes the substitution for this flesh of an appresentation to intuitive presentation, common to most phenomena: "... my primordial *ego* constitutes the other *ego* by an appresentative apperception, which, following its own specificity, neither requires nor ever tolerates fulfillment by a presentation."[11] Why can flesh in principle not be presented by intuition? Intuition presents flesh well and truly, nevertheless, but precisely as physical body—it makes me see what I can feel. As for what feels (and feels itself feeling), no intuition can make it seen to any look. It remains only to postulate, as Husserl did, that appresentation ". . . presupposes . . . a kernel of presentation *(einen Kern von Präsentation).*"[12] Flesh escapes phenomenality as such (as feeling), because only the felt can show itself by intuition. And besides, far from my flesh being able to constitute that of the other person, perhaps it [*elle-même*] can only experience its limits (thus its proper sphere) in presupposing the flesh of the other person, which, so to speak, would constitute it. The face offers a similar particularity: it is not seen as much as it [*lui-même*] sees. In effect, how can we distinguish a face from flesh in general (from any other part of an animated body)? If the face shares the privilege of flesh—making itself (be) felt, but necessarily feeling and feeling that one is felt and that one feels—it adds to it a second privilege by which we evidently distinguish it from flesh—not only to be seen, but, especially, to see. We must not only oppose the facade (visible but inexpressive) to the face (visible and expressive) but also recognize by and on this face the unique characteristic of looking without having to be looked at. But this unique characteristic, which suffices to define the face as what looks at me, dictates specifically that I cannot see it, nor look at it in

---

[11] Husserl, Hua. I, V, §54, p. 148; *Méditations cartésiennes,* p. 168; *Cartesian Meditations,* p. 119.

[12] Husserl, Hua. I, V, §55, p. 150; *Méditations cartésiennes,* p. 171; *Cartesian Meditations,* p. 122.

its turn. An empty or careless look is seen neither less nor more than a look eager to see. The look of the other person remains unable to be looked at. Further still: what do we look at in the face of the other person? Not his or her mouth, nevertheless more expressive of the intentions than other parts of the body, but the eyes—or more exactly the empty pupils of the person's eyes, their black holes open on the somber ocular hollow. In other words, in the face we fix on the sole place where precisely nothing can be seen. Thus, in the face of the other person we see precisely the point at which all visible spectacle happens to be impossible, where there is nothing to see, where intuition can give nothing [of the] visible.

If the face, such as it is—that is to say, as the look posed on me—no longer offers anything to look at itself, should we not give up looking for a phenomenon there? In short, do we not cross the limits of phenomenology? Two reasons hold us back from yielding to this conclusion too quickly. (a) *To look at* traces the Latin *intueri,* itself constructed on *tueri,* "to guard," "to watch over," "to keep an eye on." And, in fact, to watch over the visible characterizes well the mode of vision appropriate to the object, where we master by its constitution all the dimensions of its noema in a univocal and exhaustive sense.[13] But to watch over offers only one of the modes of aiming and of possible vision; there are others, since not every phenomenon is reduced to an object, no more than every visible allows itself to be mastered by its intentional aim. We have to admit that certain phenomena—for example, paradoxes—can well escape the look *(intuitus)* and nevertheless appear, but they are unable to be looked at. It remains to be defined how what our intentionality cannot keep under its watch manifests itself. (b) We are indebted to Levinas for having fixed it, in determining for the first time the mode of phenomenality proper to the face. It does not give itself to be seen in a display as one visible situated among others in the indefinite series of worldly inanimate apparitions. The face would not be distinguished from them, besides, if it only claimed to be made seen, since, at the most, it would only establish a simple difference of degree from other spectacles, at the risk of confusion. The mask and the makeup that seek to render the face more spectacular than it would be if it remained naked in fact abolish it because they substitute for it an object to see, which effaces it. No, the face is not

---

[13] See above, chapter 2, §1, pp. 56ff.

phenomenalized as such, as long as a spectacle to be looked at remains [*un spectacle regardé*]. It is therefore necessary to define it in a completely other mode: it is insofar as ". . . the face speaks"[14] that it shows itself. To speak is not necessarily the same here as making use of the physical word and the material sounds that it emits. Besides, this sonorous word never "says" anything, save if a non-said sense protects it in saving in it the welcome of an understanding, of a comprehension. Thus the word is played first in the listening and in the silence of the sense [meaning]. In this way the face speaks in silence.

How? The center of the face is fixed in the eyes, in the void of the pupils. A counter-look rises up here; it escapes my look and envisages me in return—in fact, it sees me first, because it takes the initiative. The look of the other person, precisely because it cannot be looked at, irrupts in the visible. Its word renders manifest what we could name an ethical phenomenon (following the magnificent French locution "Look, listen [to me] . . . !"): the injunction "Thou shalt not kill!" The face (that cannot be looked at) of the look of the other person only appears when I admit—submitting myself to him or her—that I must not kill. Certainly, I can kill the other person, but then he or she will disappear as a face, will be congealed into a simple object, precisely because the phenomenality of the face forbids its being possessed, produced, and thus constituted as an intentional object. Certainly, I can kill him or her, but then I will feel myself as a murderer, forever, and whatever human justice might say, the look of the other person will thus have taken the initiative and the advantage over me; it will weigh on me even after its physical disappearance. If there must be intentionality here—which can be discussed, since there is no constitution—it will not be a question, in all cases, of mine on that of the other, but of his or hers on me. If there must be intuition—which it is certainly necessary to maintain, since a phenomenon appears—it will fill no aim arising from me but will contradict instead all the object aims that I could foster. The noesis prepares no noema but instead releases an uncontrollable and unexpected noematic superabundance; since it is a question of ". . . the infinite or face . . . ,"[15] the noema appears as infinite and submerges all noesis, intuition submerges all intention. The

---

[14] Emmanuel Levinas, *Humanisme de l'autre homme* (Montpellier: Fata Morgana, 1972), pp. 47ff.

[15] Levinas, *Totalité et infini*, p. 182.

saturated phenomenon thus appears not visible, but by excess. The injunction "You shall not kill!" is enjoined, in effect, with an intuition that no concept could grasp and objectify. There is an excess of intuition because (as Kantian respect is imposed on moral consciousness) the face is imposed on me. Even and especially if I am diverted from it or if I kill it, I know then that it was a demand and a requirement; I can only despise it because I know it. Further, the face in its injunction obliges me to situate myself in relation to it. I do not adapt it to my visual devices, as I would do with an animal or a tool. I do not approach it following my intention, but following its intentionality, because it is the face that asks me not to kill it, to renounce any mastery over it, and to distance myself from it—"*noli me tangere!* [do not touch me!]." Thus it is I who submit myself to its point of view and must situate myself in the exact, precise, and unique place where it intends to appear as pure face. An anamorphosis *par excellence* is substituted for the centrifugal intentionality coming from me—a point of view come from another place, which imposes on me its angle of vision. Intuition therefore does not regulate itself according to any signification known in advance by me, but rises up as a fact of phenomenality (in the sense that Kant speaks of a fact of reason), without prior or presupposed condition. There is also excess of intuition over every meaning and concept: the face, in enjoining "You shall not kill!," does not make me understand what it nevertheless strikes me with in silence. This is, first, precisely because it does not even need to say it out loud in order for me to hear it. Next, it is because this injunction can arouse interpretations, behaviors, and thus diverse meanings, even opposed, and endlessly renewed. I can, in fact, not kill, but go on a spectrum from a contemptuous indifference to neutral respect for humanity in general, to the point of friendship between equals, or even to unconditioned love that sacrifices itself. I can also kill, but for many reasons [significations]: gratuitous barbarism, mistake, the rage of disappointed humanism, suicidal madness, ideological certitude, punishment planned by the law, the supposed "just" (or not) war, and so on. In short, the face, insofar as it appears in "Thou shalt not kill!," arouses a diversity without end of meanings, all possible, all provisionary, all insufficient. The face does not allow itself to be constituted, but this is because it imposes its phenomenon on me. It appears as not being able to be looked at, as impossible to keep under the gaze.

Nevertheless, if the ethical hermeneutic of the face accomplishes a decisive opening in the direction of its specific phenomenality and remains a definitive piece of acquired knowledge from the thought of Levinas, it must be questioned on one point. In admitting that the transcendence of the ". . . face or [of] the infinite" beyond phenomenalities of the object or of being [*étant*] is really accomplished first in ethics, does it have to depend on it exclusively? Levinas himself, it seems, ended by doubting it.[16] Ethics could simply put to work here a phenomenological deployment more originary than it, and which would consequently render possible the description of other phenomena, or of other descriptions of this same phenomenon—the face. In effect, the injunction "Thou shalt not kill!" is exercised first as an injunction, independently of its contents. One could replace it with other injunctions, just as strong, whether existentielle—"Become who you are!"; existential—"Determine yourself as the being for whom being is at stake"; religious—"Love your God with all your heart, with all your soul and with all your mind"; moral—"Do not do unto others what you would not want done unto you"; even erotic—"Love me."[17] These injunctions would impose themselves just as strongly, no doubt. They could not do so if, indeed, the injunction were not addressing a call to an authority that could hear them. But this call could not resound in this way, sometimes in silence, if it did not proceed from a particular phenomenon, the face, because more than any other phenomenon, it must appear under the form, not of an object spectacle, but of a call. The face, saturated phenomenon according to modality, accomplishes the phenomenological operation of the call more, perhaps, than any other phenomenon (saturated or not): it happens (event), without cause or reason (incident/accident), when it decides so (arrival), and imposes the point of view from which to see it (anamorphosis) as a *fait accompli*. That is why what imposes its call must be defined not only as the other person of ethics (Levinas), but more radically as the icon. The icon gives itself

---

[16] See my discussion "D'autrui à l'individu: Au-delà de l'éthique," Actes du Colloque *Emmanuel Levinas et la phénoménologie* (Sorbonne, 11–12 December 1997), appearing under the title *Levinas et le phénoménologie*, added to *E. Levinas: Positivité et transcendance* (Paris: Presses Universitaires de France, 2000). English translation by Robyn Horner, in Regina Schwartz, *Transcendence* (London: Routledge, 2002).

[17] I do not take account *here* of what Heidegger thematized under the title of *Anspruch des Seins* (GA IX, p. 319), because he does not proceed precisely from any face or any icon. It remains to be understood how he can nevertheless depend on a phenomenological structure of the call (see my *Réduction et donation*, VI, §6, pp. 294ff.; *Reduction and Givenness*, pp. 164ff., and *Étant donné*, V, §26, pp. 366ff.).

to be seen in that it makes me hear [understand] its call. One can only understand in this way that the face envisages me: its phenomenality never consists in making itself seen as one visible among others—in the face, in this sense, there is nothing to see and it remains perfectly invisible. But its phenomenality is accomplished when it is made heard [understood], when the weight of its glory weighs upon me, when it inspires respect. *To respect*—to attract sight and attention *(-spectare),* of course—but because I feel myself called and held at a distance by the weight of an invisible look, by its silent appeal. *To respect* is also understood as the counter-concept of *to look at.*

4. To Envisage

There are therefore phenomena that I call saturated, where the excess of intuition over signification censures the constitution of an object and, more radically, the visibility of a unified and defined spectacle. Among these paradoxically invisible phenomena, I have privileged the face, because the analyses of Levinas have acquired an exemplary phenomenological status for it already. I have tried, nevertheless, to advance one step further, in thinking the face as icon addressing a call, in short, as envisaging me. I therefore attain in this way a phenomenon that is invisible but which envisages me. The question becomes: Can I, in my turn envisage it? Can I attain, in return, this invisible but envisaging face as such, without lowering it to the rank of a constituted and objectivized visible, in respecting its invisibility and saluting its own phenomenality, in short, in envisaging it as it envisages me? Is it necessary to maintain that the face is envisageable or unenvisageable?

In order to respond to this difficult questioning, we go back to Husserl and to flesh, of which the face offers the extreme figure: ". . . flesh *(der Leib)* is not only in general a thing, but rather the expression of the spirit *and, at the same time, the organ of the spirit (zugleich Organs des Geistes)."* [18] The face thus expresses the spirit as its "organ." Now, as for Aristotle at least, spirit is in some fashion all things in potentiality. Its expression cannot be limited to a unique signification, as in the case of poor or common phenomena. The expression of the face ex-

---

[18] Husserl, Hua. IV, §21, p. 96; *Idées directrices II,* p. 144 (modified); *Ideas II,* p. 102.

presses an infinity of meanings. This infinity is marked first in the fact
that the features and movements of the face, even accompanied by
explicative words, cannot be translated into a concept or a finite propo-
sition. Not only do the lived experiences of the other person remain
definitively foreign to me, but, even for the other (at least I can, by
analogy, infer it from my own experience), these lived experiences
remain too complex, intermixed, and changing for a statement, even an
elaborate one, to be able to take account of them conceptually. What
the face says remains, in the best of cases, an approximation of what is
expressed there. In the strict sense, the face does not know what it says,
or, more exactly, it cannot say the meaning that it expresses, because
it does not know it itself. My incapacity to know what it expresses in a
fixed meaning does not first betray my impotence or my inattention
to seeing or understanding it, but rather its essential impossibility of
understanding and saying itself. The other person cannot know more
what his or her face expresses than he or she can see this face (because
the mirror only ever sends back an image, and an inverse image). The
possibility that this face lies to me or, as happens more often, first lies
to itself, results, as one of its possible consequences, in the irreducible
gap between expression starting from infinite lived experiences and
conceptualizable, sayable, and always inadequate significations. Only
a face can lie, because only it benefits from the dangerous privilege of
an inadequate, unobjectifiable, and necessarily equivocal expression.
The lie is absolutely not the same, from the phenomenological point of
view, as the error. The error concerns an object or a state of fact, where
intuitive fulfillment does not correspond with the signification that the
intuition aims at. In error, besides the fact that it is a matter of a common third and not of a face envisaged "face on," one always supposes
an already intelligible meaning; it is only a question of deciding if it is
confirmed intuitively, in part or totally, or if it is necessary to substitute
another one for it. In the lie, or more exactly in that of which the lie
offers an indication and result, the difficulty proceeds from the fact that
the face can never coincide with a meaning, complex or not. Moreover,
when a face expresses itself in truth, when it does not lie, this does not
imply that it delivers a signification that it would confirm by intuition.
It is only a question there of sincerity or of veracity (the will not to
deceive). This does not imply, either, that it delivers a signification that
my intuition would fill and confirm. There it is only a question of an
external confirmation, worldly, provisional for that matter, which at-

tests, in the best of cases, to the coherence of the behavior of the other person. A face only says the truth about what it expresses—truth that in a sense it always ignores—if I believe it and if it believes that I believe it. Confidence, not to say faith, offers the sole phenomenologically correct access to the face of the other person. The impossibility of constituting it in an object and a univocal phenomenon must be taken seriously: the classic definition of truth (adequation, evidence), and even its phenomenal definition (to show oneself starting from oneself), become here inoperative. For the face only shows what it expresses, but it never expresses a meaning or a complex of defined meanings. When it envisages me, it does not manifest itself. Or if it manifests itself—because in envisaging me, one can also say that it manifests itself from itself, starting from itself and insofar as itself, more than any other phenomenon manages to do so—it does not nevertheless ever say its meaning.

One could object that the face, most often and to begin with, nevertheless expresses a meaning—for example, that of its passions, which metaphysics wanted to classify as so many significations of the incarnate spirit (from Descartes to Le Brun). But if I admit that I know and understand the other person in reducing him or her to a state of mind, such that passions reconstitute the other, I only know him or her as a psychological agent, of whom I must measure the strengths, the conduct, and the intentions. I then include the other in a social strategy, constituting one element among others in such a way that I can contain or make use of him or her. But in this situation, it is no longer a question of a face that envisages me and confronts me with its call; it is a question of an animated object, which I see as I want and constitute from my point of view. All the same, when the other person finds him- or herself identified by a professional or social role (technician, notary, doctor, teacher, judge, and so on), no doubt he or she benefits from a definition and I can assign to the other a meaning; I can even consider that the person's conduct and words express this meaning. But straightaway the other disappears as a face: I cease to envisage him or her as a face, because I have no need of it in order to behave toward the other; he or she does not, besides, expect this much, and asks only to be recognized according to function and profession, which is what I most certainly do. Our reciprocal inauthenticity assures social relations very well, which standardization and effectiveness require, which anonymity guarantees. Now, precisely, social relations differ entirely from the face-to-face with the face that envisages me. The other person only appears to me starting from the moment when I expose myself to him or her, thus when I no longer master or constitute the other and admit that he or she expresses self without signification.

Must the face that envisages me remain an unintelligible phenomenon, because without signification? Not at all. For if the face lacks a conceptualizable meaning, it is not by default, but by excess. The face expresses an infinity of meanings at each moment and during an indefinite lapse of time. This endless flux of significations, which happens to the other according to the present rising up from original temporality, can never itself be reduced to the concept or be said adequately. *A fortiori* [for a still stronger reason] I cannot do it myself, either, I who receive him or her from the outside, at a distance of alterity, as an event, renewed without ceasing. To accede to this face will therefore never consist in closing it up again under the cover of what it expresses, of what it stands for, or of what it means to say, in short, under a noema. To accede to this face demands, on the contrary, envisaging it face-to-face, despite or *thanks to* its absence from defined meaning—in other words, expecting that a substitute comes to give a meaning (to constitute, Husserl would say) and a significance to the expression which, of itself, is lacking from it. This substitute is named the event, in the double sense of what happens and, especially, of what fixes the result of an action or sanctions the unraveling of an intrigue.[19] What a face means to say is not read more in its expressions than in its words, since both can deceive (voluntarily or involuntarily, it does not matter). What a face expresses is recognized in what happens to it—the act or the event that happens to it and that contradicts or confirms the spoken word or the silent expression. The truth of the face is therefore played in its story—not in what it says, but in what it does, or more exactly in what it becomes following what happens to it. To envisage a face requires less to see it than to wait for it, to wait for its accomplishment, the terminal act, the passage to effectivity. That is why the truth of a life is only unveiled at its last instant: "One must not reckon happy any mortal / before seeing his last day and that he had attained / the term of his life without undergoing suffering" (Sophocles).[20] That

---

[19] Pascal: "And these prophecies being accomplished and proved by the *event* mark the certitude of these truths and consequently the proof of the divinity of J.-C." *Pensées*, §189, p. 524.

[20] Sophocles, *Œdipe Roi,* ll. 1528–30, trans. J. Grosjean (Paris: Gallimard, 1967), p. 711.

is why the measure of friendship always remains duration. That is why to love would mean to help the other person to the point of the final instant of his or her death. And to see the other finally, in truth, would mean, in the end, closing his or her eyes.

5. HERMENEUTICS TO THE INFINITE

In this way, according to time as according to space, to envisage a face demands a hermeneutics of its apparent and infinitely numerous—thus contradictory—expressions, until the last one manages, perhaps, to strip it of all that would cover it up and deliver it in its naked truth. In fact, nothing guarantees to us that the last figure that the face of the other person takes *in articulo mortis* [in the moment of death] will open the ultimate meaning—or that the last will be the right one. That is why, in the meeting of mortal ideologies, Christian theology has the prudence and the decency to postpone this last judgment to the Last Judgment—to God, who alone can fathom the innermost parts. But at least, while we are unable to accomplish this judgment, the duty to pursue its hermeneutic without end remains to our finitude, blinded as it is by a saturated phenomenon. Or rather—and it is this that confirms our ineluctable finitude—it is once the face of the other person dies that in fact the hermeneutic without end truly commences in it, far from ending it. For it is starting from the instant of his or her death that the work of mourning begins and, indissolubly, of memory: putting together all the documents and all the memories that remain to us of the other person, discovering in them new ones by association, sifting authenticated facts from false ones, criticizing indirect information—in short, constituting the unconstitutable saturated phenomenon of the other person. Then, most importantly, trying to construct a coherent interpretation of it, or, indeed, not too coherent, in order to avoid simplifications; and then to confront the difficulty that all hermeneutics implies—yielding to an ideology or to a passion, oscillating between hagiography and disparagement, the one and the other systematic, thus insignificant. At this moment, not only can I separate myself into two distinct witnesses, but further, if the face of this other person belongs to the public, other witnesses can propose hermeneutics contradictory to mine. And so on, in such a way that the enigma of the face of the other person is going to darken in the exact measure to which hermeneutics will claim to render finally accessible in it the supposed unitary and knowable meaning. From that point on, the phenomenon saturated according to modality (the face) will cover over the characteristics, equally aporetic, of the phenomenon saturated according to quantity (the event).

In this situation, theology and philosophy follow different paths. For theology, in this world, the face of the other person remains a phenomenon of inaccessible meaning; it cannot thus be attained in the present, as long as this present is repeated and lasts. It is therefore necessary to have recourse to faith—to have faith in faith, insomuch as it is defined as "the substance of what is still hoped for, ἐλπιζομένων ὑπόστασις [*elpidzomenon hypostasis*]"—or, in almost phenomenological terms, "the index of invisible things, πράγματων ἔλεγχος οὐ βλεπομένων [*pragmaton elegchos ou blepomenon*]" (Heb. 11.1). Plainly, it is necessary for me to wait for the manifestation of the face of the other person as I must wait for the return of Christ. It is normal, besides, seeing that ". . . our life is hidden κεκρυπται [*kekryptai*]) with Christ in God" (Col. 3.3). How could the finite face of the other person rise up in the glory of its truth, outside the glorification of the infinite Face? The hermeneutic of the saturated phenomenon of the other person becomes, in Christian theology, one of the figures of faith, thus of the eschatological wait for the manifestation of the Christ. Theological faith imposes itself as the unique correct approach, because always deferred to the end of time, to the face of the other, "my fellow, my brother or sister."

On the evidence, philosophy—as it is, phenomenology—cannot claim this direct and royal way, for it cannot wait for the end of time, but only wait in time, thus endlessly. From that point, what path to follow? I suggest repeating here, while displacing it, the reasoning of Kant in favor of a certain sense of the immortality of the soul in the limits of (pure) practical reason. One is reminded of the postulate: ". . . all the other concepts (those of God and of immortality), which, insofar as simple ideas, remain without support in speculative reason, are now connected to this concept [that is to say, freedom] and acquire stability and objective reality with and by it. In other words, their *possibility (die Möglichkeit derselben)* is proven by the fact that freedom is effective."[21] In other words, the ideas without sensory effectivity of

---

[21] Immanuel Kant, *Critique de la raison pratique,* Préface, Ak.A.V, p. 4; French translation, vol. 2 (Paris: Gallimard/La Pléiade, 1985), p. 610.

God and of immortality draw, indirectly, from the effectivity of the idea of freedom (required by the fact of reason, the categorical imperative) a real, although borrowed, possibility. It remains to be established how immortality is linked with effective freedom to the point that it receives a real possibility from it. Freedom, summoned by the moral law, must aim at its perfect realization (holiness); but it unceasingly proves its powerlessness to attain this perfection, from the fact that it is there a question of a ". . . perfection of which no reasonable *Dasein* belonging to the sensible world is capable at any moment of its existence." It is therefore necessary to envisage an "indefinite progress," a progress ". . . going to the infinite," which must finally emerge in ". . . an ulterior and uninterrupted continuation of this progress, as long as its existence can last, and even beyond this life *(über dieses Leben hinaus)*"—an existence that goes beyond this sentient life.[22] Immortality is required indirectly as the necessary condition of the accomplishment of freedom in its perfect moral status. It is necessary to live "as if, *als ob*"[23] another life, an immortality, were possible to us—in order not to resign ourselves to the imperfect use of freedom in this life. In short, a fact of reason—"Act in such a way that the maxim of your will can at the same time be used as a principle of universal legislation"[24]—imposes the effectivity of an idea of reason, my freedom, but this freedom, which must become holy, can never do so in sentient life. It is therefore necessary to infer the possibility of another idea of reason, the immortality of the soul as place of an indefinite progress from freedom toward moral holiness.

I would like to suggest that it is perhaps possible to transpose this argument in phenomenological terms, suitable to the saturated phenomenon of the face of the other person. (a) The fact of reason becomes, here, no longer the categorical, universal and abstract, but this face itself, where such another person enjoins me: "Thou shalt not kill [me]!" (b) But it gives rise, on my part, to the same respect as the imperative, in claiming from me, in fact in compelling me to deploy, a way of aiming [sighting] that does not objectivize the other person

---

[22] Kant, *Critique de la raison pratique*, Préface, Ak.A.V, p. 122ff.; French translation, pp. 757–58.

[23] Kant, *Das Ende aller Dinge*, Ak.A.VIII, pp. 330 and 334; French translation, vol. 3 (Paris: Gallimard, 1986), pp. 313 and 318.

[24] Kant, *Critique de la raison pratique*, Préface, Ak.A.V, p. 30; French translation, vol. 2, p. 643.

(does not "kill"). Note well that, in French at least, "to kill" is not limited to putting to death; one also says that an ill-chosen color "kills" other colors in a painting (or in furnishings, or a bunch of flowers, and so on), that one flavor "kills" another, that a rejoinder in a public debate "kills" an interlocutor, that in society, ridicule "kills," and so forth. "To kill" thus indicates the destruction of the other person or thing, its objectivization into an insignificant term, entirely annulled, henceforth without force or proper value. In the physical annihilation of the other person, it is in fact *first* a question of this "killing," of removing the irreducible autonomy of a non-objectivizable, unknowable other person, the unforeseeable center of initiatives and intentionality. All the totalitarianisms have proved it, which have only annihilated physically certain classes of people in order, first and especially, to "kill" this irreducible humanity in them. The metaphorical sense of the word in fact delivers its proper meaning. (c) But, since it is a question here of recognizing an expression beyond all signification, a noesis without adequately correlative noema, an "idea of infinity" (Levinas), this saturating intuition goes beyond all intentionality. Thus, while it is no longer a question of will, but this time of recognition of the other person, I cannot anymore, here, attain what Kant called "holiness," obedience to the law. All that I would perceive of the other person as regards significations and intentions will remain always and by definition in the background and in deficit in relation to his or her face, a saturated phenomenon. And, therefore, I will only be able to bear this paradox and do it justice in consecrating myself to its infinite hermeneutic according to space, and especially time. For as I have already observed, even after the death of this face, hermeneutics must be pursued, in a memory no less demanding than the present vision. And it will be pursued—or at least should be—after my own death, this time entrusted to others. The face of the other person requires in this way an infinite hermeneutic, equivalent to the "progress toward the infinite" of morality according to Kant. Thus, every face demands immortality—if not its own, at least that of the one who envisages it.

Only the one who has lived with the life and the death of another person knows to what extent he or she does *not* know that other. This one alone can therefore recognize the other as the saturated phenomenon *par excellence,* and consequently also knows that it would take an eternity to envisage this saturated phenomenon as such—not constituting it as an object, but interpreting it in loving it. For ". . . love is without end. It is only love in the infinity of the loving *(in der Unendlichkeit des Liebens)*."[25] The face of the other person compels me to believe in my own eternity, like a need of reason or, what comes back to the same thing, as the condition of its infinite hermeneutic.

---

[25] Husserl, *Erste Philosophie (1923–24): Zweiter Teil: Theorie der phanomenologischen Reduktion,* Hua. VIII, ed. Rudolf Boehm (The Hague: Martinus Nijhoff, 1959), §29, p. 14; *Philosophie Première (1923–24). Deuxième partie: Théorie de la reduction phénoménologique,* trans. Arion L. Kelkel (Paris: Presses Universitaires de France/ Epiméthée, 1972), p. 20.

6

In the Name: How to Avoid Speaking of It

1. "METAPHYSICS OF PRESENCE" AND "NEGATIVE THEOLOGY"

That the two questions of the "metaphysics of presence" and of "negative theology"—questions which to all appearances come from such dissimilar provenances—should today end up encountering one another, indeed end up being by and large superimposed, could be surprising.

No doubt they have a characteristic lack in common—that of having neither precise definition nor clear-cut historical legitimacy. For instance, Heidegger never (to our knowledge) used the phrase "metaphysics of presence," a point that is all the more remarkable as he was forever radically questioning the constitution of metaphysics as well as the essence of presence (the οὐσία of the πᾰρουσία). Likewise, never, it seems to us, does Derrida himself explain exactly what can and should be understood by this phrase.[1] It follows that certain basic questions are left open: is "metaphysics" always identified as and by presence, or can it also include absence? Is presence exactly equal to onto-theo-logy, does it extend beyond, and does it even admit of being defined? Surely the indeterminacy of the "metaphysics of presence" characterizes it essentially (as essentially without essence), or even re-

---

[1] For that matter, the first occurrence (at least to my knowledge) of this phrase refers, strangely enough, to Husserl, as the thinker of ". . . phenomenology, the metaphysics of presence in the form of ideality"—Jacques Derrida, *La voix et le phénomène* (Paris: Presses Universitaires de France, 1967), p. 9; *Speech and Phenomena,* trans. David Allison (Evanston: Northwestern University Press, 1973), p. 10. It could be that it was Derrida's critical reading of Husserl during 1953 and 1954 that led him to formulate this question ("Phenomenology would no longer be master of its own house. Ontology would *already* be within it," *Le problème de la genèse dans la philosophie de Husserl* [Paris: Presses Universitaires de France, 1990], p. 117). But is it self-evident that one can legitimately count on such a "metaphysical speech of phenomenology" (La différance," in *Marges de la philosophie* [Paris: Minuit, 1972], p. 21; *Speech and Phenomena,* p. 152)?

inforces it. It does not remain less obvious, especially in the popular and polemic uses of deconstruction; and this indeterminacy perhaps also implies a fundamental imprecision, one that would inevitably be harmful to its hermeneutic efficacy. Now it also happens to be the case that the formula "negative theology" suffers from a similar indeterminacy. First because, as Aimé Solignac testifies, "To speak more accurately, Denys employs the formula 'negative theology' only once, in the title to the third chapter of the *Mystical theology.*" Even more could have been said: first because this single occurrence appears only in a chapter heading and therefore is likely to have come from the redactor; next and most importantly because it is precisely not a matter here of defining *a* or *the* negative theology but of knowing "which are the affirmative theologies [the words spoken about God] and which [are] the negative—τίνες αἱ καταφατικαὶ θελογίαι, τίνες αἱ ἀποφατικαί [*tines hai kataphatikai theologiai, tines hai apophatikai*]." Quite clearly, the plural and also the ancient meaning of the substantive must be reestablished in the rendering of this text in order not to break the parallel with "affirmative theologies";[2] but above all it must be understood that for Denys the term θελογία [*theologia*] always designates the expressions Scripture uses to say (or to not say) God, at a great distance from the concepts of metaphysics.[3] In this way, since even a great scholar, Solignac, prefers to continue with an approximation rather than break entirely with the supposedly established theme of a single "negative theology," it will not be surprising that the run-of-the-mill commentators insist on invoking this formula in authors who, to our knowledge, are ignorant of it. For neither the Alexandrian or Cappadocian fathers, nor Irenaeus or Augustine, nor Bernard, Bonaventure, or Thomas Aquinas, all of whom resort to negations when naming God and build a theory of this apophasis—none of them use the formula "negative theology." As a result, it can reasonably be sup-

---

[2] Aimé Solignac, *Dictionaire de Spiritualité,* vol. 15 (Paris: Beauschesne, 1990–91), col. 513. Under discussion is *MT* III, PG 1032d. Derrida seems aware of this difficulty when he evokes ". . . what one calls, sometimes erroneously, 'negative theology'. . . ."—*Psyché: Inventions de l'autre* (Paris: Galilée, 1987), p. 535; *Derrida and Negative Theology,* ed. Harold Coward and Toby Foshay (Albany: SUNY Press, 1992), p. 73.

[3] René Roques, *L'univers dionysien: Structure hiérarchique du monde selon le Pseudo-Denys* (Paris: Aubier, 1954), pp. 210ff.

posed that this formula is nothing but modern.[4] Consequently, we will from now on no longer consider the phrases "metaphysics of presence" and "negative theology," if by chance we have had to use them, as anything but conceptual imprecisions to be overcome or as questions awaiting answers—never as secure bases.

However, beyond such parallel aporiae, these two questions maintain a much more intimate relationship. Derrida himself recognized that they were intertwined at the center of his own work during the seminal lecture of 1968, "Différance": "And yet what is thus denoted as *différance* is not theological, not even in the most negative order of negative theology. The latter, as we know, is always occupied with letting a superessential reality go beyond finite categories of essence and existence, that is, of presence, and always hastens to remind us that, if we deny the predicate of existence to God, it is in order to recognize by God a superior, inconceivable and ineffable mode of being."[5] This,

---

[4] It will be observed that when François Bourgoin offers the modern definition of theology—". . . we must remark that there are three sorts of theology: the positive, the scholastic, and the mystical. The positive has as its object the interpretation of the Holy Scriptures. . . . The scholastic illuminates the truths of faith methodically, mixing with it some of human reasoning. And the mystical applies these truths and serves to elevate the soul to God" (*Préface* [of 1644] to *Oeuvres Complètes du Cardinal de Bérulle*, in ed. J.-P. Migne [Paris, 1856], p. 83)—he completely ignores "negative theology," or else includes it with the two other "ways" in mystical theology. On the complicated fate of this term, see Michel de Certeau, "'Mystique' au XVIIe siècle: Le problème du langage 'mystique,'" in *L'homme devant Dieu: Mélanges offerts au Père Henri de Lubac*, vol. 2 (Paris: Aubier, 1964), pp. 267ff. (where it is emphasized that Denys was at this time the mystic *par excellence*). I also want to make mine the prudent reservations of Michael Sales, "La théologie négative: Méthode ou métaphysique," *Axes* 3, no. 2 (Paris, 1970).

[5] Delivered before the Société Française de Philosophie in 1968 and reprinted in *Marges de la philosophie; Speech and Phenomena*, p. 134. I had discussed this denegation in *L'idole et la distance*, p. 318. One can even trace this preoccupation back further: "At arms with the problems which were equally the problems of negative theology and of Bergsonism, he does not give himself the right to speak, as they did, in a language resigned to its own failure. Negative theology was spoken in a speech that knew itself failed and finite, inferior to logos as God's understanding." "L'écriture et la différence," originally published in 1964 in the *Revue de métaphysique et de morale*, and reprinted in *L'écriture et la différence* (Paris: Seuil, 1967), p. 170; *Writing and Difference*, trans. Alan Bass (Chicago: University of Chicago Press, 1978), p. 116. Curiously, Levinas operates a comparable denegation with his description of the infinite: "Not all the negations occurring in the description of this 'relationship with the infinite' are confined to the formal and logical sense of negation, and constitute a negative theology!" Levinas, *Le temps et l'autre*, in a note from the revised edition of 1979 (Paris: Fata Morgana), p. 91; *Time and the Other*, trans. Richard A. Cohen (Pittsburgh: Duquesne, 1987), 33 n [Cohen's translation given here].

may it be said, is an example of a denegation. This Parisian denegation precedes by twenty years another one, made in Jerusalem, in the lecture "How to Avoid Speaking: Denegations."[6] This persistent denegation is articulated in three inseparable but not unhierarchical moments: (i) first, an explicit denegation—that by which, according to Derrida, "negative theology" says it is saying nothing positive about God; (ii) next, an implicit denegation—by which, according to Derrida, "negative theology" claims not to do what it nevertheless does all the time, namely, again say something, to predicate τὶ κατὰ τὶνος [*ti kata tinos*] of God, and thereby reinscribe God in the "metaphysics of presence"; (iii) finally, and most importantly, an explicit denegation made by Derrida—in which he denies that he himself repeats, with *différance,* the project and the failures of "negative theology." This last denegation —*différance* does not repeat "negative theology" because it alone deconstructs the "metaphysics of presence" without compromise— obviously governs the other two. For *différance* to differ from "negative theology," it must be shown that the latter always remains in submission to the privilege of presence. Derrida's criticism of so-called negative theology therefore concerns not just this particular method of discourse but first of all the dominance of *différance* in the deconstruction of presence. Here, for Derrida, it is not, as it is in his other readings of decisive moments in the history of metaphysics, a matter of deconstructing figures of presence that confess or lay claim to being as such

---

[6] Jacques Derrida, "Comment ne pas parler: Dénégations," reprinted in *Psyché;* "How to Avoid Speaking: Denials," trans. Ken Friedan, in *Derrida and Negative Theology.* See also *Sauf le nom* (Paris: Galilée 1993); "Post-Scriptum: Aporias, Ways, and Voices," trans. John P. Leavey Jr., also printed as "Sauf le nom," in *On the Name,* ed. Thomas Dutoit (Stanford: Stanford University Press, 1995), pp. 35–85. [Note that the English translation of the former essay is entitled "How to Avoid Speaking: Denials." I have chosen to render the French "dénégations" as "denegations" rather than "denials" because this seems to better capture the sense intended by the author of the present study: namely, it is not simply a matter of denying that one, be it deconstruction or "negative theology," does something, be it predicate of God or repeat "negative theology"; rather, at issue is whether or not in claiming not to speak about X, or in denying that they do Y, negative theology and/or deconstruction are in fact speaking about X, doing Y—J. Kosky] As *Psyché* made generous reference to my work (in particular *L'idole et la distance,* then *Dieu sans l'être,*), the pages that follow could be read as a response, or rather as a complementary moment, in an already old and, for me at least, quite fruitful discussion. Concerning the remarks that *Donner le temps I: La fausse monnaie* (Paris: Galilée, 1991) (*Given Time I: Counterfeit Money,* trans. Peggy Kamuf [Chicago: University of Chicago Press, 1992]) addresses to my study *Réduction et donation,* consult *Étant donné,* Book II.

but rather a matter of deconstructing a project that is already an explicit denegation of presence, thus of deconstructing a quasi-deconstruction. What is more—and this is the burning question—this quasi-deconstruction cannot be said simply to anticipate, unknowingly, the authentic deconstruction, that of *différance,* since it claims to the contrary to reach *in fine* what it deconstructs; it claims to put us in the presence of God in the very degree to which it denies all presence. Negative theology does not furnish deconstruction with new material or an unconscious forerunner but rather with its first serious rival, perhaps the only one possible. In short, for deconstruction what is at issue in "negative theology" is not first of all "negative theology" but rather deconstruction itself, its originality and its final preeminence. Thus it is strategically important to deconstruction that it deconstruct as radically as possible the twofold claim of so-called negative theology: that is, its claim to deconstruct God and nevertheless to reach God. If this were missing, the deconstruction that proceeds by means of *différance* would suffer first a rivalry (presence can be deconstructed without it) and then a marginalization (deconstruction would not forbid access to God, outside presence and without being). When deconstruction sets out to attack what it, along with the entire tradition, still designates with the imprecise title "negative theology," it is not making an attack so much as it is defending itself.

Derrida's argument therefore has nothing in common with the reproach most often made against "negative theology"—namely, that on the pretext of "honoring in silence" it in fact leads to the most radical form of atheism.[7] For Derrida, quite to the contrary, the task is to stigmatize "negative theology's" persistence in making affirmations about God (in particular the affirmation of existence)—while denying that it does so—and thereby to point out its failure to think God outside of presence and to free itself from the "metaphysics of presence." This fundamental and unified argument can be orchestrated in several objections, which I will distinguish for the sake of the clarity of the debate.

---

[7] Recently, Claude Bruaire, *Le droit de Dieu* (Paris: Aubier Montaigne, 1974), p. 21: "It is therefore necessary to assign negative theology its official place, to give it its exact status, apart from the pious sentiments which cover with a sensible outer layer, with religious scraps, the unalterable absolute, sign of the *Nothing:* negative theology is the negation of all theology. Its truth is atheism." This finds a surprising echo in Derrida: "If the apophatic inclines almost toward atheism . . ." (*Sauf le nom,* p. 18; "Post-Scriptum," p. 284). In contrast to this crude assimilation, see Henri de Lubac, *De la connaissance de Dieu* (Paris: Éditions du témoignage chrétien, 1945), c. V.

Neither Jewish, Muslim, nor Buddhist, but only Christian, and even only belatedly assigned to the conceptual hermeneutic of the New Testament alone,[8] "negative theology" could be assimilated to a Christian philosophy, indeed to what is most "Greek" about onto-theo-logy (objection 1).[9] It would even be inscribed within the horizon of being (objection 2). In effect—and this is the sole objection that seems capable of justifying the crudeness of the first two—it would always end up at a quasi-affirmation: it ". . . often calls to mind the sentence, verdict or decision, the *statement*." For "the apophatic has always represented a sort of paradoxical hyperbole" and negation ". . . [which is] everywhere, but never by itself," just like the adverb "without" "transmutes into affirmation its . . . negativity."[10] In short, "negative theology" does not annul [*ne nie pas*] the essence, being, or truth of God but rather denies [*les dénie*] them so as to better reestablish them, in something like a hyperbole (objection 3). As it could be answered that mystical theology obviously does not intend to reestablish *in fine* what it denied but rather to pass, through the way of eminence, from predication (affirmative and/or negative) to a decidedly non-predicative form of speech, namely the prayer which praises (ὑμνεῖν) [*hymnein*], the remaining task for Derrida is to disqualify the latter (ὑμνεῖν) as a

---

[8] *Sauf le nom*, pp. 69–70; "Post-Scriptum," 305 (which here, as elsewhere, depends on Raoul Mortley, *From Word to Silence*, vol. 2 [Bonn: P. Hanstein, 1986], p. 57—a work which is at once knowledgeable and profoundly foreign to what it claims to be treating, as much by its prejudices as by its omissions).

[9] *Sauf le nom*, pp. 39, 41, 69–70, 79, 84; "Post-Scriptum," pp. 293, 294, 305, 309, 310–11; and *Psyché*, pp. 564 and 573; "How to Avoid Speaking: Denials," pp. 102–3 and n. 16, pp. 136–37.

[10] *Sauf le nom*, respectively pp. 16, 70, 81; "Post-Scriptum," p. 283 (modified); p. 305, p. 310 (see in particular, on "being" and "truth," pp. 72, 80 and 82; "Post-Scriptum," pp. 306, 308–9 and 310); and *Psyché*, nn. 2 and 3, p. 542 (see 540–41) ["How to Avoid Speaking: Denials, p. 79 (see 77–78)]. This assertion too rests on Mortley, who strangely praises it in Proclus (supposedly the only true theoretician of the *via negativa*) and then reproaches Gregory of Nyssa and Denys with it: "This manoeuvre resembles [?] the positive *via negativa* [?] of Proclus [?], in that the negation is implied only [?] to allow for a positive statement of transcendence," *From Word to Silence*, p. 229). This argument is repeated by the same author with even less caution in "What Is Negative Theology?" in Raoul Mortley and D. Dockerill, eds., *Prudentia*, supplementary, 1991. It is also assumed as evident by Harold Coward and Mark C. Taylor in their respective contributions to *Derrida and Negative Theology*, pp. 176ff., 188, 200 etc. Similarly, Frank Kermode, "Endings, Continued," in *Languages of the Unsayable: The Play of Negativity in Literature and Literary Theory*, ed. Sanford Budick and Wolfgang Iser (New York: Columbia University Press, 1989), p. 89, esp. pp. 75ff.

disguised form of predication (one always praises with the title . . . or insofar as . . . , thus by naming). This is done by opposing the prayer that praises to prayer pure and simple (εὐχή) [euchē][11] (objection 4).

The crudeness of these objections—which will have to be discussed at greater length—could lead one to underestimate them and set them aside. I will not give in to this temptation, for two main reasons. First, because at least one of them (objection 3) obliges Christian theology to undertake a serious line of questioning: to what extent does negation not just function, in effect, to reestablish in the *via eminentiae* what the apophasis had apparently disqualified? In particular, wouldn't the divine eminence serve to protect, validate, and maintain the real attribution to God of being, essence, thought, and so on—in short, of all the founding concepts of metaphysics—only at the price of a hyperbolic passage (by means of ὑπέρ [hyper] and its substitutes)? Next, and more generally, we will take these objections seriously because all of them put into question the possibility, for theology, of making an exception to the metaphysical conditions of discourse. In short, can Christian theology as a theology provoked by a Revelation remove itself in principle, if not in what it really accomplishes, from the "metaphysics of presence"—or is it, in the final analysis, reducible to this metaphysics? Which amounts to asking: is Christian theology subject to deconstruction, or not?

2. THE THIRD WAY: DE-NOMINATION

The answer to such a question, or even the barest outline of one, poses such a great difficulty that we will have to proceed one step at a time. We will begin by confronting those objections to the corpus, no doubt exemplary for this debate, traditionally attributed to Denys the Areopagite—namely, that comprising *The Divine Names* and *The Mystical Theology*.[12]

---

[11] *Psyché*, pp. 572ff., n. 1; "How to Avoid Speaking: Denials," pp. 111ff., especially n. 16, p. 136.

[12] We will spare Denys the useless title "Pseudo-" which modern criticism insists on inflicting upon him, as if it were necessary to denounce a fraud in the title "the Areopagite" (classic example, Maurice Patronnier de Gandillac strenuously denouncing "the Dionysian myth" in the introduction to his translation of *Oeuvres complètes du pseudo-Denys l'Aréopagite* [Paris: Aubier, 1948 (1st ed.), 1980 (2nd ed.)]. This is obviously a religious name: Denys does not pretend *to be* the convert of Saint Paul

At the outset, one fact presents itself to us: not only does Denys not isolate "negative theology" as such (a point we have already observed), but he uses apophasis only by including it in a process that includes not two but three elements. It therefore does not contend face-to-face with the affirmative way in a duel where the last to enter the fray would be at once the victor over and the heir to the first, for both must, in the end, yield to a third way. In this way it is ". . . starting from the arrangement of beings insofar as they come from Him and contain certain icons and semblances of the divine paradigms [affirmative way] that we approach, as far as our capacities allow, the beyond of all [beings] through its way and its position and in the negation and over-coming of all [negative way], and in the cause [*Réquisit*] of all [third way]—ἐν τῇ πάντων ἀφαιρέσει καὶ ὑπεροχῇ, καὶ ἐν τῇ πάντων αἰτιᾳ [*en tē pantōn aphairesei kai hyperochē, kai en tē pantōn aitia*]." More clearly still, ". . . It is necessary at first [καὶ, *kai*] to impose and affirm [καταφάσκειν, *kataphaskein*] all theses of beings insofar as it is the cause of all [ὡς πάντων αἰτιᾳ, *hōs pantōn aitia*], then [καὶ] deny them even more radically [κυνιώτερον ἀποφάσκειν, *kyriōteron apophaskein*], as it surpasses all, finally [καὶ] let us not believe that the affirmations are the contrary of the negations, since [the cause] which is above every negation as well as every position—τήν ὑπὲρ πᾶσαν καὶ ἀφαίρεσιν καὶ θέσιν [*tēn hyper pasan kai aphairesin kai thesin*]—is still more above all privation." Also relevant here are the final lines of the final Dionysian treatise, the most formal and the most axiomatic, the *Mystical Theology*: ". . . for the perfect and unique cause of all things is above every assertion [ὑπὲρ πᾶσαν θέσιν, *hyper pasan thesin*] in the same way as what surpasses the total suppression of all things and is found beyond their totality [ἐπεκείνα τῶν ὅλων, *epekeina tōn holōn*] is also above every negation [ὑπὲρ πᾶσαν ἀφαίρεσιν, *hyper pasan aphairesin*]."[13] The game is therefore not played out between two terms, affirmation and negation, but between

---

(Acts 17:34) but assumes the name as that of a role model and patron saint. Otherwise, why would he confess his spiritual father to be not Saint Paul but "the divine Hierotheus" (*Divine Names* IV, 15–17, PG 3, 714a ff., and the paraphrase of Pachymère, 778b ff.)? It takes some naïvety to imagine Denys and his ancient readers more naïve and ignorant of monastic practices than we have become.

[13] Respectively, *Divine Names*, VII, 3, 869d–872a; *MT* I, 2, 1000b and V, 1004b [Note that all English translations of Denys have been modified in order to capture the rendering of the Greek by the author of this essay. For this reason, I have omitted citing the English page reference.—J. Kosky.].

three, different from and irreducible to each other: ἡ πάντων θέσις, ἡ πάντων ἀφαιρέσις, τό ὑπὲρ πᾶσαν καί ἀφαίρεσιν καί θέσιν [*ē pantōn thesis, ē pantōn aphairesis, to hyper pasan kai aphairesin kai thesin*].[14] It is possible not to understand, or even not take seriously, this threefold division, but it cannot be denied that Denys spoke and thought in this way.

On this threefold division, even the authors who set themselves at a noticeable distance from Denys display indisputable agreement. Thomas Aquinas begins with the names attributed negatively and then acknowledges a preeminence to the names spoken of God absolutely and affirmatively—contrary to the Dionysian way of proceeding. But even affirmation finally yields to eminence because God can be named as the cause of the perfections stated by the names—though with a causality surpassing their significations ". . . secundum modum altiorem [in a more excellent and higher way]" or ". . . secundum eminentiorem modum [in a more eminent way]" so much that it reestablishes (or rather deepens) the unknowing.[15] Still more revealing is the final position of Nicholas of Cusa. To be sure, Nicholas provides one of the rare ancient examples of the explicit use of *theologia negativa*—he even devotes the title of the final chapter of *De docta ignorantia* to it. However, he does not end up with apophasis pure and simple, but with infinity: "Et non reperitur in Deo secundum theologiam negationis aliud quam infinitas [According to negative theology, infinity is all we discover in God]." This infinity does not revert to affirmation after passing through negation but rather lays bare and circumscribes the divine truth as the experience of incomprehension: ". . . praecisionem veritatis in tenebris nostrae ignorantiae incomprehensibiliter lucere—in the shadows of our ignorance [negation] shines incomprehensibly the truth defined more precisely [eminence]." This is not a description of an hypostasized apophasis but of a third position, the sole target ever since the beginning: "That, then, is the learned ignorance for which we have been searching [Et haec est illa docta ignorantia, quam inquisivimus]."[16] The path is thus cleared for thought of the incomprehensible

---

[14] *Divine Names,* II, 4, 641a.

[15] *Summa theologiae, Ia,* q. 13, a. 2c and 3c; *The Summa Theologica of Thomas Aquinas,* vol. 1 (New York: Benziger Brothers, 1947), pp. 61, 62.

[16] *De docta ignorantia, I,* c. XXVI, in Nicholas of Cusa, *Philosophisch-theologische Schriften,* ed. Leo Gabriel, vol. 3, (Vienna: Herder, 1964), pp. 292–97; *On Learned Ignorance,* trans. Germain Heron (New Haven: Yale University Press, 1954), p. 61.

as such (Book II), opening onto a complete dogmatic theology (Book III). The Christian place of the negative way is not in doubt; it is found in the threefold character of the ways, which the eminence, cause, and incomprehensibility of God each dominate. Henceforth the task will be to assess how the establishment of a triplicity instead of and in the place of a duality modifies the status of each of the terms, and in particular the scope of the negative way. In other words, what advantage does the deconstruction of so-called negative theology draw from its ignorance (or refusal) of the threefold character of the ways? In short, what end is served, for Derrida, in denying the third way and in sticking with a straightforward opposition between affirmation and negation?

The answer can be divined by simply rereading objection (3) itself. In effect, this objection consists wholly in suspecting the supposedly ultimate and freestanding negation of implicitly and surreptitiously smuggling in and reestablishing an affirmation—"the apophatic has always represented a sort of paradoxical hyperbole"; ". . . transmutes into affirmation . . . its negativity"; "often calls to mind . . . the sentence, the decision or verdict, the *statement*."[17] The hermeneutics of suspicion always runs the risk of arbitrariness and therefore must intervene only in the last instance, when no other interpretation any longer appears possible. Now this is not the case here where the third way, however difficult to thematize it might at first seem to be, clearly indicates Denys's intention. It appears neither possible nor even useful to push the characteristics of the affirmations, by denying them, onto the negative moment because the triumphs and the failings of the first two ways are in principle overcome by a third. In other words, Denys (and the theologians who followed or preceded him on this path) has no need to overdetermine or falsify the negative moment, since he opened (or at least claimed to be open to) a final, more radical, and also more direct way, which alone leads to the end. Before going farther, let us observe that this shift to the lexicon of the mountain climber, as strange as it might be, indicates at the very least that one is attempting to undo oneself from the binary terms of the metaphysical (in fact Aristotelian) doctrine of judgment and truth: the third way is played out beyond the oppositions between affirmation and negation, synthesis and separation, in short, between the true and the false. Strictly speaking, if thesis and negation have it in common to speak the truth (and spurn the false),

---

[17] See above, note 10.

the way that transcends them should also transcend the true and the false. The third way would transgress nothing less than the two truth values, between which the entire logic of metaphysics is carried out. Therefore, if the third way is no longer about saying the true or the false, if it is precisely a matter of its not saying them, one can no longer claim that it means to affirm a predicate of a subject, not even beneath the absurd dissimulation of a negation, or that it has the least bit of interest in doing so. The third way does not hide an affirmation beneath a negation, seeing as it means exactly to overcome their duel, just as it means to overcome that between the two truth values wherein metaphysics plays itself out. Moreover, Denys thought the relation between affirmation and negation explicitly—in terms of an unambiguous hierarchy. On the one hand, negation prevails over affirmation: "The negations are true in what concerns divine things; the affirmations are unfitting."[18] That is, affirmation can give one the feeling of attaining the unattainable essence of God, while negation not only never claims as much but remains valid by denying the most remote determinations of the divine. On the other hand, negation itself submits its very own operation, and above all its duel with affirmation to the final transgression. For as we have already seen, at the very moment of recognizing the superiority of the negations over the affirmations—"and still more radically should we deny all affirmations [κυριώτερον ἀποφάσκειν, *kyriōteron apophaskein*]"—Denys still and always aims at what remains "above every negation and affirmation [ὑπὲρ πᾶσαν καὶ ἀφαίρεσιν καὶ θέσιν *hyper pasan kai aphairesin kai thesin*]" and therefore ". . . considerably above every privation [ὑπὲρ τὰς στερήσεις, *hyper tas sterēseis*]."[19]

The most elevated names (and the ones that are most theological, most directly concerned with the formulation of the Trinity itself) are in this way disqualified without looking back, without remorse: ". . . neither one nor oneness, neither divinity nor goodness, nor spirit in the sense we understand it; neither sonship nor fatherhood, nor anything else that is known by us or by any of the other beings."[20] Let it

---

[18] *Celestial Hierarchy,* II, 3, 141a. See *Divine Names,* VII, 3, 872b, and XIII, 3, 981b, and *Mystical Theology,* I, 2, 1000b.

[19] *Mystical Theology,* I, 2, 1000b [the Greek which the English translators render as "beyond" has been rendered by the author as *au-dessus,* which I translate as "above"—J. Kosky.]

[20] *Mystical Theology,* V, 1048a.

not be suggested that these negations restore, more or less subtly, disguised affirmations. Denys in fact insists explicitly that "... we cannot speak of [God]" even as goodness, nevertheless "the most revered of names [τὸ τῶν ὀνμάτων σεπτότατον, *to tōn onomatōn septotaton*]."[21] In this way, a negation by itself is never enough to make a theology, no more than an affirmation is. To speak properly of God, there is never any proper or appropriate name. The proliferation of names here amounts to anonymity: "... He who is praised manifoldly with a manifold of names [τὸν πολυύμνητον καί πολυώνυμον, *ton poluumnēton kai poluōnymon*] is called by the Scriptures ineffable and anonymous [ἄρρητον καὶ ἀνώνυμον, *arrēton kai anōnymon*]."[22] It is no longer a question of naming [*de Le nommer*], nor by contrast of not naming [*de ne pas le nommer*], but of de-nominating God [*de le dé-nommer*]—in the twofold sense that this term can have: to name (to name in view of . . . , to nominate), but with something close to a negation, and consequently also to undo [*Le défaire*] from all nomination, to release and deliver God from it [*l'en dégager et délivrer*], thwarting it [*la déjouer pour Lui*]. In its ambiguity, de-nomination bears the twofold function of saying (affirming negatively) and undoing this saying of the name. It concerns a form of speech that no longer says something about something (or a name of someone) but which denies all relevance to predication, rejects the nominative function of names, and suspends the rule of truth's two values. Denys indicates this new pragmatic function of language, aiming at the One who surpasses all nomination by being given the title αἰτία—not the metaphysical "cause," but what all those who demand [αἰτιατά, *aitiata*] demand [αἰτέω, *aiteō*] when they aim at the One from whom they come and to whom they return. The αἰτία has precisely no other function but to pass beyond every affirmation and negation: "[As] the αἰτίον [*aition*] of all things, it itself is not one of them, insofar as it superessentially transcends all things"—". . . the ungraspable αἰτία which comes from the total love beyond all things."[23] Here it is important to note that

---

[21] *Divine Names*, XIII, 3, 981a.

[22] *Divine Names*, VII, 1, 865c. See also *Divine Names*, I, 6, 596a–b in its entirety.

[23] *Divine Names*, respectively I, 5, 593c–d, and IV, 16, 713c. See also, recapitulating with αἰτία alone the overcoming of the two values of truth and predication, I, 6, 596b; I, 7, 596c; I, 8, 597c; II, 3, 640b–c; II, 5, 644a; IV, 3, 697a; IV, 7, 704a; IV, 8, 708a; IV, 12, 709b; IV, 16, 713c; V, 1, 816b; V, 2, 816c; V, 4, 817d; XIII, 3, 970c. See also my analysis in *L'idole et la distance*, p. 189; *The Idol and Distance*, p. 151 (I will not go back over this translation or the interpretation of this concept, which have not been contested).

αἰτία does not by any means claim to name or to deny a name of God; it breaks with every predicative or designative function and is limited to what each creature, as it is what it is, aims at—which is indicated by a passage to the infinite: ". . . everything may be predicated [κατηγ-ορεῖται, *kategoreitai*] of Him and yet [He is] none of that."[24] The αἰτία in no way names God; it de-nominates [*le dé-nomme*] by suggesting the strictly pragmatic function of language—namely, to refer names and their speaker to the unattainable yet inescapable interlocutor beyond every name and every denegation of names. With αἰτία, speech does not say any more than it denies—it acts by transporting itself in the direction of the One whom it de-nominates.

At this point it is necessary that we be sure of the exact scope of the adverb or suffix -ὑπέρ. First of all, is it equal to the ambiguity of "without," an adverb suspected of reestablishing an affirmation? This can be doubted: ". . . the prefix ὑπέρ '*hyper*' has a negative rather than a positive form. To say that God is *hyperousios* is to deny that God is a being of any kind, even the highest or original being."[25] That is to say, when the New Testament has recourse to the suffix ὑπέρ, it can hardly be doubted that it is understood negatively. For instance, when Paul speaks of ". . . knowing the charity of Christ who surpasses all knowledge [ὑπερβάλλουσαν τῆς γνώσεως, *hyperballousan tes gnoseos*]," it is not a matter of once again knowing charity in the guise of a formal negation, but of ". . . taking root and establishing oneself in charity" and nothing other than this (Eph. 3:18–19). The relation of knowledge to ἀγάπη [*agape*] must yield to its integration in it. Assuming that this ὑπέρ comes up quite frequently in the Dionysian corpus and plays a decisive role in it, it would still remain to be proven that it contradicts Paul's usage.[26] This is not all evident, since at least the letter of the text claims the contrary: ". . . the proposed goal of dis-

---

[24] *Divine Names*, V, 8, 824b.

[25] Kevin Hart, *The Trespass of the Sign: Deconstruction, Theology, and Philosophy* (Cambridge: Cambridge University Press, 1989), p. 202, cited by Foshay, as confirmation of my position opposite that of Derrida, "Introduction: Denegation and Resentment," in *Derrida and Negative Theology*, p. 12.

[26] See, for example, among other echoes of Paul, ". . . the good above [ὑπέρ] all logos, unsayable by all logos" (*Divine Names*, I, 1, 588b); or ". . . to know how to discover the unknown *hidden* (?) by all the knowledge which is found in all beings" (*Mystical Theology*, II, 1025b). See Maximus the Confessor, PG 91, 664 b–c; Meister Eckhart, *Sermon 83, DW*, vol. 3 (1976), p. 442, French translation, vol. 3 (1979), p. 152, following Walther Völker, *Kontemplation und Extase bei pseudo-Dionysius Areopagita* (Weisbaden: Steiner, 1958), p. 142 n. 2.

course is not to expose the superessential essence as superessential [οὐ τὴν ὑπερούσιον οὐαίαν ἢ ὑπερούσιον ἐκφαίνειν, *ou tēn hyperousion ousian hē hyperousion ekphainein*] (for it is unknown and totally unsayable, surpassing union [with the mind]); rather it is to praise the essentializing procession of the thearchy into the principle of all essence and thence to all beings."[27] ὑπέρ reestablishes neither essence nor knowledge but rather transgresses them both in view of praising what precedes and makes possible all essence.

There is at least one theologian of the divine names who saw the objection of deconstruction and responded to it explicitly, John Scotus Eriugena. I may then be forgiven for citing him at some length: "For when I consider the aforesaid designations lack the particle 'not,' I fear to relegate them to the negative part of theology. If I put them with the affirmative part, however, I recognize this does not agree with what I know of them. For when one declares [*God*] *is superessential*, one allows nothing else to be understood than a negation of essence. For one who asserts [*God*] *to be superessential* clearly denies that God is essential. And consequently, although the negation does not appear in the words, it is evident to one who considers the matter carefully that it is not lacking in the understanding. For that reason, I think, I am forced to admit the aforesaid designations which seem to lack any negation are more in harmony with negative than affirmative theology. . . . Let us conclude with this brief example: '[*God*] *is essence*'— affirmation; '[*God*] *is not essence*'—negation [*abdicatio*]; '[*God*] *is superessential* [*superessentialis*]'—both affirmation and negation. For what superficially seems to lack negation is strongly negative in meaning. One who asserts God to be *superessential* [*superessentialis*] does not say what he is, but what he is not, for he declares he is not essence, but more than essence."[28]

---

[27] *Divine Names*, V, 1, 816b. See also II, 4, 641a (cited above, note 14).

[28] *De Divisionae Naturae*, I, 14, PL 122, 426a–d; English trans. in *Medieval Philosophy from St. Augustine to Nicholas of Cusa*, ed. John Wippel and Allan Wolter, O.F.M. (New York: Free Press, 1969), pp. 130–31. As the Greek terms in columns 459–60 indicate, this is quite obviously a discussion of the Dionysian superlatives. Francis Bertin, the French translator of Eriugena's work, offers a perfect commentary: ". . . the prefixes *super* or *more than* in no way imply a way of eminence which surreptitiously reintroduces affirmations at the heart of the negations. When one says that God is Superessence, one does not at all suggest that God is an Essence situated at the apex of the hierarchy of essences, but rather that God is essentially void" (*De Divisionae Naturae*, French translation, *De la division de la nature*, vol. 1 [Paris: Presses Universitaires de France, 1995], p. 216). Let us turn, for once, to Heidegger: "For the same

It must therefore be concluded that Denys (followed by the best of his interpreters) denies first that negation by itself suffices to define a theology, next that negation opposes affirmation in a simple duel, and finally that negation reestablishes affirmation while intending to invert it. In short, Denys always thinks negation exactly as he thinks affirmation—as one of the two values truths can have, one of the two forms of predication that it is precisely a matter of transgressing completely, as the discourse of metaphysics. With the third way, not only is it no longer a matter of saying (or denying) something about something, it is also no longer a matter of saying or unsaying, but of referring to the One who is no longer touched by nomination, a matter no longer of saying the referent, but of pragmatically referring the speaker to the inaccessible Referent. It is solely a matter of de-nominating. We can therefore, at least from Denys's point of view, deny objection 3.

3. Praise and Prayer

Before moving on, it becomes possible to discuss in passing objection 4—which claims that the prayer that praises (ὑμνεῖν) [*hymnein*] should be disqualified as a disguised predication, seeing as it always praises as . . . , therefore by naming, while a prayer pure and simple (εὐχή) would have no need of naming, nor even denying a name. In fact, at least two objections can be raised against this objection.

First, it presupposes it to be unquestionable that praising—that is, attributing a name to an interlocutor, indeed dedicating to that interlocutor one name in particular—necessarily implies identifying the interlocutor in and with his or her essence and thereby submits the interlocutor to the "metaphysics of presence." Now what is proper to the proper name consists precisely in the fact that it never belongs properly—by and as essence—to the one who receives it. *Never* is the proper name a name for the essence. This rule is even more applicable in the case of a possible God than in that of the finite recipients of names (humans, or even animals). Here is not the place to develop this paradox with all its implications,[29] but we can call to mind its principal

---

reasons, the beyond of the Yes and No born of the thought of negative theology" (*Einleitung in die Phänomenologie de Religion*, GA II, 60: *Phänomenologie des religiösen Lebens* [Frankfurt am Main: Klostermann, 1995], p. 109).

[29] As I have recently done in *Étant donné*, V, §28–29, pp. 400ff.

components. First of all, the name of essence—the secondary essences, the universal—never completely succeeds in designating the individual as such because an individual cannot be individualized completely except through the indefinite nomination of accidents. Second, it is precisely this denomination by accidents that one tries to accomplish with the list of names, surnames, forenames, place-names or gentile names, and so on that make up what is accepted as *the* proper name—but is in fact the summary of a supposedly convergent but in any case indefinite series of improper names. The supposedly proper name has in fact always already been used for and by another—the family name by the whole family, the forename (Christian name) by not only all those who share it in space and time but above all by the saint (or similar) who inaugurated it. Therefore, the proper name properly has only a certain use of certain common names. Third, this use appropriates the common proper name only in a factual, not necessarily legitimate, reference which makes it function more as a deictic than as a definition. Consequently, the common/proper name implies that others besides me use it to intend me and designate me, in short, call me by it. The name I bear (that by which I call myself, name myself, and identify myself) simply reproduces after the fact the name with which others first called me (that to which I answer, by which I am known and mistaken, and which has been imposed upon me). Therefore, the experience of the proper name—received or given—never ends up fixing the essence of the individual in presence but rather always marks that, as a principle, the individual does not coincide with its essence, or its presence exceeds its essence. In short, the proper name marks the fact that an individual's presence remains anonymous in direct proportion to the degree to which its name becomes more present. In this way, supposing that praise attributes a name to a possible God, one should conclude that it does not name God properly or essentially, nor in presence, but that it marks God's absence, anonymity, and withdrawal—exactly as every name dissimulates every individual, which it merely indicates without ever manifesting. In this sense, praise in mystical theology would only reproduce in the case of divine proper names an aporia that is already unavoidable in the proper names of the finite world.[30]

Next, the objection presupposes that praise, since it names, cannot be suitable to prayer, which is supposed not to name. But can prayer

---

[30] See above, chapter 5, §4, pp. 119ff.

pure and simple (εὐχή) be accomplished without naming—giving a name, however always improper? No doubt we can contest this, seeing as no prayer can pray without giving a name, without acknowledging an identity, even and especially an improper one. Not only does naming not contradict the invocation of the prayer, but without the invocation the prayer would be impossible—what would it mean, in fact, to praise without praising anyone, to ask without asking from anyone, to offer a sacrifice without offering it to anyone? An anonymous prayer would make no more sense than does the claim to attain the proper by an (im-)proper name. This is why Denys always carries out not only his praise by an invocation *as*,[31] but prayer as well (εὐχή): "it is fitting for us to raise ourselves toward it [the Trinity] first by our prayer to it *as* the principle of goodness."[32] At issue is not so much a strict denomination, since, according to the same text, prayer does not consist in causing the invoked one to descend into the realm of our language (he or she exceeds it, but also is found always already among us) but in elevating ourselves toward the one invoked by sustained attention. The approach of prayer always consists simply in de-nominating—not naming properly, but setting out to intend God [*le viser*] in all impropriety. In this way, prayer and praise are carried out in the very same operation of an indirect aim for the αἰτία, which they never claim to name properly, but always only to de-nominate *as . . .* and *inasmuch as . . .* what this intention can glimpse and interpret of it. To a large extent, these operators—*as . . .* and *inasmuch as . . .*—anticipate in theology what Heidegger will designate the phenomenological *inasmuch as . . .*—the interpretive comprehension of what is aimed at on the basis of and to the measure of the intonation of the one who intends.[33]

As such, the de-nomination operated by prayer (and praise) according to the necessary impropriety of names should not be surprising. In effect, it confirms the function of the third way, no longer predicative (whether this mean predicating an affirmation or a negation) but purely pragmatic. It is no longer a matter of naming or attributing something

---

[31] *Divine Names,* I, 6, 596a–b, 2, 596c; II, 5 644a; V, 4, 817c; XIII, 3, 980b: "Consequently theology [Scripture] praises the thearchy, as αἰτία of all things, with the name unity."

[32] *Divine Names,* III, 1, 680b. John Chrysostom takes up this theme by confounding prayer and praise in δόξα [*doxa*] alone (*On the Incomprehensible Nature of God,* trans. Paul W. Harkins [Washington, D.C.: Catholic University of America Press, 1984], III, 37ff. = PG 48, 719).

[33] Heidegger, *Sein und Zeit,* §32.

to something but rather of aiming in the direction of . . . , of relating to . . . , of comporting oneself towards . . . , of reckoning with . . .—in short, of dealing with. . . . By invoking the unattainable as . . . and inasmuch as . . . , prayer definitively marks the transgression of the predicative, nominative, and therefore metaphysical sense of language. We find again here the affirmation of Levinas: "the essence of discourse is prayer."[34] One therefore has several reasons to oppose objection 4.

4. OTHERWISE THAN BEING

It now becomes possible to approach objection 2 and to ask if mystical theology is really inscribed within the horizon of being and, as a result, is inscribed in the onto-theo-logical figure that metaphysics imposed on it.

A preliminary remark is in order here. Even if Denys (or some other) understood the question of God on the basis of being, this simple fact would not be enough to establish that he is inscribed within onto-theology. That is, as I have tried to show in the privileged case of Thomas Aquinas, if an onto-theo-logy wants to attain conceptual rigor and not remain at the level of a polemical caricature, it requires first a concept of being, next a univocal application of this concept to God and creatures, and finally the submission of both to foundation by principle and/or by cause. If these conditions are not met, if in contrast being remains an inconceivable *esse,* without analogy, or even *penitus incognitum* [deeply unknown], then the mere fact that being comes up is not enough to establish an onto-theo-logy.[35] If this caution implies great difficulty bringing a thought as discursive and formalized as that of Thomas's into the onto-theo-logical constitution of metaphysics (and Heidegger himself shied away from the task), how much more so are our efforts to be marked with prudence when it is a question of theology—and especially mystical theology!

But in the case of Denys, prudence is not even necessary when interpreting the possibility that he determines God by being. For, in fact,

---

[34] Levinas: ". . . what is named is, at the same time, what is called"; *Entre Nous: Essais sur le penser-à-l'autre* (Paris: Éditions Grasset et Fasquelle, 1991), p. 20.

[35] See my study "Saint Thomas d'Aquin et l'onto-théo-logie," *Revue Thomiste* 95 (1995): 31–66.

such a de-nomination is clearly and precisely rejected—at least as the first, principal, and most powerful de-nomination. Once again, since this ever-so-important fact seems to have been passed over in silence, I will reiterate: for Denys, neither being [*l'etre*] nor being [*l'étant*] offers a proper, or even an improper, name of God. The major argument gives no cause for doubt: το ον [*to on*] is always preceded by τὸ ἀγαθόν [*to agathon*] because even non-beings not only "desire" the ἀγαθόν but participate in it. "If one may speak this way, even non-being desires the good which resides above all beings [τἀγαθοῦ τοῦ ὑπὲρ πάντα τὰ ὄντα, καὶ αὐτὸ τὸ μὴ ὂν ἐφίεται, *tagathou tou hyper panta ta onta, kai auto to mē ov ephietai*]." Better, ". . . even non-being participates in the beautiful and the good"; or more explicitly, "in short, all beings [come from?] the beautiful and the good, and also all the non-beings [οὐκ ὄντα, *ouk onta*] [are found] in the beautiful and the good in a mode which exceeds essence [ὑπερουσίως, *hyperousios*]."[36] Positively, it has to be said that ". . . the divine de-nomination of goodness manifests, in their totality, all the emanations coming from the αἰτία of all things and which it extends to beings as well as to non-beings [τὰ οὐκ ὄντα, *ta ouk onta*], surpassing [ὑπέρ] beings and non-beings."[37] This surpassing should not be understood simply, in the classically metaphysical meaning, in the sense that God ". . . is not a being who is in a certain way, but who is absolutely," nor even in the more radical sense that God "is not, but is himself the being of beings; not that beings alone come from the being before all time, but also the very being of beings [αὐτὸ τὸ εἶναι, *auto to einai*]." Instead, this surpassing of beings must be understood otherwise, in the decisive sense according to which God, as goodness and αἰτία, designates "the principle of beings, on the basis of which all beings whatsoever as well as being itself [καὶ αὐτὸ τὸ εἶναι, *kai auto to einai*] and every principle are characterized."[38] The theses supported by these texts thus are not tainted by any ambiguity. (i) The horizon of being remains regional, because by definition it leaves out all non-beings. (ii) It always

---

[36] *Divine Names*, IV, 3, 697a (see IV, 18, 713ff.); IV, 7, 704b; IV, 10, 705d (see IV, 19, 716c).

[37] *Divine Names*, V, 1, 816b.

[38] *Divine Names*, respectively V, 4, 818d; V, 7, 822b. See John of Damascus: "To say what God is in his essence is impossible. It is more fitting to construct a discourse through the suppression of all. For he is not among beings, not as not being, but as being above all beings and being above Being itself [ὑπὲρ αὐτὸ τὸ εἶναι, *hyper auto to einai*]" (*De fide orthodoxa*, I, 1, 4 (modified) = PG 94, 800b).

remains possible to take them into consideration, seeing as they refer to the good, even when not being, in the mode of "desire." (iii) Therefore the first (or the last) of the de-nominations of God will have to be drawn from the horizon of the good rather than from that of being—it being understood that even this de-nomination attains neither what is proper to God nor God properly.

What remains is to measure the import of these theses. It is not enough simply to declare the horizon of being to be overstepped by the authority of goodness if one wants to think this transgression. What must be understood by goodness? In contrast to the Neoplatonists, who would overcome being only for the sake of coming unto the One and would pass beyond the One only in order to retrieve it, Denys not only does not privilege the One which he paradoxically places in the last position of the divine names; he also does not accord any essential privilege to goodness—while nevertheless still granting it the title "most revered of names."[39] Goodness transcends being on principle, but it itself does not attain the essence and hovers, so to speak, between the derived names and the unnameable. Thinking God *without* being and only without being does not, however, allow it to be thought *otherwise* than being—goodness remains undetermined and, in any case, without essential impact. In the light of this, how are we not to suspect the elision of being to be insignificant? How are we not to suspect the denegation of being to reestablish being without saying it has done so, indeed without owning up to it? Since it does not succeed in thinking beyond, shouldn't it end up turning back toward being? But it is here that the objection is turned against itself. For if it is accurate to say that we cannot think beyond being—with the de-nomination goodness (or the one)—must this be held as a reproach against mystical theology and its third way? Must mystical theology be reproached for not knowing how to say, for not knowing or not wanting to say to us what this otherwise than being *is* all about—or does this reproach not at once seem a bit absurd? For if it is a question of not naming, of not reaffirming any more than denying, why be surprised that the third way cannot say anything about "without being"? If it were to predicate of it anything and everything that might *be,* wouldn't it legitimately deserve to be reproached precisely as contradictory? And more importantly, if it committed itself to saying what "otherwise than being" *is*

[39] *Divine Names,* XIII, 2 and 3, 977c–981b.

all about, would it not have to be denounced as inconsistent? On the contrary, must we not take it to be perfectly coherent, even something to be wished for, that the transgression of being and the overcoming of predication that it authorizes, and by which it is characterized, be marked by the impossibility of *saying* (of affirming or denying) anything more about what the goodness "without being" *is* or would be? For precisely as soon as it is a question of the "otherwise than being," it is no longer a matter of saying something about something, but of a pragmatics of speech, more subtle, risky, and complex. It is a matter of being exposed in one's intending a non-object, exposed to the point of receiving from this non-object determinations that are so radical and new that they speak to me and shape me far more than they teach and inform me. Henceforth, the words spoken no longer say or explain anything to me about some thing kept for and by my gaze. They expose me to what lets itself be said only for the sake of no longer permitting me to say it, but to acknowledge it as goodness, thus to love it. About this inversion in the gravity and orientation of speech—that I have been thematizing now as de-nomination, just as Denys fixed it beneath the titles ὑμνεῖν and εὐχή—it is therefore fitting as a matter of principle that one no longer be capable of saying or denying anything whatsoever. The suspension of all predication does not betray the failure of the transgression toward "otherwise than being"; rather, it attests to it.

The paradoxical importance of the objection raised by Derrida now appears fully evident: in marking that mystical theology no longer says anything more after its passage to negation, and thus runs the risk that this negation might revert to an affirmation, Derrida's objection observes that in fact, but also rightfully, the third way cannot open onto any (newly) predicated said—or non-said or pre-said. With praise, it is no doubt no longer a matter of saying but of hearing, since according to the conventional etymology that Denys takes from Plato, bountiful beauty bids—καλλὸς καλεῖ [*kallos kalei*].[40] I have therefore withstood objection 2.

5. THE PRIVILEGE OF THE UNKNOWABLE

It goes without saying that here, as is often the case, it is not simply a matter of disputing or refuting the objections raised by Derrida; rather,

---

[40] *Divine Names,* IV, 7, 701c–d. See Plato, *Cratylus,* 416c–d.

they are to be taken as the bases from which we can construct, or at least outline, the scope of the question. At this point we can begin to make out the basic thesis implicitly advanced by Derrida. It amounts to the following: (i) theology knows, according to a non-discussed hypothesis, only the two figures of metaphysical predication (affirmation and negation) and does not broach any third way; (ii) so as not to drift into atheism, the negative way inevitably compels the theologian to fall back into positivity, more or less scandalously, more or less honestly; (iii) the simply rhetorical recourse to "superessential" eminence reinforces, rather than weakens, the inscription of the question of God within the horizon of essence, thus of being; (iv) and therefore the so-called negative theology falls beneath the sword of deconstruction just like any obviously metaphysical discourse—and perhaps more so since its claim to be removed from it must also be unmasked. This argument, however, presupposes a major assumption: across all its claims to denegation, theology, and first of all Jewish and Christian theology,[41] in the end intends only the positivity of presence, envisages nothing higher, nothing more suitable, nothing more divine than the most intense presence possible. In short, theology succumbs in full to the obsession with presence. But is it so self-evident that theology suffers this fascination to such a degree? Is it self-evident that it has always thought to defend the "cause of God" so desperately that it would lash it to "metaphysical presence"? Finally, is it self-evident that the theologians did not really try to accomplish what they said they were undertaking—the third way—and that in the final analysis they again insisted on a kataphatic nomination of God? In short, must it be held as evident that, from the point of view even of Revelation, what is at issue in the question of God has something to gain by being integrated in presence in its most clearly metaphysical sense? Asked in another way: does theology not have the means, the intention, and also every reason *not* to yield banally to the "metaphysics of presence"? The advantage it would draw from such a tactic is in no way clear, but the danger, that goes without saying.

In the case of Denys, the answer to these questions leaves no room for doubt—it is the theologian who insists that de-nomination maintain God outside all proper names, without sinking into presence: "God is known through all things and also apart from all things. God is known

---

[41] That one will allow us not to separate, ever.

by knowledge and also by unknowing. . . . And it is the most divine knowledge of God that one knows through unknowing [ἡ δὶ ἀγνωσίας γινωσκομένη *hē di agnōsias ginōskomenē*]."⁴² It must be insisted here that positing this absolute principle has nothing particularly Neoplatonic about it, or anything of the hyperbolic excess of the so-called negative theology. It is first and above all a direct and inescapable consequence of the biblical thesis "No one has seen God" (John 1:18), "nobody can see my face" (Exod. 33:23). God cannot be seen, not only because nothing finite can bear the glory without perishing but above all because a God that could be conceptually comprehended would no longer bear the title "God." It is not much to say that God remains God even if one is ignorant of God's essence, concept, and presence—God remains God *only on condition* that this ignorance be established and admitted definitively. Every thing in the world gains by being known—but God, who is not of the world, gains by not being known conceptually. The idolatry of the concept is the same as that of the gaze: imagining oneself to have attained and to be capable of maintaining God under our gaze, like a thing of the world. And the Revelation of God consists first of all in cleaning the slate of this illusion and its blasphemy.

Consequently, the requirement to neither know nor name God in terms of presence traverses the entirety of Christian theology. (a) It appears in the apologists of the second century—first Justin Martyr: "No one can utter a name for the ineffable God [ὄνομα τῶ ἀρρήτῳ θεῷ, *onoma tō arrētō theō*]";⁴³ then Athenagoras: "Hear this, oh man: the form of God cannot be uttered [τὸ εἶδος τοῦ θεοῦ ἄρρητον, *to eidos tou theou arrēton*] or expressed, and eyes of flesh do not have the power to see it."⁴⁴ (b) Likewise, it shows up in the first of the Alexandrians—take the Christians, first Clement: "the First Cause is not in space [*lieu*], but above space and time and name and conception. . . . For our interrogation bears on the formless and invisible [ἀόρατος, *aoratos*]"; ". . . invisible and incapable of being circumscribed [ἀόρατος καὶ ἀπερίγραφος, *aoratos kai aperigpaphos*]"; ". . . insofar as the invisible and ineffable God [ἀόρατος καὶ ἄρρητος, *aoratos kai ar-*

---

⁴² *Divine Names*, VII, 3, 872a.

⁴³ *Apology I*, 61, PG 6, 421b [*Ante-Nicene Fathers*, vol. 1 (Grand Rapids, Mich.: Eerdmans, 1981), p. 183 (modified)]. See *Apology II*, 10, 461b, and *Dialogue with Trypho*, 127, 2 and 4.

⁴⁴ *To Autolycos*, I, 3 PG, 1028c.

rētos]."[45] Then Origen: ". . . God is incomprehensible and incapable of being measured. . . ."[46] Consider also Philo, the Jew: "It is a great good to comprehend that God is incomprehensible [ἀκατάληπσος, *akataleptos*] in terms of being and to see that he is invisible [ἀόρατος, *aoratos*]."[47] (c) And also Athanasius: ". . . God is good and the friend of men . . . is invisible and incomprehensible [ἀόρατος καὶ ἀκατάλη-πσος, *aoratos kai akataleptos*] by nature, residing beyond all begotten essence."[48] (d) Basil clearly indicates the paradox with this remark: "knowledge of the divine essence involves sensing His incomprehensibility [αἴσθησις αὐτοῦ τῆς ἀκαταληψίας, *aisthesis autou tes akatalepsias*]."[49] (e) And there is nothing surprising in the fact that Gregory of Nyssa should have repeated it almost word for word: "This is the true knowledge of what is sought [that is to say, seeing the invisible and incomprehensible God—ἀκατάληπτὸν, *akatalepton*]; this is the seeing that consists in not seeing [τὸ ἰδεῖν ἐν τῷ μὴ ἰδεῖν, *to idein ev tō mē idein*], because that which is sought transcends all knowledge, being separated on all sides by incomprehensibility as by a kind of darkness."[50] (f) John Chrysostom parses it in a slightly different form: "All the while knowing that God is, he [Saint Paul] does not know what his essence is," for "the essence of God is incomprehensible [ἀκατάληπσος]."[51] (g) Of course, John of Damascus comes next: "No one has seen God. The only-begotten Son who is in the bosom of the Father has himself taught this. The divine is ineffable and incomprehensible [ἄρρητον καί ἀκατάληπσον, *arrēton kai akatalepton*]."[52]

---

[45] *Stromates*, respectively V, 11, 71, 5, then V, 11, 74, 4 and V, 12, 78, 3 [*Ante-Nicene Fathers*, vol. 2 (Grand Rapids, Mich.: Eerdmans, 1983), p. 461, then 462 and 462].

[46] *On First Principles*, I, 1, 5 [*Ante-Nicene Fathers*, vol. 4 (Grand Rapids, Mich.: Eerdmans, 1982), p. 243]: ". . . dicimus secundum veritatem quidem Deum incomprehensibilem esse atque inestimabilem. . . . Quid autem in omnibus intellectualibus, id est incorporeis, tam praesens omnibus, tam ineffabiliter atque inaestimabiliter praecellens quam Deus? Cujus utique natura acie humanae mentis intuendi atque intueri, quamvis ea sit purissima ac limpidissima, non potest" (PG 11, 124a/b–c).

[47] *The Posterity of Cain*, 15.

[48] *Against the Pagans*, 36, PG 25, 69. Likewise, Irenaeus, *Against Heresies*, IV, 20, 5: ". . . incapabilis et incomprehensibilis et invisibilis . . ." (SC 100).

[49] *Letter 234*, 1, PG 32, 869 [*The Nicene and Post-Nicene Fathers*, vol. 8 (Grand Rapids, Mich.: Eerdmans, 1983), p. 274 (modified)].

[50] *Life of Moses*, II, 163, PG 44, 377 [*The Life of Moses* (New York: Paulist Press, 1978), p. 75].

[51] *On the Incomprehensible Nature of God*, respectively I, 1g. 293 and IV, 1g. 733 = PG 48, 706 and 733 [pp. 126 and 253] (see V, 1g. 385, p. 304 = PG 743).

[52] *De fide orthodoxa*, I, 4 (modified), PG 94, 789b (see I, 4, 800b).

(h) Nothing different from Augustine: ". . . God the highest, who is known better than knowing [de summo isto Deo, qui scitur melius sciendo]."[53] (i) Nor from Bernard: "It is not controversy, but holiness that understands things: if, that is to say, what is incomprehensible can be understood in some way—si quo modo tamen comprehendi potest quod incomprehensibile est."[54] (k) Nor even from Thomas Aquinas, for whom seeing as ". . . what God himself is remains hidden and unknown—remanet occultum et ignotum," it is necessary that we know how to unknow. Thomas therefore comments on the principle advanced by Denys in perfectly appropriate terms: ". . . what the substance of God is remains in excess of our intellect and therefore is unknown to us; on account of this, the highest human knowledge of God is to know that one does not know God—et propter hoc illud est ultimum cognitionis humanae de Deo quod sciat se Deum nescire."[55] Without going on *ad infinitum* with this anthology of citations, it seems legitimate to admit as a fact still to be explained that at least for the church fathers theology does not consist in naming God properly, but well and truly in knowing God precisely as what cannot be known properly—what must not be known, if one wants to know it as such. The known unknowability as such therefore disqualifies all possible primacy of presence over God.

There is a powerful argument confirming that it is indeed the theologians themselves who have the most extreme speculative interest in freeing God from any and all inclusion in presence. In fact, it is the heretics who claim to include God within presence by assigning God a proper name and an essential definition [*une définition d'essence*]. That is, the strong development of speculative theology in the fourth century, and first of all in the Cappadocian fathers, happens in response to the no less impressive assault of the Arians, who wanted to refute the conclusions of the Nicaean Council (325 C.E.). To demonstrate the inequality not only of Christ but of the Son to the Father, therefore to prove his non-divinity, the Arians argued for defining the divine essence as strictly unbegotten, ἀγεννησία [*agennēsia*]—being God requires being not begotten, ἀγεννητος [*agennētos*]. From this equality,

---

[53] *De ordine*, II, 16, 44, PL 32, 1015.

[54] *De consideratione*, V, 14, 30, PL 182, 805d.

[55] Respectively, *Prologue* to the *Commentary on the Divine Names* (in St. Thomas Aquinas, *Opuscula omnia*, ed. Pierre Mandonnet, vol. 2, [Paris, 1927], p. 221) and *De potentia*, q. 7, a. 5, ad 14.

it obviously followed that the Son, begotten by definition, could not be God, of the same essence as the Father. Thus Acacius, first in line in the second generation of Arians, will make unreserved use of the lexicon of the "metaphysics of presence," if such a thing can be said: "We believe that non-generation is the essence [ἀγεννησίαν εἶναι οὐσίαν, agennēsian einai ousian] of the God of all things."[56] Similarly, his pupil and the most celebrated theoretician of Arianism, Eunomius, long triumphant, will uncritically submit God to a metaphysical conceptuality: "When we say 'Unbegotten [ἀγέννητος],' we do not imagine that we ought to honour God only in name, in conformity with human invention [ἐπίνοια, epinoia]; rather, in conformity with reality, we ought to repay him the debt which above all others is most due God: the acknowledgment that he is what he is [τοῦ εἶναι ὃ ἐστιν, tou einai ho estin]. . . . But God . . . was and is unbegotten [ἀγέννητος]." Or, ". . . he is unbegotten essence [οὐσία ἀγέννητος, ousia agennētos]." And: ". . . it is not by way of privation [οὐδὲ κατὰ στέρησιν, oude kata steresin]" that these affirmations nail God to the wall of presence, but with all metaphysical violence, for ". . . his substance is the very same as that which is signified by his name [ὑπόστασιν σημαίνει τοὔνομα, hypostasin sēmainei tounoma]."[57] In effect, Eunomius, like all the Arians, holds that the (metaphysical) ideal of the equality between a word and/or a name and the concept of the essence is accomplished even (and paradoxically above all) in the case of God. It is by contrast Basil who, as a quasi-deconstructionist, interrupts this violence: "He is a liar who affirms with his sophisms that an essential distinction follows from a nominal one. For it is not the nature of things which follows that of names, but the names which are found after the things."[58] Consequently, if one of them plays the role of a metaphysician of presence, this can only be the Arian, Acacius or Eunomius. Confronted with him, the Christian theologian who practices de-nomination and is opposed to this supposed drawing of God into presence is outraged that ". . . the man dares to say that he knows God as

---

[56] Formulation reported by Epiphanius of Salamine, *Panarion*, III, t. 1, 76 (PG 42, 536, cited by Basil of Cesarea, *Against Eunomius*, I, 4, PG 29, 512b).

[57] Eunomius, *Apology*, respectively 8, 7, 8, and 12 = PG 30, 841c, 841d–844a, and 848b [*Eunomius: The Extant Works*, trans. Richard Paul Vaggione (Oxford: Clarendon Press, 1987), pp. 41–43; 41, 43 (modified), and 49].

[58] Basil, *Against Eunomius*, II, 4, PG 29, 580b. Bernard Sesboüé, in the introduction to his edition of the *Apology* (Paris: Éditions du Cerf, 1983), gives some good references supporting the inscription of Eunomius within Greek metaphysics.

God himself knows himself."[59] For the demand (and still more the pretension) to know God in an essence must be stigmatized not only as impossible but above all as indecent—it is simply not appropriate to what is at issue, because it relates to mere curiosity. Here deconstruction and theology can be in agreement, for the sake of contesting the same adversary—not the orthodox theologian, but the Arian, the sole metaphysician of presence, if there ever was such a thing.

God therefore can be known only as not being known. In contrast, to claim to know God as being known [*le connaissant*] appears to be the presupposition on which rests not only Arianism but also all conceptual—and above all metaphysical—grasp of the question of God. Just think for a moment of Spinoza's extravagant claim: "The human mind has adequate knowledge of the eternal and infinite essence of God [Mens humana adaequatum habet cognitionem aeternae et infinitae essentiae Dei]."[60] To know God by not knowing is obviously not the same thing as not knowing, nor is it the same as not knowing with the intention of knowing more (and not confessing as much). It is not a matter of a kataphasis ill-disguised in an apophasis, but of a radical apophasis which, precisely as radical, opens—by means of a paradox that is to be taken into consideration—onto knowledge of another type. To know in and through ignorance itself, to know that one does not know, to know incomprehensibility as such—the third way would consist, at least at first glance, in nothing else. But how can this be conceived? On what conditions would the renunciation of comprehension remain an authentic form of knowledge and not just a failure of knowing? Perhaps if we reason in this way: even if we were to comprehend God as such (by naming God in terms of essence), we would at once be knowing not God as such, but less than God, seeing as we could easily conceive an other still greater than the one we comprehend. For the one we comprehend would always remain less than and below the one we do not comprehend. Incomprehensibility therefore belongs to the formal definition of God, since comprehension would put God on the same level as a finite mind (ours), would submit God to a finite conception, and would at the same time clear the way for the higher possibility of an infinite conception, beyond the comprehensible.[61]

---

[59] *On the Incomprehensible Nature of God*, II, 1g. 158–59, PG 48, 712.

[60] *Ethics* II, §47.

[61] Descartes, *Réponses aux V objections*, AT VII, 368, 1–3.

Comprehension suggests adequate knowledge as long as one is dealing with things of the world. But as soon as one tries to catch sight of God, the relation must be inverted—knowledge holds only if comprehension ceases. Except for incomprehensibility, it is no longer a matter of what one intends when one says "God": "Of God, we say: what wonder is it if we do not comprehend him? For if you comprehend it, it is not God. . . . To touch some part of God through one's mind is a great blessing. To comprehend him is entirely impossible [De Deo loquimur, quid mirum si non comprehenderis? Si enim comprehendis, non est Deus. . . . Attingere aliquantum mente Deum, magna beatitudo; comprehendere autem, omnia impossibile]."[62] In the case of God, knowledge cannot rise up to itself except by transgressing itself until it becomes an unknowing, or rather until it becomes one that is capable of acknowledging the incomprehensible, and thereby respects the operative, pragmatic, and endlessly repeatable de-nomination of God as *that than which nothing greater [better] can be thought [id quo majus (sive melius) cogitari nequit].*[63]

De-nomination, therefore, does not end up in a "metaphysics of presence" that does not call itself as such. Rather, it ends up as a *pragmatic theology of absence*—where the name is given as having no name, as not giving the essence, and having nothing but this absence to make manifest; a theology where hearing happens, as Paul remarks, ". . . not only in my presence but also in my absence [μὴ ἐν τῇ παρουσίᾳ μου μόνον, ἀλλὰ πολλῷ μᾶλλον ἐν τῇ ἀπουσίᾳ μου, *mē en tē parousia mou monon, alla pollō mallon en tē apousia mou*]" (Phil. 2:12). But if essence and presence, and therefore *a fortiori* ground and the concept of being, are missing from this name, one can no longer speak of onto-theo-logy or of metaphysics or even of a "Greek" horizon. And besides, can one ignore the fact that the work of the Greek fathers consisted precisely in freeing the Christian theological concepts from the Greek (and perhaps metaphysical) horizon where they first

---

[62] Augustine, *Sermo 117*, 3, 5, PL 38, 663. See *Sermo* 52, 6, 16: "Si enim quod vis dicere, si capisti, non est Deus; si comprehendere potuisti, cogitatione tua decepisti. Hoc ergo non est si comprehendisti: si autem hoc est, non comprehendisti" (PL 38, 663).

[63] *Proslogion*, XIV, ed. Franciscus Salesianus Schmitt, vol. 1 (Edimbourg, 1938), p. 111. This formulation, which comes from Augustine (*De Trinitate*, V, 2, 3, etc.) and Boethius (*De Trinitate*, IV), will be taken up by Bernard: "Quid est Deus? Quo nihil melius cogitari potest" (*De Consideratione*, V, 7, 15, PL 182, 797a).

arose?[64] No ground, no essence, no presence. In this way I have stood up to objection 1.

By "pragmatic theology of absence," therefore, I mean not the non-presence of God but the fact that the name that God is given, the name that gives God, which is given as God (each of these going hand-in-hand, without being confused), serves *to shield God from presence*—weakness designating God at least as well as strength—and to give God precisely as making an exception to it. Gregory of Nyssa saw and described this perfectly: "What is the significance of the unnameable name [ἀκατονόμαστον ὄνομα, *akatonomaston onama*] of which the Father speaks [when he says] 'Baptize them in my name,' without adding the signification uttered by this name? On this matter, here is our opinion: we grasp all the beings in creation through the significa-tion of their names. Thus, he who says 'sky' conveys to the mind of the one who is listening the creature shown by this name; and if one mentions 'man' or one of the living things by his name, his form [εἶδος, *eidos*] is at once impressed upon the one who is listening. And likewise all the other things are, by the names that they are given, inscribed on the heart of him who receives, through listening to them, the denomination imposed on the thing in question [τὴν προσηγορίαν τὴν ἐπικειμένην τῷ πράγματι *tēn prosēgorian tēn epikeimenēn tō pragmati*]. In contrast, only the uncreated nature, which we believe [to be] the Father, the Son, and the Holy Spirit, surpasses all signification that a name can convey [κρείττων πάσης ἐστὶν ὀνομαστικῆς ση-μασίας, *kreittōn pasēs estin onomastikēs sēmasias*]. This is why the Word, in saying this name, did not add to the tradition of faith what it is [τὸ τί, *to to*] (how could he have found a name for a thing above all names?). But he gave our understanding the power to set about piously to find, according to its capacity, a name which indicates [ὄνομα ἐνδεικτικόν, *onoma endeiktikon*] the supereminent nature and which is equally fitting to the Father, the Son and the Holy Spirit. . . . And this, it seems to me, is what the Word decreed by this formula [that is to say, to say 'the name' without saying which one]—in order to con-vince us that the name of the divine essence is unsayable and incom-prehensible [ἄρρητον καὶ ἀκατάληπτον, *arrēton kai akatalēpton*]."[65]

---

[64] See, among other works, Endre von Ivanka, *Plato christianus* (Einsiedeln: Johan-nes Verlag, 1964).

[65] *Against Eunomius*, II, §14–15, ed. Werner Jaeger, vol. 2, pp. 301–2 = PG 45, 471d–3c. "The use of the uniformative term 'name' is deliberate," acknowledges

The Name does not name God as an essence; it designates what passes beyond every name. The Name designates what one does not name and says that one does not name it. There is nothing surprising, then, in the fact that in Judaism the term "Name" replaces the Tetragrammaton, which must and can never be pronounced as a proper name, nor that, amounting to the same thing, in Christianity it names the fortunate and necessary "absence of divine names" (Hölderlin). For the Name no longer functions by inscribing God within the theoretical horizon of our predication but rather by inscribing us, according to a radically new praxis, in the very horizon of God. This is exactly what baptism accomplishes when, far from our attributing to God a name that is intelligible to us, we enter *into* God's unpronounceable Name, with the additional result that we receive our own. This pragmatic theology is deployed, in fact, under the figure of the liturgy (which begins with baptism), where it is never a matter of speaking *of* God, but always of speaking *to* God in the words of the Word. The Name above all names therefore de-nominates God perfectly, by excepting God from predication, so as to include us in it and allow us to name on the basis of its essential anonymity. The Name does not serve knowledge by naming but by including us in the place de-nomination clears out. The basket never overflows except with bread that first was lacking. In this way, mystical theology no longer has its as goal to find a name for God but rather to make us receive our own from the unsayable Name. Concerning God, this shift from the theoretical use of language to its pragmatic use is achieved in the finally liturgical function of all *theo*-logical discourse.

Whence this absolute rule of the pragmatic theology of absence, by which it is opposed to the "metaphysics of presence" at least as much as deconstruction is: "our best theologian is not he who has discovered the whole, for our present chain does not allow of our seeing the whole, but he who has better pictured or represented in himself the image of the Truth, *or its shadow or whatever we may call it.*"[66] Or: ". . . God as such cannot be spoken. The perfect knowledge of God is so to know

Raoul Mortley (*From Word to Silence*, p. 181). This can be compared to the argument for the comprehensibility of ἐστί in the predications concerning God in III, 5, n. 60, t. 2, p. 172 = PG 45, 764.

[66] Gregory of Nazianzus, *Fourth Theological Oration 30*, 17, PG 36, 125c [*Nicene and Post-Nicene Fathers*, vol. 7 (Grand Rapids, Mich.: Eerdmans, 1983), p. 316 (modified)].

him that we are sure we must not be ignorant of Him, yet cannot describe Him [Deum ut est, quantusque est, non eloquetur. Perfecta scientia est, sic Deum scire, ut, licet non ignorabilem, tamen inaerrabilem scias]."[67] The theologian's job is to silence the Name and in this way let it give us one—while the metaphysician is obsessed with reducing the Name to presence, and so defeating the Name. The dividing line has been established by an inescapable formulation: ". . . between creator and creature no likeness can be recognized which would be greater than the unlikeness that is to be recognized between them [inter creatorem et creaturam non potest tanta similitudo notari, quin inter eos major sit dissimilitudo notanda]."[68]

6. The Saturated Phenomenon *Par Excellence*

We have thus wound up with a complete reversal of the initial problematic. To observe this by examining the theological tradition of mystical theology and reconstructing its logic is one thing, but it is quite a different matter to describe the phenomenon to which it is trying to do justice. The remaining task, then, is to conceive the formal possibility of the phenomenon that seems to demand an "absence of divine names" and our entering *into* the Name. It is a matter of conceiving its formal possibility—but nothing more, since phenomenology cannot and therefore must not venture to make any decisions about the actuality of such a phenomenon—this is a question entirely beyond its scope. Phenomenology is to make decisions only about the type of phenomenality that would render this phenomenon thinkable.[69] The question is to be formulated in this way: if that with which the third way of mystical theology deals in fact is revealed, how should the phenomenon be described, such that we do justice to its possibility?

Let us suggest a response. If one admits, with Husserl, that the phe-

---

[67] Hilary of Poitiers, *De Trinitate*, II, 7, PL 10, 36 [*Nicene and Post-Nicene Fathers*, vol. 9 (Grand Rapids, Mich.: Eerdmans, 1981)].

[68] Fourth Lateran Council (1215) in H. Denzinger, *Enchiridion Symbolorum*, §432. Despite its title, Erich Przywara's *Analogia entis* (Einsiedeln: Johannes Verlag, 1962) has indicated this in an exceptionally strong fashion.

[69] Concerning this distinction, see "Métaphysique et phénoménologie: Une relève pour la théologie" ["Metaphysics and Phenomenology: A Relief for Theology" (see chapter 1, note 38)]; and *Étant Donné*, §24, only speaking here of Revelation as a ". . . possible figure of phenomenology as such" (p. 326).

nomenon is defined by the inescapable duality of appearing and what appears [*l'apparaître et l'apparaissant*] and that this duality is deployed in terms of the pairs signification/fulfillment, intention/intuition, or noesis/noema, one can imagine three possible relationships between the terms at issue: (i) The intention finds itself confirmed, at least partially, by the intuition, and this tangential equality defines adequation, therefore the evidence of truth. (ii) In contrast, the intention can exceed all intuitive fulfillment, and in this case the phenomenon does not deliver objective knowledge on account of a lack. The first case would correspond to the first way, kataphasis, which proceeds through a conceptual affirmation that justifies an intuition. The second would correspond to the second way, apophasis, which proceeds by negating the concept because of an insufficiency in intuition. Husserl (in this following Kant) admits only these two hypotheses and thus remains stuck within the horizon of predication, and therefore of a possible "metaphysics of presence." But a third possibility remains. (iii) The intention (the concept or the signification) can never reach adequation with the intuition (fulfillment), not because the latter is lacking but because it exceeds what the concept can receive, expose, and comprehend. This is what we have elsewhere called the saturated phenomenon.[70] According to this hypothesis, the impossibility of attaining knowledge of an object, comprehension in the strict sense does not come from a deficiency in the giving intuition, but from its *excess,* which neither concept nor signification nor intention can foresee, organize, or contain. This third relation between the two inseparable facets of the phenomenon—in the occurrence of the saturated phenomenon—can perhaps allow us to determine the third way, where mystical theology is accomplished. In this third way, no predication or naming any longer appears possible, as in the second way, but now this is so for the opposite reason: not because the giving intuition would be lacking (in which case one could certainly make a favorable comparison between "negative theology" and atheism or establish a rivalry between it and deconstruction) but because the excess of intuition overcomes, submerges, exceeds—in short, saturates—the measure of each and every concept. What is given disqualifies every concept. Denys states this to the letter: "It is stronger than all discourse and all knowledge— κρείττων ἐστὶ παντὸς λόγου καὶ πάσης γνώσεως [*kreittōn esti pan-*

---

[70] See *Étant donné*, §§24–25.

tos logou kai pasēs gnōseōs]—and therefore surpasses comprehension in general and therefore [is also excepted from] essence [ὑπὲρ οὐσιὰν, *hyper ousian*]."[71] Indeed it is precisely by means of this undoing of the concept and intentionality that the theologians reach de-nomination. For example, Athenagoras: "On account of his glory, he cannot be received [ἀχώρητος, *achōrētos*]; on account of his greatness, he cannot be comprehended [ἀκατάληπτος, *akataleptos*]; on account of his sublimity, he cannot be conceived [ἀπερινόητος, *aperinoētos*]; on account of his strength, he cannot be compared; on account of his wisdom, he can be referred to nothing at all; on account of his goodness, he cannot be imitated; on account of his goodwill, he cannot be described."[72] The undoing of knowledge here arises explicitly from an excess, not from a lack. Likewise, John Chrysostom: "We therefore call him . . . the unutterable, the inconceivable, the invisible, and the incomprehensible, he who conquers the power of human language [τὸν νικῶντα γλώττης δύναμιν ἀνθρωπίνης, *ton nikōnta glōttēs dynamin anthrōpinēs*] and goes beyond the comprehension of human thought [ὑπερβαίνοντα διανίας κατάληψιν, *hyperbainonta diavoias katalēpsin*]."[73] Excess conquers comprehension and what language can say. We have already heard from Gregory of Nyssa: ". . . the uncreated nature . . . surpasses all signification that a name could express [κρείττων πάσης ἐστιν ὀνοματικῆς σημασίας, *kreittōn pasēs estin onomatikēs sēmasias*]."[74] This text describes a shortcoming, and a shortcoming that results from a lack of utterable signification, not of intuition. In short, God remains incomprehensible, not imperceptible— without adequate concept, not without giving intuition. The infinite proliferation of names does indeed suggest that they are still there, but it also flags as insufficient the concepts they put in play and thereby does justice to what constantly subverts them. Consequently, the third way cannot be confused with the sufficiency of the concept in the first way or with the insufficiency of intuition in the second; rather, it registers the ineradicable insufficiency of the concept in general. The de-

---

[71] *Divine Names,* I, 5, 593a.

[72] *To Autolycos,* I, 3, PG 6, 1028c.

[73] *On the Incomprehensible Nature of God,* III, PG 48, 720 (see also, among other examples, III, 713 and 723). Likewise, "The invisible, the incomprehensible . . . he who surpasses all understanding and conquers every concept [νικ´ν πάντα λογισμὸν]" (*Sermon "Father, if it is possible . . . ,"* 3, PG 51, 37).

[74] *Against Eunomius,* II, §15, ed. W. Jaeger, t. 2, p. 302 = PG 45, 473b.

nomination that puts us *in* the Name has nothing in common with one or the other possibility opened by predication and nomination.

No doubt a final objection will be advanced: how, without resorting to a meaningless and even mad paradox, can the excess of giving intuition in the case of God be considered plausible, when the evidence attests that precisely and *par excellence* God is never given intuitively? Rigorously considered, this objection does not deserve a response, since it no longer concerns the formal possibility of a phenomenon corresponding to the third way but is already concerned with its actuality. Nevertheless, I will address it, since it reflects a quite common point of view. It will be noted first of all that there is nothing mad about having recourse to paradox in this matter, since this is precisely a case of a phenomenon that arises from the particular phenomenality of the paradox. For it is by no means self-evident that every phenomenon must be submitted to the conditions of possibility for experiencing objects and cannot sometimes contradict them. It could even be the case that this is a requirement proper to the phenomenality of God— supposing one admits its formal possibility, and what right does one have to exclude it? Next, one should keep in mind that even in the case when the positive form of the giving intuition would be missing, apparently or factually, this intuition is not wholly submerged beneath two of its undeniable figures, even if we can describe them only negatively. First, the excess of intuition is accomplished in the form of stupor, or even of the terror that the incomprehensibility resulting from excess imposes on us. "God is incomprehensible not only to the Cherubim and Seraphim but also to the Principalities and the Powers and to any other created power. This is what I wished to prove now, but my mind has grown weary. It is not so much the great number of arguments that tires me, but a holy terror at what I had to say [τῇ φρίκῃ τῶν εἰρημένων, *tē phrikē tōn eirēmenōn*]. My soul shudders and becomes frightened [τρέμει γὰρ καὶ ἐκπέπληκται, *tremei gar kai ekpeplēktai*] since it has dwelt too long on speculations about heavenly matters."[75] Access to the divine phenomenality is not forbidden to us; in contrast, it is precisely when we become entirely open to it that we

---

[75] *On the Incomprehensible Nature of God,* III, p. 214 = PG 48, 725 [English trans., p. 108 (modified)]. I refer to the wise and well-argued suggestion made by Jean Daniélou, who interprets the theme of the "holy terror" (and all the conjoint terms) as attesting the excess of divine intuition, which subverts all our expectations and our capacity (*Introduction,* III, pp. 30–39).

find ourselves forbidden from it—frozen, submerged, we are by ourselves forbidden from advancing and likewise from resting. In the
mode of interdiction, terror attests the insistent and unbearable excess
of the intuition of God. Next, it could also be that the excess of intuition
is marked—strangely enough—by our obsession with evoking, dis-
cussing, and even denying that of which we all admit to having no
concept. For how could the question of God dwell within us so
deeply—as much in our endeavoring to close it as in our daring to open
it—if, having no concept that could help us reach it, an intuition did
not fascinate us?

The question of the names of God is never about fixing a name to
God or opposing a "non" to him. "Name" and "non," when heard [in
French], sound the same sound, and nothing responds to the one any
more than to the other. The "non" of the so-called negative theology
does not say the Name any more than do the "names" of the affirmative
way. For if no one must say the Name, this is not simply because it
surpasses all names, passes beyond all essence and all presence. In
fact, not even not saying the Name would suffice for honoring it, since
a simple denegation would still belong to predication, would again in-
scribe the Name within the horizon of presence—and would even do
so in the mode of blasphemy since it treats it parsimoniously. The
Name must not be said, not because it is not given for the sake of our
saying it, even negatively, but so that we might de-nominate all names
of it and dwell in it.

The Name—it has to be dwelt in without saying it, but by letting it
say, name, and call us. The Name is not said by us; it is the Name that
calls us. And nothing terrifies us more than this call, ". . . because we
hold it be a fearful task to name with our proper names the One '. . . to
whom God has bestowed the gift of the name above all names'—ὅτι
φοβέρον ἡμιν ἡμετέροις αὐτόν ὀνόμασι προσφνεῖν, ᾧ ἐχαρίσατο
ὁ θεὸς τὸ ὄνομα τό ὑπὲρ πᾶν ὄνομα [hoti phoberon hēmin hēmeter-
ois auton onomasi prosphōnein hō echarisato ho theos to onoma to
hyper pan onoma]."[76]*

---

[76] Phil. 2:9, in Basile de Césarée, *Contre Eunome*, II, 8, PG 29, 585 b = ed. B.
Sesboüé, p. 30.

*Jeffrey L. Kosky translated the bulk of this chapter. Marion's additions and changes
have been inserted, and the whole chapter lightly revised to reflect the translation style
of the rest of the book.—Trans.

INDEX

Lightning Source UK Ltd.
Milton Keynes UK
UKOW01f0855080916

282513UK00001B/30/P